THE MEDITERRANEAN THEATER, 1939

0 100 200 300 400 500
Miles

Hungary
Romania
BLACK SEA
France
Italy
Yugoslavia
Bulgaria
Albania
Greece
Turkey
Portugal
Spain
Toulon
Corsica
Sardinia
Taranto
MEDITERRANEAN SEA
Sicily
Syria
Tangier
Gibraltar
Bizerte
Tunis
Matapan
Cyprus
Sp. Morocco
Tunisia
Pantelleria Is.
Malta
Crete
Palestine
Trans-Jordan
Port Said
Morocco
Algeria
Tripoli
Benghazi
Tobruk
Alexandria
Suez Canal
El Alamein
Sidi Barrani
Cairo
Tripolitania
Cyrenaica
Nile R.
RED SEA
Libya
Egypt

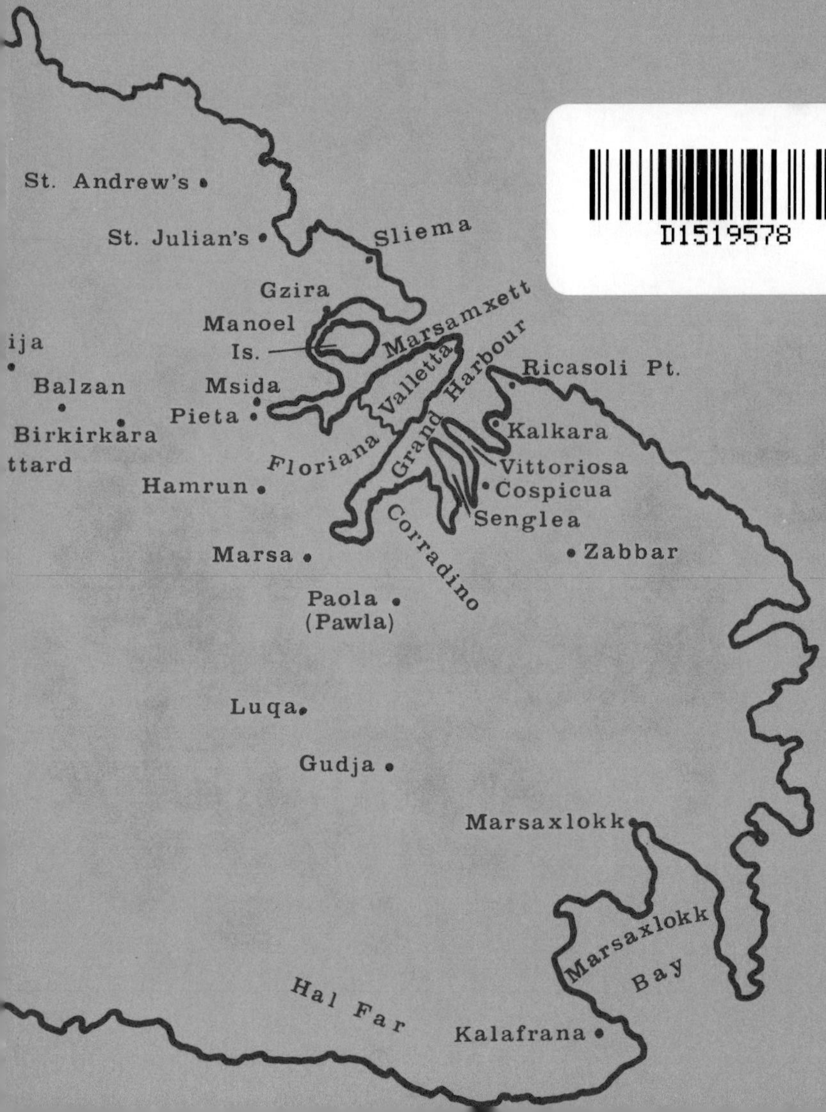

St. Andrew's
St. Julian's
Sliema
Gzira
Marsamxett
Manoel Is.
ija
Balzan
Msida
Valletta
Grand Harbour
Ricasoli Pt.
Pieta
Birkirkara
Kalkara
ttard
Floriana
Vittoriosa
Hamrun
Cospicua
Senglea
Marsa
Corradino
Zabbar
Paola (Pawla)
Luqa
Gudja
Marsaxlokk
Marsaxlokk Bay
Hal Far
Kalafrana

Besieged

Recipient of the
University of New Hampshire
Book Prize for 1984

Besieged The World War II

Published for the University of New Hampshir

Ordeal of Malta, 1940-1942

Charles A. Jellison

y University Press of New England, 1984

University Press of New England

Brandeis University
Brown University
Clark University
Dartmouth College
University of New Hampshire
University of Rhode Island
Tufts University
University of Vermont

The publisher gratefully acknowledges the support of the Andrew Mellon Foundation in the publication of this book.

Printed in the United States of America

Library of Congress Cataloging in Publication Data

Jellison, Charles A. (Charles Albert), 1924–
Besieged : the World War II ordeal of Malta, 1940–1942.

Bibliography: p.
Includes index.
1. Malta, Battle of, 1940–1943. I. Title.
D756.5.M35J45 1984 940.54'21 84-40305
ISBN 0-87451-313-8

To Pauline

And they blessed Thee on their knees,
When they learned Thy Grace and Glory
under Malta by the sea.

—*Kipling*

Contents

Preface

The following account centers on the early years of World War II, when the once-mighty British naval base of Malta stood alone and virtually naked in a hostile sea. Set upon from all sides by a determined and resourceful enemy and often neglected or abused by its friends, the little island was subjected during that time to prolonged periods of physical and psychological torment seldom equaled on any other occasion in recent history. How it managed not only to survive but to rise up time and again to play a major role in deciding the course of the war in the Mediterranean theater, and perhaps beyond, is the main burden of this story.

I am grateful to the United States government's program for the International Exchange of Scholars for providing me with the financial support and to the University of New Hampshire for the released time that enabled me to live for a year on Malta, where most of the material for this book was gathered. I am also indebted to many people here and abroad for helping me prepare this account of life on Malta during those desperate days of more than forty years ago when the odds were so long and the stakes so high. Among my principal collaborators: Ambassador and Mrs. L. Bruce Laingen, Harry and Ellen Radday of the United States Information Service in Valletta, and Professor Richard Beck of the University of Malta, who used their knowledge of the island and its people to point me in the right direction; my colleagues in the Department of History at the University of Malta, whose counsel, so freely given, proved invaluable, especially on matters of background and bibliography; Philip Vella of Malta's National War Museum Association, Richard Mifsud of the Union Press in Valletta, and Father Joseph Micallef of Luqa, all of whom directed me to sources I would otherwise have missed; Simone de Brincat, whose translations from the Maltese language were professionally and cheerfully rendered; the staff of the Melitensia Room at the University of Malta, where amid extensive records of Malta's past much of my research was conducted; and dozens of other islanders, from all walks of life, who were generous enough to share with me their personal recollections of wartime Malta. Many are mentioned by name in the pages that follow. Finally and foremost there was my wife, Phyllis, who besides helping to prepare the maps and charts for this book, read the manuscript in progress, offered her gentle criticism, and constantly cheered me on—as she always has.

Besieged

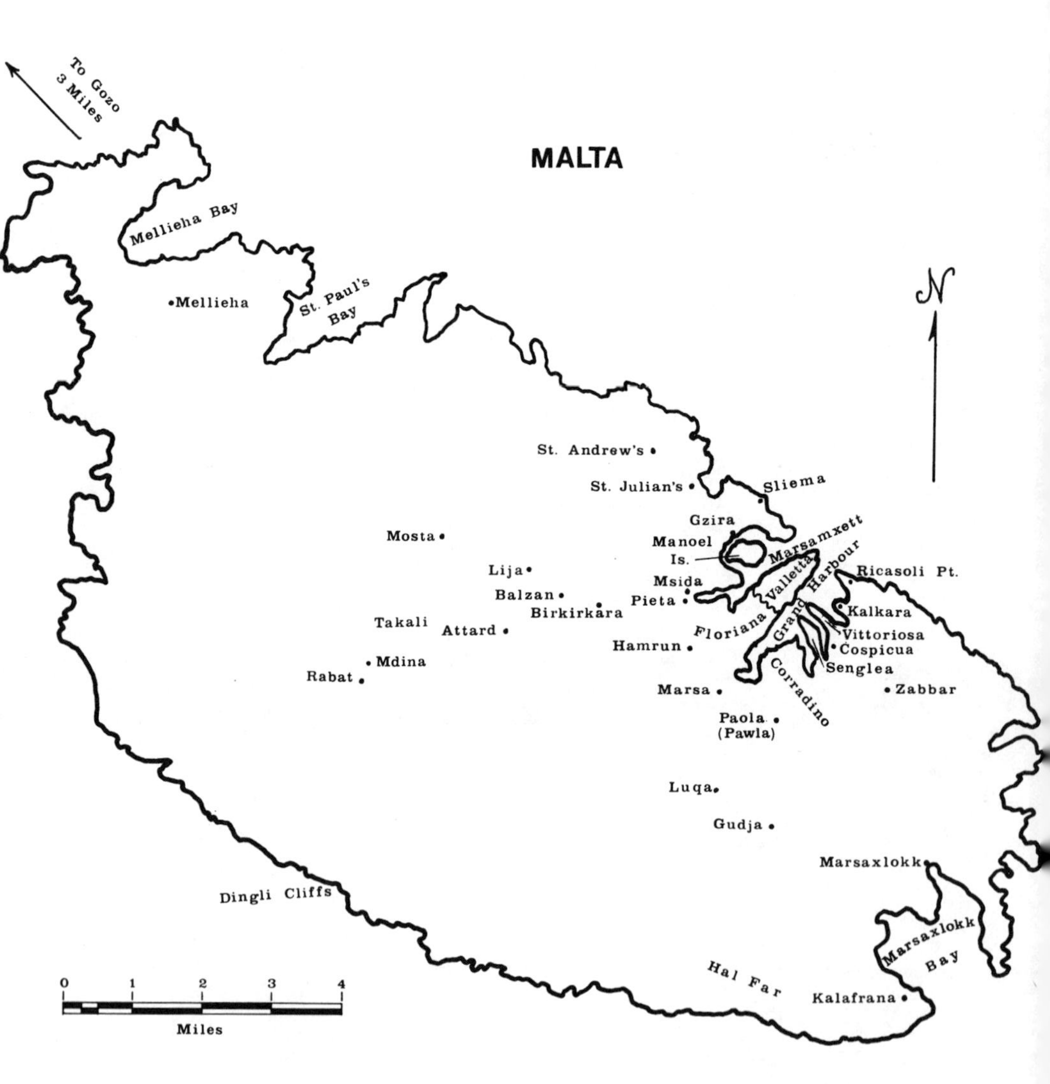
MALTA
To Gozo
3 Miles
Mellieha Bay
•Mellieha
St. Paul's Bay
N
St. Andrew's
St. Julian's
Sliema
Gzira
Manoel Is.
Marsamxett
Mosta
Lija
Balzan
Birkirkara
Msida
Pieta
Valletta
Grand Harbour
Ricasoli Pt.
Kalkara
Takali
Attard
Floriana
Hamrun
Vittoriosa
Cospicua
Senglea
Mdina
Rabat
Corradino
Marsa
Zabbar
Paola
(Pawla)
Luqa
Gudja
Marsaxlokk
Dingli Cliffs
Marsaxlokk Bay
Hal Far
Kalafrana
0
1
2
3
4
Miles

1 *Genesis*

Lying like a golden leaf in the narrows of the central Mediterranean, the tiny island of Malta has known many masters through the ages. Indeed, until independence finally came in 1964, there was scarcely a moment of its long and eventful history when it was not under the control of one foreign intruder or another—which helps explain the highly composite character of the Maltese people and their institutions.

It may be that Cro-Magnon man roamed the island in search of game and berries during the Upper Paleolithic period, but as far as can actually be determined, the first permanent inhabitants arrived no earlier than 3800 B.C. These were Neolithic farmers who had crossed over from Sicily, some sixty miles to the north. On Malta they built communal villages, grew cereals, and kept livestock, while worshiping simple, animistic gods. As the centuries passed, these Stone Age settlers were absorbed by successive waves of invaders from Sicily and the toe of Italy. The newcomers brought with them copper and bronze, together with more sophisticated gods for whom they erected megalithic temples and other holy places, the ruins of which may still be seen today.

By perhaps as early as 1000 B.C. civilization of a kind had come to Malta with the arrival of the Phoenicians, a seafaring Semitic people from the region around Palestine, whose records mention having put in at Maleth (meaning "shelter") in the course of their travels through the central Mediterranean. Soon after 800 B.C. they established a permanent trading base on the island—an outstation of sorts for their North African colony of Carthage some 250 miles to the west near the site of present-day Tunis. During the next five hundred years, as Carthage prospered and came to dominate the western and central Mediterranean, thousands of Carthaginians migrated to nearby Malta, carrying their skills and customs with them. It is to these people—Phoenicians really—that the modern Maltese trace their ethnic roots.

The defeat of Carthage in the Second Punic War, shortly before 200 B.C., ushered in a period of more than a thousand years during which Malta was under the control of Rome and its successor state, the Byzantine Empire. But the Romans were more interested in ruling the island than in settling it. So were the Byzantines—with the result that, despite its longevity, the Roman-Byzantine presence left few imprints upon either the land or its inhabitants. In fact, at the end of this long stewardship in the late ninth century, the people of the island were still speaking a basically Phoenician language. This much may be said for the Roman period, however: In the year 60 A.D. the Apostle Paul, on his way to Rome to stand trial for crimes against the state, was shipwrecked on Malta. During the following three months, while a prisoner there, he succeeded in Christianizing the island's "chief man," who in turn converted the rest of the islanders. Thus, Malta became the first country in the world to adopt the new religion. The Romans may also have left a mark of a different kind: They called the place Melita (meaning "honeyed" or "honeylike"), and it is generally believed that it was from this, rather than the earlier Maleth, that the island derived its present name.

In 870 A.D. the Arabs came, riding the crest of a religious fanaticism that would carry the power of Islam halfway around the world. What little is known of the ensuing period seems to indicate that it was a time of prosperity and benign rule. A rare reference to Malta found among the chronicles of its new masters suggests that they thought highly of the island: "Malitah . . ., rich in everything that is good and in the blessing of God."[1] During their more than two hundred years of occupation the Arabs introduced a variety of commercial and agricultural improvements and, perhaps most important of all, helped shape the modern Maltese language, which, although a mixture of many tongues, has remained since then more Arabic than anything else. Despite the preferred status of Islam, Christianity was tolerated and continued to be adhered to openly by many of the subject people.

By 1100 A.D. Arab power had receded from the central Mediterranean, and during the next four hundred years Malta was controlled by a succession of European princes, who proceeded to uproot Islam and introduce a modified type of Western manorialism. Meanwhile, the island neared the final stages of denudation. Long centuries of destroying its trees to make room for fields and pasture, together with overgrazing and abusive methods of crop production, had produced a familiar sort of ecological disaster: With nothing left to shield it or hold it in place, the topsoil of the ages had been gradually stripped from the rolling countryside by the persistent Mediterranean winds or washed into the sea by torrential rains. Eventually, when it was almost too late, the land was terraced behind checker-board patterns of stone walls that helped preserve a precariously thin covering of powdered dirt over parts of the island. But only in the sheltered ravines and gullies, where the topsoil had not only remained but in some cases had accumulated to a depth of ten feet or more, could crops any longer be grown in significant quantity. The damage done the land was incalculable and irreversible. The onetime verdant and wooded landscape of Malta had been transformed into the nearly naked outcropping of tan and yellow rock that it remains today.

In 1530 Malta's most famous visitors arrived to take over the island. These were the Knights of Saint John of Jerusalem, an international monastic order composed of the flower of European nobility. Some four hundred years old, the Order had been founded during the First Crusade to provide hospital care for Christians in the Holy Land and to wield the sword in their defense if the occasion called for it. The occasion often did, with the result that the Order soon became more widely known for its fighting prowess than its treatment of the sick. With their expulsion from Palestine by the Moslems near the end of the thirteenth century, the Knights of Saint John moved first to Cyprus and then Rhodes. Here in this distant outpost of Western Christendom they remained for more than two hundred years, tending their hospital and enhancing their wealth and prestige by raiding Moslem commerce. With the rise of Turkish power, however, their position on Rhodes became untenable, and in the early 1500s they were once again forced to move—this time with no place to go. After several years of wandering about the central and western Mediterranean from one temporary base to another, the Knights finally struck an agreement with Charles V, king of Spain, whereby they would be granted Malta in fief provided they would defend it. Not long thereafter the Knights of Saint John of Jerusalem entered the barren beauty of Grand Harbour to take charge of the island. Compared with Rhodes, the Order's new home was a bitter disappointment, but it would have to do until some better place could be found.

Almost immediately after their arrival the Knights resumed their practice of raiding Moslem commerce, this time directing their efforts mainly against the Turkish vassal states in North Africa. It was too much to expect that the Turks, who were now sweeping everything before them in their drive westward, would delay for long in wiping out this nest of Christian vipers. In fact, even if the Knights had behaved themselves, it would have been only a matter of time before the Turks turned their attention to Malta because of its obvious advantages as a staging area for an invasion of southern Europe. Thus, after several preliminary probes and years of extensive preparations, a Turkish fleet of some 200 ships carrying an army of 40,000 men arrived off the island in mid-May of 1565. Against this awesome force of infidels stood the 800 or so Knights of Saint John together with perhaps 7000 native Maltese troops—all under the command of Grand Master Jean Parisot de la Valette who, although in his seventies, would prove more than a match for his Turkish counterpart in courage, tenacity, and downright cruelty.

"Nothing is better known than the siege of Malta," Voltaire wrote in the mid-1700s. But that was more than two centuries ago, and today the heroic story of how the Knights of Saint John saved Malta (and perhaps the rest of Western Christendom) from "the unspeakable Turk" is all but forgotten. For nearly four months the island's outmanned, outgunned defenders held the fanatical hordes of the sultan at bay, inflicting fearsome casualties from their heavily fortified positions. Finally in early September, worn down by death, disease, and the utter futility of it all, the Turks broke camp and sailed for home, leaving behind, either dead, dying, or enslaved, nearly three-quarters of their once magnificent army.

The defeat of the Turks ushered in the golden age of the Knights of Malta, as they were now commonly called. Showered with riches from grateful princes and churchmen of western Europe, they proceeded to spend lavishly on the beautification and overall improvement of their tiny domain, especially the Grand Harbour area, where the Order's presence and activities had from the first been centered. In 1566, the year after the siege, the Knights began construction of a new city situated on the slim, humpbacked peninsula called Sciberras that juts out for more than a mile between Grand and Marsamxett harbors and commands the entrance to both. They named the place Valetta (now Valletta) in honor of their doughty old grand master, and it was here, in what Disraeli would describe nearly three centuries later as "a city for gentlemen built by gentlemen," that the Knights established their new headquarters.

As the years passed, the Grand Harbour area, and Valletta especially, took on a majestic elegance and grace scarcely matched anywhere else in the world. Magnificent churches, law courts, theaters, hospitals, and auberges to house the various language groups of the Order were erected with little regard for expense and adorned with precious art treasures imported from various parts of Europe. At the same time, with almost boundless energy the Knights applied themselves to the task of strengthening the island's defenses against the anticipated return of the Turk. Huge ditches and dry moats were dug; ramparts and watchtowers were erected; and in the soft limestone beneath Valletta a complex network of tunnels was constructed by thousands of Moslem slaves. Dozens of deep caverns for storing grain were hollowed out of the rock. This time Malta would be ready. But the Turks never came. The Germans did instead, more than three centuries later, and had it not been for the elaborate defense preparations just described, the island would have fared considerably worse at their hands.

The reign of the Knights came to a sudden and inglorious end in the summer of 1798 when, weakened by their own opulence and internal intrigues, they succumbed without a fight to a French force under Napoleon and were unceremoniously hustled off the island. The Maltese people were not sorry to see them leave, for although the Knights had done wonders in improving the economic and cultural life of Malta, in their later years they had become insufferably arrogant, and in some instances oppressive. It soon grew apparent, however, that the French were even worse—so much so that before long the usually docile Maltese rose up in arms against them, and with a major assist from the British fleet forced their withdrawal after a stay of barely two years. Although free now for virtually the first time in their history, the Maltese were not bemused into thinking that they could long remain that way. They therefore invited the British to stay on as their permanent protectors. The British agreed, but only after much indecision: The island would be expensive to administer and defend and in Lord Nelson's view (which he later altered) was poorly suited for the needs of the Royal Navy. Still, there was no denying that Malta would be a handy asset to have at a time when opportunities for the expansion of trade in the Mediterranean were already exciting the imagination of British merchants. Thus, in the early 1800s the Union Jack was raised over the palace of the grand masters in Valletta, and Great Britain assumed its role as new ruler of Malta.

Despite their original misgivings, the British soon came to realize what a rare prize they had acquired. With its excellent location, and its dockyards and fine harbors, Malta enabled Britain to enhance its commercial and political influence throughout the Mediterranean and for the first time to become a major power in that part of the world. But the best was yet to come: With the advent of coal-burning ships in the mid-1800s, followed a short time later by the opening of the Suez Canal and the reduction of Egypt to a British dependency, the importance of Malta grew immensely. Suddenly the little island found itself no longer merely a distant outpost in an inland sea, but

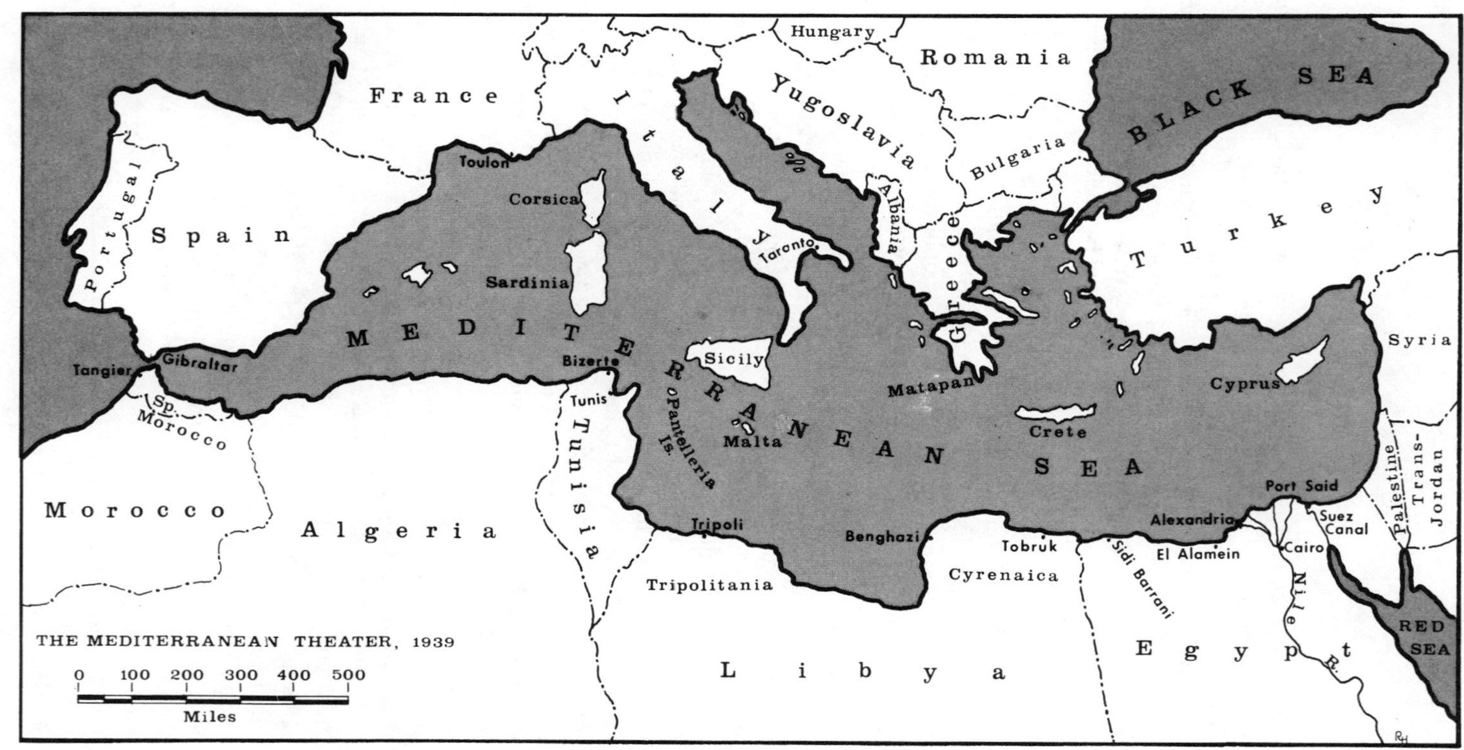

THE MEDITERRANEAN THEATER, 1939

a linchpin in the British overseas empire—a vital way station along Britain's new lifeline to India and the Far East. In 1869 a British naval base was established at Grand Harbour.

Situated about halfway along the 2000-mile stretch between the two great British bases at Gibraltar and Alexandria, Malta now bustled with activity as ships of the Royal Navy and commerce-carriers from a dozen or more nations put in for coal or repairs or to deliver the mountains of supplies needed to keep the island in business. Most of the larger vessels tended to congregate in Grand Harbour and neighboring Marsamxett, less than half a mile to the northwest on the other side of Valletta. Both are excellent, spacious ports, but of the two, Grand Harbour is much superior in all respects. It is, in fact, one of the finest natural harbors in the world. Nearly two and a half miles long and at its widest point slightly less than a mile across, it is penetrated from the side opposite Valletta by several well-defined promontories separated from one another by deepwater creeks. Here in these little backwaters, which lie almost perpendicular to the harbor proper, safe shelter can be found on even the roughest days. And here, mainly in French and Dockyard creeks where the Knights once kept their galleys, the British erected drydock and repair facilities capable of tending to the nautical needs of virtually anything afloat, including the mighty leviathans of their new steel navy. Well before the turn of the century Malta had developed into one of Britain's most valuable and active strategic assets. It had also become the headquarters of the British Mediterranean Fleet.

Throughout the eaarly decades of the twentieth century Malta continued to play an important but unobtrusive role in the affairs of the empire, as the Great War came and went and the 1920s slipped quietly by. But then in the autumn of 1935 the little island was suddenly thrust center stage when Italy launched its unprovoked attack upon Abyssinia, a naked act of aggression carried out in direct contravention of the covenant of the League of Nations. It should have been nipped in the bud. But it wasn't. Instead, Mussolini was permitted to swallow all of Abyssinia, with precious little done to prevent him. Although the League can be blamed for its timidity, and the French for their indecision, it was the British who were most at fault for not bridling the beast. They were, after all, in the best position to do so. They needed only to order their Mediterranean Fleet to close the Suez Canal to Italian military shipping or interdict the Duce's oil supplies.

But such a hard-line approach would have involved a certain element of risk. Frustrated and humiliated, Italy might have gone to war, and although the British government did not doubt a favorable outcome, the cost would likely have been high—probably six battleships, according to the Admiralty.

Besides, with England still reeling from the depression and Japan making unpleasant sounds in the Pacific, Whitehall had problems enough. Finally, after months of angry remonstrances, during which Italy proceeded to carve up its prey, the British abandoned even the pretense of counteraction and allowed the Duce to deal with Abyssinia as he saw fit.

Meanwhile in Malta, less than twenty minutes flying time from Sicily, a simple people who had never known war were issued gas masks and warned to be ready for an attack against their island at any time. Curious as to Malta's visibility from the air at night, the Admiralty, after much publicity in the newspapers and on radio and wall-posters, arranged for all lights to be turned off or covered at a predetermined time while reconnaissance planes circled overhead in a series of observation runs. Thus, the island came up with an arrangement that within a few years would become a standard feature of life in much of the world. The *London Times* called it a "trial occultation of lights." Malta had invented the blackout.

These were anxious times for Malta, but they would soon pass. By the early months of 1936 it was becoming apparent that there would be no war after all, and although at the time this was generally considered cause for rejoicing, within a few years the tragic reality of what had happened began to be understood. It was a peace too dearly bought. The men in London would have done well to have listened to the advice of their Mediterranean Fleet Command. "It was exasperating," Adm. Andrew Cunningham wrote some years later. "Had we stopped the passage of Italian transports through the Suez, and the import of oil into Italy, the whole subsequent history of the world might have been altered." But this was not the course chosen by those who decided on such matters, and as Cunningham ruefully noted: "It was not any business of ours to ask why."[2]

2 *Malta on the Eve*

Abyssinia should have been an object lesson for the British. But it was not. Instead of preparing for an inevitable showdown with Mussolini, Whitehall persisted in believing that he could be tamed and proceeded to conduct its Mediterranean affairs accordingly. Even after Italy's bloody collaboration with Germany in the Spanish Civil War and Mussolini's subsequent signing of the Pact of Steel with Hitler in the spring of 1939—indeed, up to within a few days of Italy's entry into the war in June of 1940—the British did their best to accommodate the Duce. On the very day that Italian troops invaded Albania, Good Friday of 1939, units of Great Britain's Mediterranean Fleet were in various Italian ports paying courtesy visits. And all the while great care was taken to avoid any action that might offend the Duce. It was for this reason the British maintained virtually no intelligence-gathering apparatus in Italy during those critical years just before the war and therefore had only a vague, and often badly distorted, idea of Italy's fighting capabilities and intentions.

In the meantime, as Europe approached the abyss, life in Malta remained pleasant, leisurely, and on the whole characteristically unruffled. How could it have been otherwise in such a picture-book setting, where the sun shone benignly and sheep did safely graze?

The tiny Maltese archipelago is composed of five tightly clustered islands, of which Malta itself is by far the largest and most important. Three of the other four are little more than rocks with names, naked outcroppings of less than a square mile each. At the time of the war they were totally uninhabited and without significance except as practice targets for the Royal Navy. The remaining member of the group is Gozo, an engaging land of rolling hills three miles northwest of Malta, where Ulysses is said to have been pleasantly detained for several years by the nymph Calypso. Some distance removed from the prime target areas of the main island and with no military or naval importance of its own, Gozo would be left virtually untouched by enemy attacks during the long battle to come. It would, however, share in the hardships of the blockade. It would also figure prominently in the story of Malta's survival, for here on this little island of barely twenty-five square miles, much of Malta's wartime food would be raised. Here too over 30,000 evacuees, mostly from in and around Grand Harbour, would find refuge after the bombs began to fall. Since Gozo already contained 25,000 people of its own, making for a population density of 1000 per square mile, the job of accommodating such a heavy influx of newcomers, many of whom stayed on for years, represented no small sacrifice by the Gozitans.

But as for direct involvement in the hostilities, the main island of Malta would bear the brunt of the attack, and it is difficult to imagine a less likely setting for the coming carnage. Malta may or may not have been, as George Bernard Shaw once pronounced it, "the finest heap of rock in the world," but it was surely a land of striking loveliness, especially in the countryside, where one encountered a strange, muted beauty. The soft undulations of its many hills, the little fields with their stone walls and ancient shepherds' huts, the crumbling watchtowers from an earlier age, and everywhere the dominance of yellow limestone set against the backdrop of a cloudless sky—all these combined to present a scene of almost biblical enchantment. It was not this pastoral hinterland that the Axis raiders had in mind, however, when they came to drop their bombs.

At this time the main island, with an area of just under a hundred square miles (roughly the size of the District of Columbia), had a population of approximately a quarter of a million people, all but 3 or 4 percent native Maltese. According to the 1937 census, most of the inhabitants lived within four miles of Grand Harbour, where the population density was more than six times that of the island as a whole. Among the most congested spots was the city of Valletta, political and military capital of the island, as well as its commercial and cultural center. Here in this onetime fortress of the Knights, 23,000 people lived in an area slightly larger than a quarter of a square mile. Across Grand Harbour in the so-called Three Cities, where the dockyards were located and the Admiralty had its headquarters, 28,000 more were packed into roughly half a square mile. It was in these two tiny areas, Valletta and the Three Cities, with their crowded warrens of one- and two-story row houses, that the heaviest and most sustained concentration of bombing in all history would take place.

The Three Cities comprise Senglea, Vittoriosa, and Cospicua. The first two occupy fingerlike peninsulas on either side of Dockyard Creek, probably the finest berthing place in all of Grand Harbour. The third, Cospicua, forms a crescent-shaped link between them at the head of the creek. On the eve of the war the Three Cities provided much of the 4000-man workforce for the dockyards and were therefore somewhat more prosperous than their neighbors, but in other respects they were much the same.

For one thing, they were not really cities at all. There were no political subdivisions in Malta. The entire island (along with Gozo) was centrally run from Valletta. The various communities might choose to call themselves cities, towns, or villages, depending on their size or pretensions, but they actually possessed no political authority or organization of their own—a situation that would give rise to considerable administrative awkwardness once the heavy demands of war began to be felt. Malta's communities were, in fact, nothing more than expanded neighborhoods, which helps explain the absence of clear-cut boundaries among them, as well as their diminutive size. At the time of the war none of the seven so-called cities and towns fronting on Grand Harbour covered as much as two-thirds of a square mile, and where one of them left off and the next began was no easy matter for even the most discerning stranger to determine. In the more rural areas this situation was less pronounced, but even there amid the open fields the countryside was dotted with dozens of tightly settled little towns, separated by boundaries that were largely a matter of opinion.

To the people who lived in these little communities, none of this was at all strange. It had never occurred to them that a town was supposed to be a political entity or that there was any merit in size. The town was a social unit, made up in most cases of all those people who attended the same church. Ideally, therefore, it should be small enough to enable even the most elderly of its inhabitants to walk to worship as often as they liked. As for fixed boundaries, there was no need for them. The people knew well enough how far the town extended. It extended as far as the homes of those who worshiped at a different church.

For the individual Maltese, whether urban worker or farmer, there was a strong feeling of attachment to his town. Like the ancient Greek he was a nonperson when absent from it. Although, as was often the case, he might have to earn his living elsewhere, it was only in his hometown that he had a sense of real identity and meaning. For here were the things that mattered most in his life: the church that his grandfather, the stonemason, had helped build with his own hands; his family, which might include as many as four generations living under the same roof; his neighbors, with whom he would sit and smoke on his doorstep or on one of the stone benches beside the church; and his social club, which he visited from time to time for a glass of wine or a game of snooker. It may not have been the most exciting life imaginable, but it was pleasant, familiar, and secure—unthreatened by sudden or dramatic change. Or so it seemed at the time.

The dominant feature of the town, physically and in other respects, was the church. No other building was allowed to rival it in height or grandeur, and in some of the older towns all streets radiated outward from it like spokes in a wheel. Built by the townspeople themselves with savings painstakingly accumulated over the years, the church stood as a monument not only to the glory of God but to that of the town as well. It was a source of immense pride among its parishioners. In it were housed those holy icons and relics so precious to the community, together with life-sized figures of Christ, the Virgin Mary, and the town's patron saint. On religious feast days (*festas*) it was customary to parade these figures shoulder-high through the streets, as the people cheered, fireworks rattled, and the town band, resplendent in its finery, blared away.

The church was the main gathering place for the town. Here the people met frequently to exchange news and views and to listen to public announcements read from the front steps overlooking the square. Here too they assembled to attend the baptism of a neighbor's child, or a wedding, or to bid goodbye to an old friend. Above all, however, the church was a place of prayer and communion with God, where all members of the community found spiritual sustenance and absolution. To these deeply devout people religion was as much a part of their lives as the air they breathed, and religion included being able to attend their own church, sometimes as often as three or four times a day, beginning with a four o'clock mass before work in the morning. To such people life without a church of their own was unthinkable. And yet, by mid-1942, nearly seventy-five churches on this tiny island would be either totally or partially destroyed, over fifty of them in the southeast quadrant alone.

On the eve of conflict the Maltese people were, by and large, a simple, conservative lot, among whom home, family, and traditional values loomed large. So too did class distinctions and deference to authority. The manner and tempo of their lives suggested an earlier age, and for the most part they seemed disinclined to seek out newer ways or to quicken the pace. In general their standard of living was low in comparison with that of Western Europe, but aside from a few urban slums, there was little of that appalling poverty so common in nearby Sicily and other parts of the Mediterranean world. Although adults as well as children often went barefoot (but not in church), rarely was anyone seen dressed in rags.

By their very temperament the Maltese seemed ill prepared for the war ahead. Despite the pressures caused by their modest means and crowded living conditions, or perhaps because of them, they were uncommonly considerate and good-natured. When crossed, they could be peevish and sometimes slow to forgive, but the idea of committing an act of violence against a fellow human was almost beyond their comprehension. More than that: In keeping with their religious beliefs, they went out of their way to show kindness to others, not only to family and friends but to outsiders as well. The loving attention lavished on the children, the consideration and respect given the elderly and infirm, the generous spirit of cooperation among neighbors and even strangers—all bespoke a high degree of civility and human warmth. Once the initial shock of battle had passed, these qualities would assert themselves and serve the Maltese people well during the hard days ahead.

Like Saturday's child, the Maltese had to work hard for a living. While the women kept house and tended to their numerous children, their menfolk generally put in long hours at poor pay. The great majority of them were farmers or shepherds, like their fathers before them, or day laborers who worked in the limestone quarries or at some menial job in town, such as wrestling cargo on the docks. There was also a fairly sizable group of skilled and semiskilled artisans, including carpenters, stonemasons, and mechanics, whose services were usually in demand, particularly at the shipyards. A notch above these in the class structure were the island's petty shopkeepers and civil servants for the colonial administration, who together accounted for most of Malta's small white-collar class. By and large the Maltese were good workers—steady, conscientious, and, although small by European standards, generally strong and hardy. But, as already noted, their traditional ways of doing things often proved awkward and time-consuming. Furthermore, most were functionally illiterate, and only one in five could either speak or understand English, which made communication difficult. Still, one way or another, they got the job done, and that was the important thing, especially once the bombs began to fall.

Superimposed upon this broad base of lower- and middle-class Maltese, who together represented some 95 percent of the island's total population and most of its productive labor, was a thin layer of native elite. Consisting mainly of business and professional leaders and a smattering of old-line

Maltese nobility whose titles dated back as far as the Middle Ages, this group was generally well-to-do and socially prominent. Most of them had been educated in England or Italy, traveled extensively, lived in splendid old town houses or country villas, and were fluent in several languages. Some held high political positions. Some had even been knighted by the king. Although few in number, they wielded a heavy influence, not only in Malta itself but also in London, where several of them had important friends. And relatives as well. Over the years a considerable amount of intermarriage had taken place between them and suitable members of the small British community on the island. The Stricklands, for example, were descended from a mid-nineteenth-century union between an officer of the Royal Navy and a young Maltese noblewoman. At the time of the war the Stricklands were perhaps the most powerful family on the island—powerful enough to make their voices heard as far away as Whitehall.

Well armed with money and the social graces, these upper-crust Maltese families mingled freely with members of the British governing class, attending the same teas, concerts, and bridge parties and, in most cases, subscribing to common views and fashions. In *most* cases but by no means all: Among the Maltese elite was a small but eloquent minority, made up mainly of intellectuals and members of the higher clergy, who showed a distinct preference for things Italian.

The differences between Malta's pro-British and pro-Italian factions went back a long way, but it wasn't until the early 1920s, after the island had been granted internal self-government, that the factions formed political parties and began vying with one another for support among the newly enfranchised masses. The central issue, while generally not explicitly stated, was Great Britain's future role in Malta. On the one hand was the Constitutional Party. Created and controlled by the Stricklands, it stood foursquare for maintaining close imperial ties. On the other was the Nationalist Party, whose members shared a sense of dissatisfaction with British stewardship as it then stood, and favored the development of a closer relationship with Italy. How much closer and how soon were questions that gave rise to bitter divisiveness within the party. Most members were willing to settle for the creation over the long run of stronger cultural and economic ties with the Italians while maintaining at least a nominal political allegiance to the British Empire. A small but vocal group, however, called for complete and immediate independence from Great Britain, followed by political annexation to Italy. Much depended upon one's attitude toward Mussolini and his fascist regime. As a prominent Nationalist later explained:

Only a small minority of the party actually favored Mussolini, mainly the more radical elements. They were impressed by the new orderliness he had brought to Italy. The trains really did run on time, you know. And, of course, he was recognized as a great enemy of communism, which was very important to the clergy. But most of our members were suspicious of him and what he was up to. This doesn't mean, though, that they loved Italy any the less, if you can understand how that could be.[1]

The Nationalists had little trouble acquiring a sizable following among the island's rank and file, who, whatever their attitude toward the British may have been, had warm feelings of affection for the Italians. After all, Italy was Malta's next-door neighbor and for centuries the two had experienced close and usually cordial relations. People and goods had passed freely between them in general disregard of immigration and customs restrictions, and intermarriage had occurred at all levels of society. Long before the British arrived, the Maltese had become at least partially Italianized, in many of their ways, including their preferences in music and art. Even their stubbornly Semitic language had acquired many Italian words and expressions as well as a heavy Italian inflection. In addition, the shared Roman Catholic faith of the two peoples caused many of the Maltese to feel a closer kinship to the Italians than to the British, whom they had known for scarcely more than a century and with whom they really had very little in common.

Whether the Nationalist Party actually posed a serious threat to Britain's future in Malta is questionable, but the British thought it did. Thus, in the early 1930s when the Nationalists finally triumphed over the Constitutionalists at the polls and took control of the government, London revoked Malta's constitution and returned the island to colonial rule. Neither political party took kindly to this "fancy bit of despotism," and both said as much, but it was understandably the Nationalists who were the more sorely affronted. Outraged at having their electoral victory snatched from them, they became increasingly surly and more willing to listen to those members who favored rejecting English rule altogether and seeking political union with Italy.

Not content with chopping the Nationalists down politically, the British embarked upon a calculated campaign to de-Italianize the island. Years later an aging Nationalist would remember those days with a sense of loss and sadness:

Before the war the Italians had been very active on the island in helping and befriending the Maltese. They had two fine schools, where the arts were taught. They had a Boy Scout organization. They had a program that sent Maltese children to Italy for two weeks of camp in the mountains. But the British couldn't abide Italy's popularity and drove all those people out. They even stopped the use of the Italian language in the law courts and other parts of the government.[2]

For the Nationalists and their pro-Italian friends this was all very distressing, but there was little they could do about the situation. Whatever chance they may have had to muster popular support and bring pressure to bear against the British all but disappeared with the coming of the Abyssinia scare in 1935. When this occurred, Italian stock took such a drastic dip on the island that the Nationalist Party found itself stripped of much of its popular backing and was forced to defend itself against cries of "treason" and "fascisti," even from many of its former members.

In 1939, after six years of arbitrary rule, the British granted Malta a new constitution. With war appearing ever more likely, the Home Government thought it advisable to institute a "less antagonistic" type of political administration for the island. Thus, on the very eve of World War II, representative government reappeared on Malta, although in a barely recognizable form. The Council of Government, as the new governing body was to be called, would be composed of members elected by the people plus an equal number appointed directly or indirectly by the royal governor and responsible to him. The governor himself would preside over the meetings and cast the deciding vote in case of a tie. This meant that the elected members could never constitute a majority, even if they were to vote as a bloc. So nothing had really changed. Here was semblance without substance—a sham put forward by the British like a cigar store Indian to bemuse the people. Both of Malta's political parties were shocked. They had expected more from the new constitution. Even the Stricklands labeled the document "something of a disappointment." The Nationalists had stronger words for it. But when the time came for the first general election under the new roof, both parties put forward full slates of candidates, perhaps because they reasoned that as bad as the constitution was, it was at least a move in the right direction.

The British referred to the new government as "an harmonious accommodation." It was hardly that, but it did provide a forum where the elected representatives could at least air their views. As will be seen, some of these views proved highly useful to the colonial administration in its dealings with the civilian population. At the same time, the opportunity to present them before the Council gave the Maltese people a sense of participation in the governing of the island, although it was clear that in the final analysis all power resided with the British. Not that it mattered much, but the general election of that summer resulted in a landslide victory for the Constitutionalists, who wouldn't be apt to cause their British masters much trouble, even if they could. Thus, Malta approached the war with its political house in order, well insulated from any unwanted interference by the natives. True, there were a few unreconcilable Nationalists about who were making a nuisance of themselves with their pro-Italian grumblings, but they were being carefully watched and, if necessary, could be dealt with when the proper time came.

Political vagaries aside, life in Malta was good during the years just before the war, especially so for the regular British residents, who accounted for about 1 percent of the island's total population. Civil administrators, businessmen, military retirees, they basked in the still-warm glow of a dying Western imperialism, and, let it be said, they basked with considerable style. Seldom overburdened by work or confronted by challenge, they lived out their days in a sedate little world of changeless routine: midmorning tea and biscuits at the office in Valletta; a leisurely lunch at the club; an afterwork splash of Scotch at the Osborne Hotel on South Street, which served the best drinks on the island, followed by a dinner of native pork or fowl at home; and perhaps a rubber of bridge with friends. The weekends, of course, were special, with tennis and bowls and sometimes a chukker of polo at the Marsa playing field, along with the usual Saturday night dinner dance at the fashionable Union Club. It was not a very stimulating life, but it was pleasant and tidy. Several years later a Maltese noblewoman would recall her British neighbors during those days:

> They were really a decent, civilized lot. I knew a great many of them here on the island and I liked them. I think most of us did. But looking back now on those days, I honestly can't remember a single thing they ever did for us. I mean, for the Maltese people. Every road they built went to one of their bathing clubs or a polo field; every monument was of a *British* admiral or a *British* statesman. They were so rich and we were so poor, and yet they were miserly toward us. Even the free school system they were so proud of having introduced was paid for by Maltese taxes. Their idea of generosity was giving pennies to children who danced for them in the streets. They didn't oppress us, you understand. There was none of that. They let us lead our own lives, but, oh, they took so much from us and gave so little in return. Of course, we didn't see those things back then in the same light we do today. If we had—well, who can say how differently we might have behaved when the war came.[3]

3 Naked unto Its Enemies

During those fading months of peace in the late 1930s, even the appeasers at Whitehall must have seen that war with Italy was at least a strong probability and that, if it came, Malta would surely be a part of it. Indeed, given the island's position directly astride Italy's main supply line to its North African colonies and the fact that here was a British base practically within cannon shot of Italian shores, it seemed likely that Malta would come under immediate attack once Italy entered the war. And yet, despite all this, the island was left in a state of almost total unpreparedness—with the result that when the Duce finally decided to join the conflict, he could have seized Malta before lunch if he had chosen to do so. The fact that he didn't would prove to be a military blunder of the first order.

When Mussolini declared war on England and France in June 1940, Malta's garrison was badly undermanned and underequipped. Its troop strength consisted largely of four infantry battalions of British regulars assigned to protect some thirty miles of coastline where any seaborne invasion would be most apt to occur, and also to guard the island's three aerodromes in case the Italians should decide to fly in. For the most part these troops were deployed along the northern beaches, where the shallow, sandy harbors were ideal for a landing operation. Here they had sown the approaches with antipersonnel mines, strung out dozens of miles of barbed wire, and then sat back in their hastily constructed concrete pillboxes to await the enemy. For weapons they relied mainly on the aging Enfield rifle, the Vickers machine gun, of which there were perhaps sixty on the entire island, and a few field pieces left over from the Great War. There were also ten or twelve tanks somewhere about, but they were fakes, wooden mock-ups meant to deceive the enemy's aerial reconnaissance. "We had very little, you know," commented a British officer looking back a generation later on those anxious days. "We were even low on ammunition, and our transport was mostly bicycle. It does seem that something more could have been done for us."[1]

Besides these four infantry battalions, together with a few support units of sappers (engineers) and antiaircraft personnel, the island's garrison included two territorial regiments: the Royal Malta Artillery (RMA) and the King's Own Malta Regiment (KOMR). Both were made up entirely of Maltese troops commanded, with few exceptions, by Maltese officers. However, although one battalion of the RMA had been kept up to strength and was on active duty manning the coastal guns when World War II began, the regiment's other battalions had fallen away to cadre size. The KOMR, an infantry outfit, was in even worse shape. Deactivated for many years, it had become little more than a paper organization.

With the outbreak of war against Germany in September 1939, hurried efforts were made to bring both these regiments up to full strength, beginning with the commissioned ranks. Years later a Maltese author would recall walking through the streets of Valletta and seeing old friends who had never done an hour's soldiering or even held a rifle, now suddenly decked out in officers' uniforms. "Commissions were as cheap as cigarette cards," he reported. "Everywhere were captains and majors. They strutted about vain as peacocks, and the girls made little tin gods of these untried heroes."[2] Finding men for them to command would prove considerably more difficult, however. The reservists were called up, but time had so reduced their ranks that recruitment became necessary. Despite concerted campaigns in the press and over the government-controlled rediffusion (cable) radio, this too fell short of the mark. The idea of leaving home and village for a gun pit or a pillbox on some remote beach had little appeal for most Maltese. Only the poorest farm boys, won over by the prospect of their first pair of shoes and a shilling a day, came forward in any number—and far too few of them. In June, when the bombs began to fall, the RMA was still well understrength, and the KOMR could field only one battalion, which the colonial governor generously described as "temporarily not at its fighting peak." Altogether—British and Maltese, infantry, artillery, and support personnel—troop strength on the island, as the battle was about to begin, fell somewhat short of 5500. This was not a very imposing force with which to fend off the might of the Italian Empire.

Sources differ on the number and type of antiaircraft ordnance on the island, but according to the newly appointed colonial governor, who was certainly in a position to know, only sixteen guns were available when he arrived on April 28, 1940.[3] This was only six weeks before the Duce unleashed his first air attack against Malta, and there is nothing to indicate that the island's gun strength increased significantly during the intervening period. There were also two dozen searchlights and a primitive radar set that sometimes worked and sometimes didn't. All of the guns were heavies, except for a few make-believe ack-acks that had been constructed out of wood by British sappers and stuck around the Grand Harbour area like stage props. Without any light AA the island was virtually defenseless against low-level attack. Enemy planes could simply have flown in under the minimum range of the heavies. But, either because the Italians weren't aware of it or, more likely, because they preferred to stick with their well-rehearsed plan for high-level precision bombing, they would fail to take advantage of this situation.

The coast artillery was not much better off than the AA. Its guns were up-to-date, in good working order, and manned by highly trained crews of the RMA with a reputation for excellent marks at target practice. However, there were only fourteen pieces in all, and most of them were positioned for the defense of Grand Harbour. As a result, much of the coastline was left unprotected. Fortunately the entire south side of the island and some of the west are rimmed by an almost unbroken barrier of cliffs, rising in places to a height of 400 feet. But the north and northeast are not, and here in this sector where an invasion now seemed most likely to occur, there was little if any gun coverage. Years before, while modernizing Malta's coastal defenses, London had clung to its earlier belief that if an attack came it would be a bombardment of Grand Harbour by enemy naval units. A shelling of the island at some other location had been considered unlikely, and the idea of an actual landing operation against the home base of the British Mediterranean Fleet was too farfetched even to contemplate.

As it happened, however, the British fleet was nowhere near Malta when the war finally came to the island. In October 1939, with Italy still neutral and showing no signs of causing trouble in the near future, the combined Anglo-French fleet had left the Mediterranean to help out in the Atlantic. Not until the following April, after Mussolini had begun to make ominous sounds, did the British fleet pass back through Gibraltar—but not to Grand Harbour as expected. For several years a running argument had gone on within the British Admiralty over the navy's ability to withstand attack by enemy aircraft. Here was a factor that had never been confronted in any previous conflict—an imponderable in the military equation. Most senior officers believed that the navy could take care of itself in such a situation, but were nonetheless reluctant to put the matter to a test, least of all to invite one. Thus, with Italy known to have several squadrons of planes on nearby Sicilian airfields, the Admiralty ordered the British Mediterranean Fleet to move to the safety of Alexandria, nearly a thousand miles away. This meant that at the worst possible time Malta was stripped bare of its naval protection, except for a few submarines and the monitor *Terror,* which had recently arrived from the East to help with the antiaircraft defenses. When the Maltese questioned this new arrangement, they were assured that the island could be defended just as well from Alexandria as from Grand Harbour. This, of course, was not true, and not many people supposed it was.

As poor as the island was in troop strength, guns, and naval protection, it was poorer still in air cover. When war began with Italy in 1940, Malta had three airfields, which would become increasingly important as the conflict progressed. The oldest of these, Hal Far, was situated on the south side of the island near the port of Marsaxlokk (or Marsa Scirocco as it was then known). When construction was begun on the field in 1918, the entire scheme was rejected by many people as foolish and costly: Malta had no need of an airfield, and even if it had, it would be impossible to build one anywhere on the island. The land was much too hilly. There were too many gullies and outcroppings. The winds were too strong. Besides, it was inconceivable that on this tiny island where food production was already so limited, dozens of small farms would be destroyed for such a frivolous purpose. In the end, however, engineering know-how and dogged determination won out, and after an enormous amount of leveling, including the removal of seventy-five miles of stone walls, Hal Far opened shortly after World War I as a base for the fleet air arm. Even by the standards of those times it wasn't much—a single, grass-covered runway, with cliffs on one side dropping off sharply into the sea and a deep ravine on the other. On certain days throughout the year strong crosswinds forced the suspension of all flights, and during the rainy season the field usually turned to mud and had to be shut down for weeks at a time.

About eight miles to the northwest, in almost the exact center of the island, was another and somewhat newer aerodrome. This was Ta Qali (or, as the British called it, Takali), which in some respects was even less suitable for air operations than Hal Far. Situated on a broad depression of level grassland that had once been the basin of a prehistoric lake, the field was partially obstructed by nearby hills and plagued by tricky wind currents that often made for difficult landing approaches. Even more than Hal Far, it had a mud problem and was unusable during much of the wet season. Although more of a meadow than an airfield at the outset of the war, Takali would eventually come to serve as the main base for the Royal Air Force fighter command on Malta.

About halfway between Hal Far and Takali was Luqa, the newest and best all-purpose aerodrome on the island. Begun in 1938, construction had proceeded nicely for nearly two years, despite enormous problems created by the uneven terrain and the need to sequester hundreds of acres of cultivated fields and pasture. Suddenly, however, the sappers conducting the operation were called to France in early 1940, with the result that work was suspended and the field was still uncompleted at the time of Italy's entry into the war. The runways, for instance, were only 1200 yards long, less than three-quarters of their intended length, and several of the taxi strips were still in a rough state. Nevertheless, unlike the island's other fields, Luqa had cross runways that allowed aircraft to take off and land in any direction. Perhaps even more important, these runways were surfaced with a thick layer of tarmac that would enable them to accommodate heavier planes. It would also help serve as protection against the erosive effects of the weather and the wear and tear of an increasing volume of traffic as the war progressed. Hal Far, Takali, and Luqa: From these three wind-swept little aerodromes, all in or near the southeast quadrant of the island, the enemy would get more than it bargained for in the bloody years ahead, although at the beginning of the war there wasn't a single British military plane within 800 miles of any one of them. At least none to speak of.*

Thus, with the curtain about to go up in the late spring of 1940, Malta offered the strange spectacle of a naval base without a fleet, airports without planes, a pitifully small garrison of ill-equipped troops, virtually no antiaircraft protection, and coastal guns that were too few and pointed probably in the wrong direction. It is perhaps not unreasonable to ask why.

The answer is not hard to find. Although no official document says as much, it is clear that sometime during the years immediately preceding the war the British government reached the decision not to defend Malta in the event of a conflict with Italy. Since the mid-1930s, when the Abyssinian crisis had brought the whole matter to the fore, British Army and RAF planners had been cautioning the government that because of Malta's proximity to enemy naval and air bases it could be held against an Italian assault only at great cost, and probably not even then. It would be better to let the island go. The Royal Navy, and its good friend at court, Winston Churchill, dis-

*See below, pp. 46–50.

sented vigorously: Malta, with its strategic location, excellent harbors, and first-rate dockyard facilities, was invaluable as a base for Mediterranean naval operations. It was one thing to withdraw the fleet to Alexandria as a precautionary measure, but to surrender the island to the enemy without a determined effort to save it was unthinkable. In the end, though, the government concluded that under the circumstances a defense of Malta would be inadvisable—which at the time certainly seemed a reasonable decision. The Italians were known to have 6 battleships (2 of them brand new), 19 modern cruisers, 120 destroyers and torpedo boats, and over 120 submarines, all within easy striking distance of the little island. Furthermore, it was estimated that the Regia Aeronautica had 1500 combat planes, many of them poised on bases in Sicily and southern Italy. Altogether this was a formidable force, vastly superior in size to any the British could muster against it. To engage it in battle anywhere would be risky enough, but to do so in the enemy's home waters would be nothing short of foolhardy.[4]

Of course, the Italians might not attack the island at all. With their overwhelming advantage in naval and air units, all of which could operate effectively out of North Africa and Sardinia as well as Italy itself, the enemy might decide instead to cut off Malta's supplies and thereby squeeze it into surrender. This shouldn't take much doing, for few if any people in Europe were more dependent upon imports than the Maltese. At the start of the war the island produced only 30 percent of its food (some sources say as little as 10 percent), and less than 5 percent of all other necessities, including such vital commodities as clothing and fuel. Only in rock, salt, and water was it wholly self-sufficient. To make matters worse, many of the island's imports, such as commercial fertilizers, manure, animal fodder, and a full 70 percent of all outside food, came from Italy and its North African colonies. Given this situation, the British government had good cause to question its ability to keep Malta supplied in case of war with Italy—which may have been another factor in its decision not to try to hold the island.[5]

Despite these sobering arguments, however, the men at Whitehall might still have decided to risk an all-out defense of the island had they not been persuaded by their army and RAF advisers that Malta was expendable, for the simple reason that it was superfluous for British needs. Granted, in a war with Italy the island could offer important advantages, but these same advantages could be had elsewhere. What was really at stake here was control over the central Mediterranean, and there was nothing that could be done from Malta toward achieving and maintaining this objective that could not be done just as effectively from well-established French bases in North Africa, Corsica, and southern France. At the same time, a fallback to these less-exposed French bases would involve far fewer risks in men and matériel than trying to hold onto Malta and would free the British from having to keep the island supplied. Simply stated then, to back off from Malta in favor of such bases as Toulon, Tunis, and Bizerte would cost England very little and at the same time probably spare it a great deal of grief. As for Malta itself, even if it were taken over by the Italians, it would be of little strategic benefit to them. The Duce's arm would scarcely be lengthened because of it.

Once the decision had been made not to hold Malta, it would have made no sense for the British to have strengthened its defenses—which perhaps explains why in fiscal 1939–40, as Mussolini was obviously preparing to enter the war, military spending for the island dropped to less than 40 percent of what it had been three years earlier.[6] In August 1939 a shipment of 112 new antiaircraft guns originally authorized for Malta was quietly diverted elsewhere, presumably out of fear that if sent to the island the guns would end up as gifts to the Italians. Stores of critical supplies upon which the life of the island depended not only were not increased but in many instances were not even kept up to normal peacetime levels. Coal, for example, the main source of Malta's electricity, was seriously low, as were certain basic foodstuffs, such as edible oils. Although in the spring of 1940 the island's lieutenant governor assured the Council of Government that the supply situation had never been better, the truth is that food reserves were down to less than five weeks. This was not a very adequate stockpile for a people about to go to war, especially the Maltese with their almost total dependence upon imports. "Although we couldn't see it then," a Maltese military officer later remarked, "It is clear enough now what the British were up to. It is dead right that they had written the island off."[7]

On the other hand, the British government had no intention of surrendering Malta without at least some show of resistance. It was one thing not to make a serious defense of the island, but quite another to present it as an outright gift to the enemy. There was the matter of pride and tradition to consider, or, as a British officer later stated, "We couldn't let the Eyeties just wade ashore, now could we."[8] Thus, Malta's meager garrison was expected to stand and deliver as best it could before hauling down the flag. "Bloody British fools," remarked a Maltese businessman years afterward. "For the sake of appearances they were willing to get the whole island blown to pieces. If they wanted to get themselves killed, that was up to them, but what gave them the right to take us with them?"[9]

So it appeared that there would be a scrap after all. Not much of one, most likely, but probably enough to call down the wrath of the Italians upon the civilian population. This being the case, it might be argued that the British should have felt morally obligated to provide for the protection of the people. Little was done toward this end, however, and virtually nothing that cost money. Consider, for example, the following set of official figures: During fiscal 1939–40, which ended just prior to Italy's entry into the war, Malta's colonial government spent only a tiny fraction of 1 percent of its budget on civil defense. During the following year, however, after the British had decided not to abandon the island after all, the figure soared to 35 percent, and in the year after that to more than 50.[10]

It wasn't as if the Maltese failed to express concern over the matter. Since the first meeting of the Council of Government under the new constitution in the summer of 1939, opposition members had repeatedly called upon the colonial administration to start digging deep underground shelters to protect the civilian population against high-explosive attacks. Even the Constitutionalists registered surprise that the government was doing so little in the construction of "dug shelters," or rock shelters as they soon came to be called. But the colonial administration refused to be pushed, with the result that between the outbreak of war in September 1939 and Italy's entry into it the following June, only three rock shelters were started, and none finished, at a total cost of £322 (about $1300). This was less than one-twelfth the amount spent during the same period for maintaining the boys' reformatory.[11]

The government's position was that rock shelters were unnecessary because people would be just as safe in their own homes. "The houses of our towns are solidly built and will stand anything but a direct hit," declared a civil defense pamphlet that had been prepared and distributed during the Abyssinian crisis some four years earlier. Now, as if Barcelona and Warsaw had never happened, it was being recirculated in its original form. According to the pamphlet, even a direct hit could be survived if people took a few simple precautions, such as standing under an archway to protect themselves against a falling ceiling.[12] Years later a retired schoolteacher would remember a meeting that he and other members of the recently created Special Constabulary had with the governor only a few days before the war:

> He was not at all worried about the civilian defense situation. He said: "Now, tell the people not to be afraid of bombs. We tested your houses and they are very strong. Unlike our houses in England yours are built of strong materials and won't be damaged by bombs." Then he told how he personally had gone to a farmhouse with a demolition team and put bombs all around it, and when they were exploded the house wasn't hurt a bit. In fact, even the rabbits out back kept nibbling at their lettuce. "Private homes are the safest places to be," he said. "Tell the people not to leave them under any circumstances."[13]

For those who happened to be caught outside during a raid, however, public shelters were available—a total of thirteen, all in the Grand Harbour area. Actually these so-called shelters were nothing more than ordinary buildings with hand-lettered signs to identify them as places of refuge. Some, like the Auberge d'Auvergne, which housed the law courts, were government owned, while others, such as Mamo's Garage and Bonaci's Premier Bakery, were private places of business that, perhaps for the free publicity, had been made available at no cost to the government. Until just before the war none of these buildings was supported by sandbags or structural reinforcements of any kind. Few even had first-aid equipment.[14]

But, as the colonial administration was wont to point out, all this worry about high explosives was probably irrelevant anyway. When the Italians came, they would most likely come not with high explosives but with gas, and the people would do well to forget about bomb shelters and prepare themselves for this much more deadly and horrifying weapon. From the beginning the British authorities seemed to have had little doubt that Italy would rely mainly on gas, and they proceeded to direct their civil defense efforts (such as they were) accordingly. Ask any person who remembers life on Malta just before the war, and he or she will attest to the almost evangelical fervor of the government's campaign to ready the island for gas, to the virtual exclusion of all other protective measures. "Everything was gas, gas, gas in those days," recalled a Maltese professor a generation later. "The British could think of scarcely anything else. I suppose it was due to the fact that Italy had used it in Abyssinia, or it might have been their bad memories of the 1914–18 war. Whatever the reason, they were positively fixated on gas."[15] A Maltese noblewoman agreed:

> It is simply incredible that we were left so vulnerable and uninstructed. It is hard to know whether to attribute this to stupidity or criminal negligence. In any event, it was inexcusable. . . . The British cared nothing for anything but gas, and I will say that they went to some lengths to protect us against it. We were all issued respirators [gas masks], of course, which I suppose were the same ones we had been given during the Abyssinia days. I recall that each one came in a box and was awkward to carry around, but the authorities insisted that we take it everywhere with us—even to bed. It was really a great nuisance, and, as you know, we never did have to use it.[16]

Unlike the shelter program, which was scarcely mentioned, the government's antigas crusade was given a great deal of publicity through pamphlets and circulars, the press, wall-posters, and rediffusion radio—all aimed at instructing the people on the proper care of their respirators and the best means of defense against an attack. A dozen or so "safety centers" were set up, again all in the Grand Harbour area. As with high explosives, however, the home was supposedly the safest place to be, provided it were properly prepared. Excerpts from a government circular tell how this could best be accomplished:

> Have a special gas-protected room selected and ready in your home . . . of the proper size to accommodate the number of people likely to use it. The room should be on an upper floor, NOT on the ground floor, for gas sinks to the ground level and stays there.
>
> The selected room . . . should have the least number of openings (doors, windows, fireplaces, etc.); these as well as joints and cracks should be stopped up with rags, papers or similar materials. The room should be divided from the rest of the house by solid walls . . . and should face away from prevailing winds.[17]

Wet blankets were to be hung over all doors and windows opening onto the room in order to sop up any gas that might leak through. It was also recommended that a supply of certain medicines and other precautionary items be kept on hand, including chlorinated lime as a disinfectant. When it was discovered, however, that chlorinated lime when wet gives off a poisonous gas of its own, it was quickly stricken from the list.

By following these instructions the islanders would supposedly be able to protect themselves from gas within the walls of their own homes. In actual fact, though, for most Maltese families the instructions were not very realistic: In more homes than not, there was no upper floor to repair to; nor, for that matter, was there any room (downwind or otherwise) that could be spared from the needs of everyday living; or blankets; or the extra money to purchase the recommended medicines and other supplies. Here, as would so often be the case during the war, the British authorities showed surprisingly little awareness of the actual conditions of life for most people on the island, and their Maltese assistants, either out of diffidence or embarrassment, did little to enlighten them.

Still, insofar as gas was concerned, the British made an honest effort to protect the people. Or did they? There were those, especially among the Nationalists, who thought not, and still do. According to them, the respirators that were issued were leftovers from the Abyssinian crisis. In many cases the rubber had become porous, the stitching had begun to give way, and the filters needed replacing. Worst of all, there weren't enough of them. A head schoolteacher then living in Valletta remembers having only four respirators for his family of seven. "The authorities were very good about telling us what we should do in case of gas, with their directives and what have you, but there simply weren't enough respirators to go around, and this caused great concern among the people."[18] A Maltese doctor recalls being in charge of one of several teams sent around the towns and villages to demonstrate a special respirator to be used for infants too young to be fitted for masks. Great care was taken to instruct mothers in its use, and yet when the war came, there were not more than a half-dozen of these devices on the entire island.[19] "It was all just camouflage, you know," declared a retired Maltese cable operator in looking back on those days a generation or so later:

> The British had decided that Malta was untenable and they didn't want to go to great expense in protecting something they were going to lose. I've always thought that they concentrated on gas because that was the cheapest way out for them. All this business with the respirators and the like was just a token. A camouflage.[20]

Perhaps so. The point can be argued either way, but the larger point cannot: Whether out of callous intent or unthinking negligence (or possibly both), the British failed to provide adequately for the safety of the civilian population. As the war drew perilously near, the Maltese people still had no casualty centers, no first-aid stations, no emergency medical plans, no paid civil defense workers of any kind, no effective plan for evacuating the principal target areas, no special provisions for the safety of their children while in school, and, finally, no rock shelters to repair to in case of high-explosive attacks. All this was, of course, consistent with Britain's plan for an early and inexpensive surrender of the island, and therefore, like the absence of a proper military force, made a good deal of sense. It was not, however, a very nice way to treat old friends.

4 The Hand That Held the Dagger

It is doubtful whether during those few months just before Italy's entry into the war many of the islanders had a clear understanding of the danger facing them, or even gave much thought to it. Caught up in the routine of their daily lives, the Maltese left such alien matters as military strategy and civil defense to the authorities and, by and large, believed them when they said there was no need to worry. Events outside the island during most of this time did little to create alarm. After Hitler's lightning takeover of Poland in September 1939, fighting remained at a standstill, as the opposing armies glowered at one another from behind their heavily fortified positions on the western front. For more than six months this so-called phony war, or sitzkrieg, continued, with no indication from Mussolini that he had any intention of joining forces with Hitler. In fact, at the very beginning of the conflict the Duce had announced that Italy would "take no initiative in military operations," and throughout that autumn and winter he lived up to his word, as he watched with the eye of a vulture to see which way the fortunes of war would turn.

Meanwhile, after a brief flurry of excitement following the outbreak of hostilities between Germany and the western Allies, life in Malta had resumed its normal course, or virtually so. Although a blackout remained in effect throughout this period, gradually the curfew and other restrictions that had been imposed at the outset of the war were lifted or relaxed. Christmas passed in peace, and the early months of the new year were generally untroubled. Business returned to its prewar tempo, and except for the absence of the fleet, shipping came and went as before, with only an occasional reminder of the still faraway conflict: One day the trooper *Mariette Pacha* steamed dolefully into Grand Harbour, its bow badly mangled by a collision at sea. The ship was loaded with African troops, many of whom had been killed or maimed in the accident. Workers at the docks were sickened by the sight and smell of so much death and by the groans of the dying. On both sides of the harbor people lined the heights to catch sight of these strange, dark-faced creatures who sat huddled together on the deck, stunned by their experience. "In their small red fezzes," a Maltese writer reported, "they looked like a troop of circus monkeys caught in the spotlight."[1]

Spring came on warm that year, with a resplendence of wild flowers and oleander. Now, more than ever, war was only a word, a distant anomaly that people read about in the papers and saw depicted in British newsreels at the cinema in Valletta or Sliema. Despite sporadic scolding from the authorities, respirators were left at home to mildew in the closet, and the anxieties of the previous September were all but forgotten. But suddenly, beginning in the second week of April, a shattering sequence of events would put an end to the island's make-believe world and plunge Malta into a cruel struggle for survival. First came Hitler's easy conquest of Denmark and Norway. Then in early May the Wehrmacht began its relentless surge through the Low Countries that would drive the British into the sea at Dunkirk, demoralize the French army, and set the stage for the fall of France a few weeks later.

To these events Mussolini reacted about as expected. Like a jackal sniffing the scent of blood he grew increasingly bold with each new German success, and increasingly concerned lest Italy not be on hand to share in the kill and, of course, partake of the spoils. "We Italians are already sufficiently dishonored," he told his son-in-law and foreign minister, Count Galeazzo Ciano, in mid-May. "Any delay is inconceivable. We have no time to lose. Within a month I shall declare war. I shall attack France and Great Britain in the air and on the sea."[2] Two weeks later the Duce informed Hitler that he would enter the war on June 5.

The Führer was not overjoyed. He would have appreciated Mussolini's aid earlier to relieve some of the pressure on the western front, but now, with the French army falling back in disarray and victory over France expected within a few weeks at most, Italian involvement would probably prove more of an embarrassment than a help. Therefore, Hitler politely suggested that Italy could best serve the common purpose by waiting in the wings until a more appropriate time. But Mussolini would not be dissuaded. He did agree to put off his attack, but only until June 10, leading the Germans to assume that the Duce had "something brewing" for that date. When informed by Gen. Enno von Rintelen, their military attaché in Rome, that he knew of no major military or naval operation planned by the Italians. the Germans concluded that Mussolini had gone to great lengths to keep the whole thing secret. Obviously he had something special in mind. To both the German High Command and Abwehr (German Intelligence) an invasion of Malta or Tunisia, or perhaps both, seemed the most likely possibility.[3]

When the day came, however, it soon became apparent that the Duce had no such surprises to offer. Aside from, as President Roosevelt put it, plunging the dagger into the back of his neighbor France, he had neither prepared for nor even drawn up plans for any immediate strike against the enemy. The Germans were appalled. At the very least they had expected Mussolini to seize Malta, which with the collapse of France would soon take on a new (and critical) strategic importance for the British. His failure to do so was as incomprehensible to them as it was stupid and inexcusable. "Italy's missing the chance to occupy the island at the start of hostilities," German Field Marshal Albert Kesselring later reported, "will go down in history as a fundamental blunder."[4]

But the Duce had his reasons. For years this posturing little man, with his bombastic talk of restoring the Roman Empire, had somehow succeeded in convincing the rest of the world that under his leadership Italy had become a major military power. It hadn't, of course, and no one was more aware of this than the Duce himself. At the time of Italy's entry into the war he had little confidence in the Italian army and not much more in the navy.

The army was particularly suspect. Besides those units stationed in Africa, it contained forty divisions, which, according to Marshal Pietro Badoglio, Italian chief of staff, were totally unfit for battle. They had few vehicles of any kind, no heavy tanks, and an insufficient supply of ammunition. "We don't even have shirts for our soldiers," he told Mussolini not long before the war, and he might have added that there was also a serious shortage of shoes. "War is suicide," the marshal warned. None of this came as any surprise to Mussolini, who was fully aware of the army's sorry state of readiness but was nonetheless determined to take Italy into the war in time to pick up some easy plunder in the form of French territory. "You see the war only from the narrow military point of view," he told Badoglio. "I look upon it in its general and political aspects."[5]

The Italian navy was something of an anomaly. In many ways it was very impressive; in others, sadly deficient. Compared with the British Mediterranean Fleet, which, with France gone, would be its only naval adversary during the battle for Malta, the Italian navy had a decided advantage in overall tonnage, number of ships, and firepower. Of the British vessels only the *Warspite,* flagship of Admiral Cunningham, who had recently succeeded to the Mediterranean command, could fire effectively at a range equal to that of any of the six Italian battleships. Furthermore, the Italian navy had excellent speed and maneuverability (except for its submarines) and, at the outset of the war, first-rate communications and gunnery systems. Perhaps its greatest asset lay in the number of its lighter ships, especially its destroyers and torpedo boats, in which it greatly outweighed the British. Add to this a submarine force at least five times as large as the enemy's, and the Italian fleet seemed very menacing indeed.

But, like the army, the Italian navy was badly flawed. For the sake of speed and economy its ships were not so heavily plated as those of the British and therefore less able to withstand enemy fire. They were also short of modern detection equipment and antiaircraft predictors. More important was the lack of an air arm, including a total absence of carriers, which not only limited the offensive capabilities of the fleet but also left it vulnerable to enemy air attack beyond the 200-mile range of land-based fighter protection. For years the Italian navy had been calling for carriers, or, failing that, at least a few land-based planes under its own command. However, these requests had been repeatedly turned down by the Duce, who accepted the air force's argument that the fleet had no need for carriers, since it would be unlikely to go beyond the reach of fighter cover from Italy or the North African colonies. As for having its own land-based planes, the navy would do well to stick to its ships and let the air force take care of the flying.

Thus, without any air support of its own, the Italian navy was forced to go to the air force, hat in hand, whenever it wanted help overhead. This was an awkward and, for the navy, a humiliating arrangement that would cause much ill feeling between two sister services frequently called upon to work closely together. Relationships were not improved when at the Battle of Punta Stilo early in the war, Italian pilots spent six hours bombing their own fleet instead of the enemy's, while the fleet blasted back at them and the British looked on in disbelief. "The battle was not a fight between British and Italians," Count Ciano noted ruefully in his diary, "but a dispute between our sailors and our aviators."[6] When Supermarina (the naval high command) complained once again to the Duce about this intolerable situation, it was told not to worry: The war would be over within six months.

Another problem facing the Italian navy was its submarine fleet, which, although among the largest in the world and generally manned by well-trained crews, was inferior in most other respects. Its vessels were slow, cumbersome, and not very versatile. Compared with German submarines of equal size, they had a surface speed of several knots less, took twice as long to dive, and were unable to descend as deeply or stay down as long. These deficiencies made them highly vulnerable to attack, especially in the clear waters of the Mediterranean, where, even at their maximum depth, they could often be spotted by enemy aircraft. To make matters worse, their periscopes were not long enough, so that in order to fire their torpedoes they had to come dangerously close to the surface. Given these circumstances, it is not surprising that as the war progressed and his submarines suffered increasingly heavy losses, the Duce tended more and more to keep them at home. When Hitler questioned Mussolini about the inactivity of his underwater fleet, the Duce complained that the Mediterranean was not a fit place for submarines to operate, which, as far as the Italian subs were concerned, was true. Had it been otherwise, the battle for Malta would almost certainly have had a different outcome.

By far the greatest weakness of the Italian fleet, however, and one over which it had little control, was the shortage and uncertainty of its fuel supply. With no domestic production to speak of, Italy had to import virtually all of its petroleum, an all but impossible task once the war broke out. Thus, after exhausting their meager reserves early in the conflict, the Italians were almost always short of oil, so much so that in order to keep them in the war Germany would be forced to send them periodic allocations from its own supplies. Even so, Italy seldom had enough oil to meet its needs, including those of its navy. Time and time again, often for several weeks running, capital ships were forbidden to leave port, and when permitted to do so, were usually under orders limiting their range and speed. Similar but less stringent restrictions were imposed on the smaller vessels. These and other difficulties arising from a lack of fuel help explain why the Italian fleet missed so many opportunities to engage the enemy at an advantage, why it sometimes broke off contact when victory seemed all but won, and why it failed on more than one occasion to intercept thinly protected merchant ships with their thousands of tons of precious cargo bound for Malta. As the conflict wore on, this oil shortage became increasingly serious. By the autumn of 1941 the allocations from Germany had dwindled to barely one-third the promised amount, and left the Italian fleet virtually paralyzed at the very time the battle for Malta was about to enter its most critical phase.[7]

So the Italian navy had its share of problems, which in the long run would reduce it to near impotency. Nevertheless, at the outset of hostilities many of these problems had not yet made themselves felt, at least not enough to interfere seriously with an invasion of Malta. At that time, and probably for some months into the war, the Italian fleet should have been able to support a landing operation against the island with a minimum of difficulty and risk. Fuel was not then the worry it would later become, nor, with land-based aircraft available from nearby Sicily, would the lack of carriers have been a concern. Best of all, the British fleet probably would not have intervened. British Foreign Secretary Anthony Eden might boast that "an attempted invasion of Malta supported by the Italian fleet would surely give the Royal Navy the opportunity of which it has dreamed,"[8] but it was unlikely that the British would choose to engage the Italian navy in a major encounter so close to the enemy's home bases and the main might of its air force—which is why the Mediterranean Fleet had withdrawn from Malta in the first place. As for the landing operation, while the Italian army left much to be desired, it could surely have fielded a sufficient force to seize an almost totally undefended island. In other words, when the war broke out in June 1940, and for some time thereafter, Malta was ripe for the picking. Mussolini needed only to reach out for it, and not very far at that.

But perhaps all this is clearer now than it was at the time. Basing their calculations on reports from Italian Intelligence (which grossly overestimated the strength of Malta's defenses), Mussolini's military advisers informed him that the assault force should consist of no fewer than 40,000 well-trained, well-equipped troops, supported by light field pieces. Even then there could be no guarantee of success. Much would depend upon getting the men ashore quickly, and since the navy had only a limited number of landing craft, problems could easily arise, especially if the sea came up rough. Still, it seemed probable that the island could be secured within forty-eight hours. Meanwhile, the fleet would be expected to stand offshore in support of the operation.

When projected in these terms, an invasion of Malta might have seemed not altogether inviting to the Duce. Obviously there would be an element of risk. What if the British defenses were stronger than reported? What if the wind or sea failed to cooperate during the landing? How would the Italian troops, who had not performed with great distinction in Abyssinia or Spain, fare against hardened British regulars? And the biggest question of all: What if the Mediterranean Fleet should receive advance word of the operation and return to the island? Instinctively the Duce feared the British fleet, perhaps because he understood something of the deficiencies of his own. One of his guiding principles throughout the war would be to avoid naval encounters with the British except in the most "predictably favorable" circumstances—and the circumstances confronting Italian ships having to remain stationary for forty-eight hours while supporting a landing operation could hardly be considered "predictably favorable." Perhaps for this reason, more than any other, the Duce passed up the proffered gift of Malta, which would probably have won the battle of the Mediterranean and North Africa for the Axis.

On the other hand, there is reason to believe that Mussolini had never actually given serious thought to a land invasion of the island. Since the mid-1920s the Duce had been an avid disciple of fellow-Italian, Major (later General) Giulio Douhet, generally recognized as the world's leading philosopher and prophet of strategic air power. According to Douhet, whose writings on the subject would revolutionize modern warfare, future conflicts would be characterized by an increasingly defensive role for conventional land and naval forces, while air power, with its unique ability to strike swiftly and with deadly results at long range, would be "the solely effective offensive weapon." Armies and navies would be helpless before it; the enemy's factories and transportation systems could be reduced to rubble; and, most important of all, the will of the civilian population could be undermined by unremitting waves of attackers. "A people who are bombed today as they were bombed yesterday and who know they will be bombed tomorrow and can see no end to their martyrdom, are bound to call for peace in the end." In addition to high explosives, Douhet recommended a liberal use of poison gas, which no doubt contributed in some measure to the gas fixation of the British authorities on Malta.[9]

During the 1930s Mussolini proceeded to build the Regia Aeronautica into a formidable weapon. By the time Italy entered the war, its aircraft numbered somewhere between 2500 and 3000, of which more than 1500 were operationally ready combat machines. While not especially well designed or constructed, these planes did have many superior features and on balance were probably competitive with anything the British might send against them, as well as being vastly more numerous. There is no question that the Regia Aeronautica was the apple of the Duce's eye. He fawned over it like a doting parent, referring to its pilots, including his own son Bruno, as "my young eagles." With Italy poised to enter the war, an estimated 350 bombers and 200 fighters stood ready on Sicilian bases only twenty minutes flying time from Grand Harbour. Here was the weapon Mussolini had determined to use in his campaign against Malta. In keeping with Douhet's formula, he would simply bomb the island into impotency. In that way he could avoid the complications and risks of a landing operation and also spare himself the trouble of occupying the place and perhaps having to defend it at some future time against enemy counteraction. After all, Malta had no positive value for Italy, strategic or otherwise. The important thing was to nullify any worth it might have for the British, and this could be accomplished by rendering it unusable as a base of any kind. As the Duce himself repeatedly stated, Malta must be "neutralized"—an objective perfectly suited for the special talents of his young eagles.

By the beginning of June it was apparent that Italy was about to enter the war. On the first day of the month, a Saturday, the influential Roman publication *Relazione Internazionale* announced: "The moment we have been waiting for for fifty years has arrived. The Italian people will fight their French and British enemies with the greatest determination until final victory." It was expected that Mussolini would make the official declaration on the following day, or possibly Monday. But both days passed, and several after that, with no word forthcoming from the Duce. On June 6 Count Ciano's Leghorn newspaper, *Il Telegrafo,* declared, as if referring to a soccer tournament rather than a war, that it was unthinkable for "a people like ours, with all our energy, to remain outside of a great contest like the present one in which all the great peoples of Europe are participating."[10] On the following day all Italian merchant ships were ordered to head immediately for friendly or neutral ports, and in Valletta the Italian consul general closed shop and left for home.

Meanwhile, the full gravity of the situation had finally caught up with the people of Malta, who, after those first few anxious weeks of the previous autumn, had by and large come to view the war as only a distant abstraction that, like all others before it for nearly 150 years, would somehow pass them by. Despite blackout precautions and respirators and talk of prime target areas, the idea of actual involvement in the war had never seemed entirely real. But now suddenly with the events of early June, all this changed, and the mood of the island grew sober and apprehensive. Churches were filled to overflowing all day long, every day. Religious processions were seen in the streets of every town and village. Newspapers were snapped up as soon as they reached the stands, and people huddled around their radios, awaiting the latest word from Rome.

Even the authorities were at last stirred to action, although not to the extent of spending much money: Schools were ordered closed until further notice and the buildings turned into reception centers for casualties; doctors were registered for emergency service; some first-aid equipment was provided for the public shelters; and, civilian volunteers were organized to serve as air raid wardens and rescue workers. A curfew was imposed, which forbade any person from straying more than five yards from his front doorstep during the hours from dusk to dawn, and special ordinances against looting were put into effect. All road signs and milestones were ordered taken down or defaced, perhaps with the idea in mind that if the invading troops couldn't be turned back by military action, they might get lost. When the government received the report (false, as it turned out) that the Italians had assembled paratroop units in Sicily, it called upon the island's bird hunters to register for possible action against chutists. On the first day two thousand men arrived with shotguns. Finally, with time running out, the authorities agreed upon a warning system for enemy raids, and then, through a mix-up, classified it secret and temporarily withheld it from the people.[11]

A good deal of attention was given to the danger, real or imagined, of disloyalty. On the eve of the war about sixty of the more prominent Nationalists on the island were rounded up and placed in detention centers, where, without anything even resembling a trial, they were kept in close confinement until most of them were deported to Uganda nearly two years later.* Among those arrested were many of Malta's most illustrious political and intellectual figures, including the island's chief justice, an elected member of the Council of Government, and several university professors, newspaper editors, and high-ranking members of the clergy. The rest were for the most part laborers from the Three Cities who had been under suspicion for some time as leaders of pro-Italian elements among the dockyard workers. According to the colonial authorities, security required that these persons be detained. Some islanders saw things differently, however. To them, the arrests represented another move by the British and their Constitutionalist stooges to destroy the Nationalist Party. "I don't doubt that some of those who were seized might have been a bit of a nuisance if left loose," a relative of one of the detainees explained some time later:

> But I can assure you that most of the higher types among them would *never* have considered doing anything to jeopardize the safety of the island. Still, you see, this was too good a chance for their political opponents to pass up. The war provided them with an excellent pretext, and they made the best of it.[12]

In retrospect it does seem that the authorities were overzealous in their search for "quislings" (now a common noun), and not only among pro-Italian elements. Instructions to police and civil defense personnel contained frequent reminders to be attentive to all reports and even rumors of disloyalty or defeatism and to forward the identity of any suspect to the commis-

*See below, pp. 154–57.

sioner of police, "but in no case will the name of the person giving the information be divulged."[13] Many years later a Maltese doctor would recall those days when the people of the island were "set against one another":

> The government deliberately created a climate of fear and distrust. The point was soon reached at which good friends hesitated to confide in one another, and of course enemies were given a perfect opportunity for settling old scores. People were so afraid of being thought disloyal that they sometimes tried to prove their patriotism by reporting a neighbor's slightest indiscretion. The whole thing was vicious and unforgivable.[14]

Nevertheless, it worked. Not once during the war was there a known instance of espionage or sabotage on the island, nor were there any serious incidents of defeatism—or so at least the official records read. According to British accounts, the Maltese were from start to finish solidly behind the war effort and unwavering in their determination to sacrifice what they must in order to win. "Oh, they behaved very well, very well indeed," a British resident of the island remarked long after the smoke had cleared. "Many of my friends would say to me at the time: 'Just wait; you'll see it.' But I told them: 'No you won't see it.' And I was right. The Maltese were with us all the way."[15] This was certainly true, but as some of the natives later observed, they really didn't have much choice. Said one:

> I wouldn't want to say that the British held a pistol to our head, but they certainly succeeded in impressing upon us, sometimes in not very subtle ways, how we were expected to behave, and as a timid people who were used to being told what to do, it would never have occurred to us to step out of line. If things had been left up to us, however, I'm sure we would have acted differently. In fact, I doubt that Malta would have gone to war in the first place. After all, we had no argument with the Italians, nor they with us. I think most of us felt that it would be nice if the British simply left and took their war with them. . . . But, being a subject people, we were in no position to decide on such matters, or even voice a very loud opinion.[16]

Shortly after six o'clock on the evening of June 10, 1940, the Duce appeared on the balcony of the five-hundred-year-old Palazzo Venezia, headquarters of his Fascist government in the center of Rome. Dressed in a Black Shirt uniform, with the red stripes of an honorary corporal in the Fascist militia, he announced to the wildly cheering thousands crowded into the piazza below and to the world at large, that on the following day Italy would enter the war. "With you," he exclaimed, hands on hips and jaw thrust forward in seeming defiance of all creation, "the whole world is a witness that Italy has done all that is humanly possible to avoid the hurricane that is overwhelming Europe, but all was in vain. . . . We must break off the territorial and military chains that are strangling us." And then: "I solemnly swear that Italy does not intend to drag other people who are her neighbors by sea and by land into the conflict. Switzerland, Yugoslavia, Greece, Turkey, and Egypt must take note of my words."[17]

No mention was made of Malta.

5 The Opening Round

The first day of the war with Italy came on clear and warm, with only a slight breeze and barely a blemish in the intensely blue Mediterranean sky. From dozens of lookout stations on the main island and Gozo there was no sign of enemy aircraft or ships. By 6:30 many of the island's housewives had finished their daily haggling at the outdoor markets and were headed for home. Just like any other day. Most of their menfolk had already left for work, including the more than 3000 who were due at the dockyards at 7:00. Shortly before 6:50 the island's radar picked up a number of tiny specks several miles to the north. A call went in by field phone to Defense Command Headquarters in Valletta, and a moment later the sirens began to wail—a baleful overture to the first air attack of any consequence ever launched against the British Empire.

There were ten planes in all, flying in V formation at an altitude of nearly 14,000 feet. Although scarcely visible to the naked eye, through binoculars they were recognizable as tri-engine Savoia Marchetti 79s, Mussolini's best. While still some distance out at sea, three of them peeled off from the rest and headed for Hal Far aerodrome on the south coast, where they unloaded their bombs harmlessly upon the empty landing strip and the workshop complex of the fleet air arm at nearby Kalafrana. The other seven flew directly toward the Grand Harbour area, while all about them little puffs of white and gray began to appear as the island's heavy antiaircraft guns vainly thundered their defiance. One of the first bombs scored a direct hit on Fort St. Elmo near the tip of Valletta, killing six soldiers of the RMA—Malta's initial casualties of the war. Other bombs fell on nearby Msida and Pieta. But it was Cospicua in the Three Cities that suffered the greatest damage. Years later a British resident of the island would still remember the terrible fear and commotion of that first raid on Cospicua:

> At 6:50 A.M., . . . when congestion at the dockyard gate was at its highest, the siren sounded. The crowd looked anxiously at the sky. "Practice," muttered some of the workers, as if to quell the fears of the others. "Manoeuvers," muttered another one, with an air of satisfaction. Then someone came running from behind the crowd. "Air raid!" he shouted. "Come on, run!" It was that shout that set the crowd in motion, the words that many were expecting but were afraid to utter.[1]

Like a herd of frightened animals the workers surged through the gate and rushed for shelter inside the dockyard compound. Here many found safety in tunnels dug centuries earlier by the Knights to house their galley slaves. Others crowded into the partially completed deep-rock shelter that Adm. Kenneth Mackenzie had ordered constructed for the workers shortly after he took over command of the dockyards in 1939. Perhaps he hadn't been told, or refused to believe, that the island was to be written off, or perhaps he thought he should do what he could to protect the lives of his workers—just in case. At any rate, with a foresight rare in the Malta of those days, the admiral had opted to dig in. "The high rock wall which surrounds the dockyards is a God-given gift," he had declared. "Let us make the most of it."[2]

Outside the dockyard gate the regular residents of Cospicua were not so fortunate. For them there were no safe shelters to go to, and when the bombs turned out to be high explosives rather than gas, the people streamed out of their homes in panic and started running toward the Corradino highway tunnel nearly half a mile away. By now the raid had ended, but the frenzied flight continued. As they passed by scenes of death and devastation and the acrid odor of cordite tore at their lungs, a people unaccustomed to violence became terror-stricken and began stampeding mindlessly toward the tunnel. When old people fell or fainted, it was imagined they had been machine-gunned by the enemy, and they were stepped over and left to fend for themselves. Overhead thousands of pigeons swarmed out of the Three Cities on their way inland to escape the noise and the columns of thick yellow dust that had risen to a height of a hundred feet or more above where the enemy bombs had landed.

For some time after the raid, life throughout the entire harbor area was at a standstill. Buses stopped running. The streets were empty and silent. Inside the Corradino highway tunnel and in the inner recesses of thousands of homes, people remained huddled together like cornered animals—frozen in fear and disbelief. A few minutes before 9:00, however, the spell was broken when Mussolini's young eagles returned with another load of bombs. Shortly thereafter small groups of evacuees began leaving the communities adjacent to the harbor—the vanguard of what would soon become a mass exodus. Later the colonial governor, William Dobbie, would say of the people's conduct on that first day: "In the trying circumstances in which they found themselves they behaved beautifully, as I knew they would," a generous remark but not a very truthful one.[3] Actually they behaved about as might be expected, considering that the British had done so little to prepare them for what was almost certain to come, sooner or later.

As far as anyone could recall, not a single air raid drill had been held, either for gas or high explosives. In many instances the people hadn't even been properly informed about the warning signal, and some of the outlying towns, such as Mellieha, were not notified of the first air raid until half an hour after the enemy planes had returned to Sicily.[4] Although the all-volunteer Air Raid Precaution Corps (ARP), dating back to the Abyssinian crisis, had been reactivated a few days before the war, its wardens and other members had received virtually no training in the actual performance of their duties, and in some cases had been provided with incomplete or conflicting instructions. As a result, once the bombs began to fall there was confusion on all sides, with no one really qualified to step forward and take effective charge of the situation. "Much of the suffering and panic of that first day could have been avoided if the British had given us a clearer idea of what to expect and what to do when the time came," a Senglea doctor later remarked. "Everyone thought afterwards that the authorities should have done more to prepare us."[5]

In the matter of evacuation, the colonial government seemed especially unconcerned. As far as can be determined, no measures were taken to provide for the prior removal of civilians from areas that were likely to come under attack. In fact, there is nothing to suggest that pre-evacuation was even considered. Nor, for that matter, was any other kind of organized removal until the very eve of the war. As late as May 31, only ten days before the first raid, the following general instructions were sent out to the island's Special Constabulary:

EVACUATION: The evacuation of any particular town is not envisaged; it is however anticipated that the public may voluntarily evacuate some places after heavy bombing. In this contingency special constables will shepherd the people and try to avoid panic and confusion.[6]

During the final days preceding the war the government finally gave some thought to postattack evacuation and went so far as to draw up plans for residents of bombed towns in the Grand Harbour area to be moved, if they wished, to safe sister towns in the interior. For example, if the occasion should arise, the people of Floriana would be sent to Mosta, and those from Sliema would go to Birkirkara, where temporary accommodations would be found for them. By the time of the outbreak of the war, however, these plans had scarcely progressed beyond the paper stage, with the result that when the bombs came, most of the refugees simply headed out on their own.

The largest exodus, and the most frantic, was from the Three Cities and nearby Paola (Pawla). From midmorning until well after curfew the roads leading out of the area were clogged with thousands of people, vehicles, and animals, all headed for the greater safety of the interior. There in strange new surroundings the refugees, many of whom had never before set foot outside their own village, would find lodgings with relatives or friends, or, in some cases, total strangers. A Cospicua shopkeeper recalls having fled with his family to Rabat, six miles inland from Grand Harbour, where he had never been before and knew no one: "Eventually we found a house in a narrow street. It belonged to an old man and his two daughters. They were very pleased to put us up." Their host was kind, and the shopkeeper and his family were most grateful to him and, of course, to the Blessed Virgin. But it was not like being home in their own village where they belonged: "I have always liked my house, but now all of a sudden I find myself imposing on other people, whom I have never seen before."[7]

Some of the refugees traveled by car or bus, with their most treasured household belongings strapped to the top. The majority went by bicycle or on foot, however, carrying what they could on their backs. A few of the more fortunate, like the Jaccorinis of Senglea, had their own donkey carts. Fr. Mario Jaccorini, then a boy of twelve, would remember helping his father and younger brother pile the cart sky-high with furniture and other family valuables:

We had arranged beforehand to go to an uncle's in Oormi. But it was very hard to decide what to take and what to leave behind. Our cart was not very big, and our little donkey could pull only so much. But *this* had to go, and *that,* and we couldn't leave Papa's chair behind. Finally, when we tried to put a mattress on top of everything else, the cart tilted back and the poor donkey went up in the air. That was when we knew we had a full load.[8]

Once out on the main road heading west, the Jaccorinis found themselves caught up in a pushing, shouting stream of frightened people. Pregnant women hurried along with little children clinging to their skirts so as not to get separated in the confusion. Occasionally an elderly person would cry out in despair and collapse in the road. When the bombs began to fall again, even though now a safe distance to the rear, some of the refugees became hysterical and rushed off in all directions. Others, especially the elderly, fell to their knees and became transfixed in prayer. Scattered among the crowd were several macabre figures who had been caught out in the earlier raids and were covered with limestone dust from the blasts, so that everything about them except their eyes had taken on the eerie shade of ocher. A few were wounded and were still trickling blood, which kept their powdered faces and limbs streaked with bright red markings and left them looking like creatures from the dance of death.[9] Along the way the older children would occasionally scuffle with one another over splinters of spent antiaircraft shells found along the roadside—treasured souvenirs that would soon be among the most plentiful items on the island. Somewhere in this grim procession was Angelo Grima, a shepherd from nearby Tarxien, who with his wife, twelve children, and fifty goats, was headed for Rabat, where they would all spend the next two years living in the stable of a stranger.[10]

The road leading south from the Three Cities was much the same. A man then living near Zabbar remembers hearing the people coming from some distance away:

There was a sound, a shuffling crescendo sound, as of a big herd of cattle coming nearer and nearer, and soon this sound revealed itself. It was not cattle, but human beings coming from the nearby city of Cospicua in a state of great distress. Many were crying in despair because they had left neighbors and loved ones behind, buried beneath the debris.[11]

Just outside the Zabbar Gate lay four dead bodies, swollen from the heat and covered with flies. As the refugees hurried by, they crossed themselves and began to wail like wounded animals. By nightfall the Three Cities were all but deserted. Later, Archpriest de Brincat of Senglea, who stayed behind with what remained of his flock, estimated that during the early days of the war with Italy, all but 300 of his 8,000 to 10,000 parishioners fled, most of them during the first twelve hours. "I well remember the horrors of those terrible days in which everybody waited for death to come without knowing what war meant."[12]

There were eight raids that day. The last and largest occurred an hour or so before twilight and centered on Marsamxett Harbour, on the other side of the Valletta peninsula, where the main submarine base was located and the monitor *Terror* was tied fast alongside the shore. During the raid the waterfront towns of Gzira and Sliema were struck repeatedly by enemy bombs, which destroyed dozens of buildings and would have caused heavy casualties if most of the residents had not already fled from the area. "And on this note," one of the islanders would recall years afterward, "the first day came to a close. The civilians of Malta had had their first taste of war, and as darkness fell we all went to bed, with the fervent hope that the Italians would not be able to fly at night."[13] Some time later, after families had been reunited and the ruins inspected, a more or less official estimate was made of the damage done civilian property and personnel on that first day: over 200 buildings completely or partly destroyed; 36 people killed, 22 of them in the Three Cities area during the first raid; and 130 injured seriously enough to require medical attention.

Given the amount of physical damage, casualties were surprisingly light—a tribute to the good sense of the people, who chose to run rather than remain shut up in their gasproof rooms. The Regia Aeronautica also helped hold down the carnage by dropping only light bombs (mainly 50 kilograms), which in contrast to what would come later, had a limited blast effect. Or, as a British officer explained: "Their bombs go 'pop,' when they should go 'bang.' " Even so, it was a day of great suffering and sadness for the Maltese people. A shame that they would soon forget some of the lessons so painfully learned by them during those early hours of the war, thereby setting the stage for far greater horrors to come in the not-too-distant future.

During the first two days of the war, between 60,000 and 80,000 people fled the Grand Harbour area. Some communities, most notably the Three Cities, Gzira, and Sliema, became virtual ghost towns. Others, such as Valletta and Floriana, where the bombing had been less severe, retained only a small fraction of their normal population, barely enough to keep them going. On the third day an evacuee of Cospicua returned to the town and found "the wilderness of a desert." Houses were locked and shuttered, shops closed, and the streets deserted except for scattered squads of ARP volunteers—and cats, hundreds of them crying pitifully for food and water. The ARPs were working their way slowly through the remains of a hundred or so demolished buildings. Occasionally the members of a crew would cry out in excitement as they discovered a body, living or dead, amid the debris. Halfway down Oratory Street an ARP team heard what sounded like a puppy whimpering beneath a pile of rubble. Upon removing several large blocks of limestone, they found two small children, hungry and frightened but unharmed, trapped under the partially open lid of a large wooden trunk, where they had apparently been placed for protection when the bombs came. Beside them was the dead body of their mother. "Surely it must at least have occurred to the authorities," a Maltese government worker remarked years later when it was no longer dangerous to say such things, "that the enemy might use high explosives and that, if they did, all our preparations against gas would be worthless."[14]

Meanwhile the Gzira-Sliema waterfront presented a similar picture of desolation. Here too, except for the cats and ARP workers the area was all but deserted. Many families had left notes on their front doors telling where they could be found: "Gone to B'Kara. St. Pawl Road. God bless all of you who remain." But very few did remain. One of the last to leave would recall walking the entire length of the esplanade on the morning after that first evening's raid without seeing another living soul. Where only the day before yesterday families and young lovers had strolled by the hundreds along the shore, taking in the cooling breeze and watching the gentle swell of the sea against the sloping ledge below, there was nothing now but solitude and foreboding silence.

Although the first day's raids had left a heavy mark on the civilian population, they had inflicted little military damage. Only minimal harm was done the harbor facilities, and even less to Hal Far aerodrome and the maintenance sheds at nearby Kalafrana. Nevertheless, the day had clearly belonged to the Regia Aeronautica and the ghost of Guilio Douhet. Through repeated bombing attacks those civilians living in the most populous and strategic part of the island had been demoralized and put to flight. For the time being, activity in the immediate vicinity of Grand Harbour had been brought to a virtual standstill, and by any reckoning that represented a good day's work for the Duce's young eagles. There was only one discordant note: Returning from the first raid, the trail bomber was ripped through the fuselage by a surprise burst of machine-gun fire—which is how the Italians came to discover that Malta had an air force.

Not much of one, to be sure, but the island's defenders counted themselves fortunate to have any at all. The whole thing had begun as a mistake when in early April the carrier *Glorious,* ordered from Alexandria to the North Atlantic, left the Mediterranean in such a hurry that it neglected to stop by the Kalafrana slipway and pick up eight disassembled fleet fighter aircraft that had been assigned to it as reserves. Eventually news of the passed-over planes reached Malta's air officer commanding, F. H. M. Maynard, a quiet but forceful New Zealander who did the unheard-of thing of asking the navy to turn them over to the Royal Air Force for defense of the island. In Alexandria, Fleet Admiral Andrew Cunningham had already received word from London that the fighters would soon be taken on by another carrier. Still, he agreed to stick his neck out halfway and let Maynard have four of them, even though, as he was later reminded, giving away navy property was not considered good form, even for an admiral. "It is almost unbelievable," Cunningham wrote some time afterward, "but a month or two later a signal was received from some Admiralty department asking why I had permitted Fleet Air Arm spares to be turned over to the Royal Air Force. I wondered where the official responsible had been spending the war."[15]

The four planes were speedily assembled at the Kalafrana workshops and towed a mile or so to the airstrip at Hal Far, where they were immediately concealed in hangars. In those days, right up to the eve of the war, an Italian commercial airliner flew into Malta every afternoon, ferrying spies in and out and taking hundreds of pictures of the harbors, aerodromes, gun emplacements, and anything else of possible military interest. Since Italy was still officially a friendly country, there wasn't much the British could do to prevent this. They did mean to see to it, however, that their new fighter planes remained a secret for as long as possible. Remarkably enough, in spite of the dozens of workers involved in assembling and servicing them, and who can say how many nearby farmers and shepherds who saw them take off and land several times daily in training exercises, no word of the four planes reached the enemy. Their appearance in the skies over Malta on that first day of the war came as a complete surprise.

Finding men to fly the planes presented no problem. At that time there were perhaps as many as a dozen qualified pilots stationed on Malta, most of them in administrative positions. Although none had flown fighters, all volunteered to serve. Seven were eventually chosen and were assigned at once to an intensive training program. Fortunately there was nothing fancy or notional about their planes. They were the old reliable single-seater Gloster (or Gloucester) Gladiators, the last and best of the British biplanes. Although then being phased out of service in favor of faster and more maneuverable craft, such as the Hurricanes, the Glads were still excellent equipment, capable of giving a good account of themselves in any fight—provided they managed to get there on time. There is no denying they were slow, with a top speed of less than 240 miles per hour. They were also rather clumsy. But with their all-steel fuselage and powerful 840 horsepower Bristol Mercury engine, they were exceptionally rugged. Furthermore, their four Browning .303 machine guns, two of them synchronized through the propeller and two mounted under the lower wing, gave them a wide and effective field of fire. The men who flew them likened them to flying tanks. The Maltese called them "carts," because from the ground their silhouettes looked more like donkey carts than planes.

During the first few days of the war, three of the Gladiators were sent up to meet each of the attacks, while the fourth was kept in the hangar to be cannibalized for replacement parts. With the Italians reappearing day after day, however, damage to Malta's tiny air force began to mount, which meant that more and more time had to be spent on the ground for repairs. There was also the attritional effect on the pilots, who, because of fatigue and nervous strain, were soon put on three shifts of two each, with an alternating backup man. Thus, after the first week the number of Glads in combat at a given time was never more than two, and sometimes only one.

Many tales have been told (and still are) about the three brave little planes that came to be known as *Faith, Hope,* and *Charity*—in honor of Saint Paul, who had such special meaning for Malta. Over the years their exploits have been enormously magnified and embroidered. It has been said that they shot down as many as forty enemy planes. Actually they probably accounted for no more than five. They have also been credited with so unnerving the attacking planes by their daring and skill that Italian bombs were often aimed too hurriedly and fell harmlessly into the sea. The truth is, however, that the Glads were seldom able to break through the curtain of Macchi fighters that accompanied enemy bombers after the initial raid. In fact, it is unlikely that in a strictly military sense the presence of the Gladiators made any appreciable difference. But their effect upon the islanders' morale was incalculable. "They made us feel that we were fighting back," a Maltese businessman later explained, "and that was terribly important to us during those early days of the war when everything seemed so dark. They gave us something to cheer about."[16]

And they were well worth cheering—*Faith, Hope,* and *Charity,* and the men who flew them. Day after day for weeks running, at least one of the three Gladiators would be in the air for every raid, challenging an enemy force of sometimes fifty planes or more. At first between raids the on-duty pilots stayed in a shack by the side of the runway, but so much time was lost getting to their aircraft that they soon took to remaining in their cockpits. Here they would sit, often for hours at a time, with parasols shielding them from the blistering sun, while they leafed through magazines or wrote letters home, and crewmen worked around them replenishing the planes with fuel and ammunition and patching them up as best they could. When the siren sounded, the Glads would be off in no time, climbing to as high as 20,000 feet, from where they could help compensate for their lack of speed by diving down upon the enemy raiders. For the pilots there were no rules, save one: Bring the plane back. And somehow they did, for longer than anyone would have thought possible. With their fuselages riddled with holes, their wing staves shot off, and large pieces missing from their rudders, the stubby little planes would come fluttering home for a few hours' respite, and then fly off to do battle again with the cream of the Italian air force.

This was sheer madness, of course, but all the same it was tremendously stirring to see those brave men go aloft time after time against such impossible odds. After the first few days thousands of Maltese in the outlying communities would rush to their rooftops at the first sound of the siren to watch their heroes in action and cheer them on. The little planes became objects of great affection and pride, while the men who flew them were lionized with an almost religious veneration. Wherever they went, they were mobbed by an adoring public, hoping to get near enough to touch them or hear them speak. In hundreds of homes newspaper pictures of one or more of them hung on the wall beside those of Jesus and Mary. And when after five incredible weeks the first of the sparrows fell, all Malts wept.

Three years later the cannibalized carcass of *Faith* was found in an abandoned quarry. It was all that remained of that little band of Gladiators listed in the records as Station Fighter Flight #1, the rest having been shot to pieces or otherwise destroyed without a trace. After pounding out its dents, replacing several missing parts, and applying a coat of black and gray paint, the RAF presented it in a fitting ceremony to the people of Malta as a remembrance of things past. Today it may be seen in the National War Museum in Valletta, wingless but otherwise looking much the way it did in the wartime skies over Malta.

As for the seven pilots, such uncommon men deserve to be remembered. They were:

Pilot Officer Peter Alexander	Killed in action, flying out of Gibraltar, 1942.
Flight Lieutenant George Burgess	Survived
Flying Officer Peter Hartley	Shot down over Malta, July 31, 1940. Survived, but badly burned over much of his body.
Flight Lieutenant Peter Keeble	Killed in action over Malta, July 16, 1940.

Squadron Leader A. C. "Jock" Martin	Killed in action over Belgium, 1941.
Flying Officer J. L. Waters	Survived
Flying Officer W. J. "Timber" Woods	Killed in action over Greece, 1941.

Ad astra per ardua. To the stars the hard way.

6 *Guerra Lampo*

The surrender of France in late June, only two weeks after Italy's entry into the war, drastically altered the power equation in the Mediterranean theater. With the French fleet and air force now neutralized, the British would have to carry the entire burden of Mediterranean defense. Worse than that, they would have to do without the use of those French bases in North Africa and France itself that they had counted on so heavily in their prewar strategy planning. Once France left the war, the Italians automatically assumed a commanding and seemingly unassailable position in the Mediterranean, with their naval and air bases in Sicily, Sardinia, and Libya, and on the tiny island of Pantelleria at the choke point of the Sicilian narrows. Opposed to this, Britain had Malta as her only foothold between Gibraltar and Alexandria, and needed desperately to hold onto it if she hoped to prevent the Mediterranean from becoming an Italian lake. Thus, the little island that had so recently been written off as indefensible or not worth the effort, now suddenly became indispensable to Great Britain's plans, and perhaps her very salvation.

All this more or less vindicated what Britain's new prime minister, Winston Churchill, had been saying all along. Churchill, who had taken over from his doddering predecessor in early May, had never reconciled himself to the expendability of Malta. Regardless of French fortunes, he had always looked upon the island as essential to Britain's power in that part of the world: not only could it offer a haven for British vessels at their most vulnerable point along the Gibraltar-to-Alexandria run, but it could also provide an excellent forward position for offensive thrusts against enemy shipping, bases, and supply depots in the central Mediterranean. He referred to Malta as "our unsinkable aircraft carrier" and, within a month after taking office, reversed the policy of his predecessor and ordered the island held at all costs. "It is a duty compulsive upon us," he declared. And to those who argued that Malta would be too hazardous to defend, he answered that he for one was not impressed by the fighting qualities of the Italian fleet, despite its strength on paper. He didn't doubt that there would be a considerable risk involved, especially from enemy aircraft, but "from time to time . . . this risk will have to be faced. Warships are meant to go under fire." Top priority was to be given to bolstering Malta's antiaircraft defenses and getting fighter planes there as soon as possible.[1]

But how soon would that be? Britain may have thrilled the free world by snatching its men safely from the beaches at Dunkirk, but it had left behind virtually everything else and was now desperately short of matériel with which to defend the home island against a German invasion expected at any time. Therefore, regardless of Churchill's good intentions, Malta would get precious little in the way of military equipment for some months to come. In fact, aside from a few Swordfish torpedo planes flown in from nearby French bases in late June, and four lonely Hurricanes that Malta's AOC Maynard practically kidnapped on their way to Alexandria, the island received no help at all for several weeks. Finally in early August a squadron of fighters were flown into Luqa off the ancient aircraft carrier *Argus*.

These twelve new fighters, all Hurricanes, were a most welcome addition. The Hawker Hurricane was an excellent plane in almost every respect. A single-seater with an underslung wing and a 1000 horse power Rolls Royce engine, it could climb rapidly and despite its heavy ordnance was highly maneuverable, especially at medium altitudes. The first of the British fighters to carry eight machine guns, the Hurricane had a combined firepower of 2500 rounds. This was not the plane that would finally win the contest for the skies over Malta. The Spitfire, an even classier aircraft, would do that. But until the Spitfires arrived in the spring of 1942, the Hurricanes would be the mainstay of Malta's fighter force, such as it was.

The arrival of the twelve new fighters that August certainly helped, but they were far too few to be a serious deterrent to the overwhelming numbers of aircraft the Italians could send against the island. Even RAF figures, which tended to be self-serving, conceded that Malta-based fighters "destroyed, seriously damaged, or slightly damaged" only thirty-two enemy planes during the first five months of the war—an average of one and a half a week, which was hardly an impressive showing.[2] The most that could be said for the island's fighter force at this time is that its presence served as a continuing reminder to the Regia Aeronautica that its visits would not go unchallenged aloft. The big question, of course, was how long before more fighters would be flown in, and during the late summer and autumn of 1940, with Britain battling for its life against the Luftwaffe, the prospects of any kind of fighter reinforcements in the foreseeable future were not very bright.

In the meantime, despite repeated pleas from the colonial governor for more troops and antiaircraft equipment, no help was received until early September, when three merchant ships laden with several thousand tons of food and military matériel reached Grand Harbour under naval escort from Alexandria. This was the first of the famous Malta convoys of World War II, and like so many of its successors it arrived bloodied by the enemy, although on this occasion with its cargo intact. Included in the shipment were eight heavy AA guns and ten Bofors (light AA), along with supporting equipment.[3] This was a move in the right direction, but not much of one. At this rate it would be a long time, perhaps too long, before Malta's antiaircraft defenses would be able to put up much of a showing. And where were the troops?

Where indeed? Since July, Churchill had been trying his best to get troop reinforcements to Malta. At first he had asked for four battalions but was persuaded by the War Office to settle for two. "But we must have two *good* ones," he insisted. Some time later, however, he learned that the two battalions he had expected to be sent to Malta had been assigned instead to Freeport in the Bahamas. The prime minister was not pleased and, after some difficulty and delay, managed to get the troops rerouted to Malta. Shortly thereafter, in late September, he wrote to the secretary of state for war, expressing his "dismay":

> It is now agreed that the two battalions will be sent as reinforcements; but after how much haggling and boggling. . . . Do you realize that there is no command of the sea at Malta, and that it might be attacked at any time by an expeditionary force of twenty or thirty thousand men from Italy? Yet it was proposed that these two battalions should go to Freeport to complete the brigade there, although no enemy can possibly attack Freeport while we have command of the Atlantic Ocean. You will, I am sure, excuse my putting some of these points to you.[4]

Thus, throughout the long summer of 1940 Malta stood alone and, in the words of its colonial governor, "unbelievably weak, both in men and matériel, hopelessly, even ludicrously, inadequate." Fortunately, though, the Italians persevered in their course of missed opportunities by failing to take advantage of the island's continuing vulnerability. Instead of occupying Malta, they proceeded to pick away at it with high-level bombing, confident that Giulio Douhet's doctrine of unremitting air attack would eventually reduce the island to surrender—or impotence. And perhaps it would have if implemented properly, but what the Duce liked to call his *guerra lampo* turned out to be a far cry from the German blitzkrieg upon which it was modeled. In fact, after the first week, during which there were thirty alerts resulting in some 250 casualties, the frequency of the raids fell off dramatically. By mid-July there were fewer than eight alerts a week. For the entire month of August the number was down to twenty-two, with only five or six resulting in any real damage; and, for a period of about two weeks during the early part of that month, there were only three actual bombing attacks against the island. It was almost as if the Regia Aeronautica had become bored with Malta. Furthermore, as the summer wore on, the size of the raiding forces tended to be smaller, generally no more than five bombers with an escort of perhaps a dozen fighters.

The reason for this slackening off is not clear. Some of the islanders boasted that the cowardly Italians were afraid of Malta's guns and fighters, but this was just talk and few people really believed it. More realistically, the dwindling attention given the island by the Italians that summer may have been due to their impression that they had already successfully neutralized it and that, aside from an occasioanl "refresher" raid to remind the people of exactly how matters stood, no purpose would be served by further bombings. Except for fishing boats and other small craft, the harbors had become completely emptied of shipping. The *Terror* had departed for safer waters soon after the first raids, and even the few submarines that had been on hand at the outset of the war had left Marsamxett Harbour for Alexandria. As for the aerodromes, by mid-July they had been bombed repeatedly for over a month, and hardly warranted further attention. True, the dockyards had not been entirely eliminated, but according to Italian reconnaissance, they had been badly damaged and, with no ships to attend to, had become irrelevant anyway. Meanwhile, with each passing day the island's reserves of food and other supplies were further depleted. Under the circumstances it could be argued that the Italian air force showed good sense by biding its time, conserving its energies until Malta gave it ample cause to renew its *guerra lampo*.

But if this were indeed the reason for the Italians' low level of activity during those early months, why, later when it clearly behooved the Regia Aeronautica to come down hard against the island, did it fail to do so? Why on several occasions that autumn did it allow Malta to be reprovisioned without making a determined attempt to prevent it? Why were precious cargoes permitted to reach Grand Harbour intact, and, even more mystifying, why were they permitted to be unloaded virtually unmolested by Italian bombs? From mid-October to mid-November, while Malta's harbors were astir with incoming traffic, the number of air alerts dropped to seventeen. For eighteen days during that period not a single enemy aircraft approached the island. On only three days was there more than one raid.[5] At the same time, despite Hitler's polite demurrer that they really weren't needed and probably could be used to better effect elsewhere, Mussolini insisted upon sending two hundred of his finest first-line planes to assist the Luftwaffe in the Battle of Britain, presumably in order to share center stage.

This unaccountable lack of attention, while certainly welcome to the Maltese, was also a bit worrisome. Could the Italians be up to something? In the late summer a terrifying rumor swept over the island that enemy submarines were secretly chipping away at the three (some said four) underwater limestone columns that supposedly supported Malta like a giant table top. This meant that at any moment the entire island might go plummeting to the bottom of the sea—which is probably as good an explanation as any for the strangely nonchalant behavior of the Italian air force during the summer and autumn of 1940 when Malta lay practically helpless before it.

Even on those increasingly infrequent occasions when the Italians raided the island, they failed to accomplish much. Not that they weren't good at their job. They were, in fact, very good. Some day perhaps the cliché of the cowardly, fumbling Italian soldier will be permanently put to rest. When well led, well equipped, and well motivated—which admittedly was not often the case during World War II—the Italians were first-rate fighting men, and the young eagles of the Regia Aeronautica were among the bravest and the best. According to all who actually engaged them in combat, they were excellent pilots and, given the altitude at which they operated, were highly accurate with their bombing. Admiral Cunningham, who came up against them on more than one occasion, had the greatest respect for the daring and ability of the Italian airmen, especially during the initial stages of the war before their cream had been killed off. "It is not too much to say of those early months," the admiral later wrote, "that the Italian high-level bombing was the best I have ever seen, far better than the German."[6]

This is not the same as saying, however, that the Italians were very effective with their bombing. Because of their rigid adherence to high-level attacks and their inferior ordnance, they seldom succeeded in inflicting significant damage. The main problem was the size of their bombs, which were simply too light to unleash much of a blast effect. To destroy a specific target of any size or sturdiness, Italian bombadiers had to score a direct hit on it, and although they were good, at 12,000 to 14,000 feet they weren't *that* good. To make matters worse, a substantial number of their bombs, perhaps as many as 10 or 15 percent, failed to explode at all.[7]

The situation was made still more difficult for the Italian raiders by the fact that, Guilio Douhet notwithstanding, they obviously took great pains to limit their bombing to military objectives. On several occasions ground monitors reported overhearing enemy airmen cautioning one another not to harm the civilian population.[8] Perhaps this was part of a calculated campaign to reassure the Maltese people of the Duce's good intentions toward them and possibly loosen their ties to the British, or perhaps it was simply a compassionate gesture toward old friends. Whatever the reason, by all accounts Italian planes did not "go for the people." Indeed, to avoid doing so they tended to shade their bombing toward the least congested segments of their target areas, with the result that an estimated one-third to one-half of all Italian bombs landed in the sea. This naturally led people to believe that the Italians were poor marksmen. It also created great opportunities for Maltese fishermen, who would rush out in their boats immediately after enemy bombing runs and skim huge harvests of dead and stunned fish from the surface of the water.

Only twice during the summer and autumn of 1940, that period commonly referred to as the first Italian phase, did the enemy raiders deviate from their set pattern of high-level, precision attacks with light bombs: Once in August and again in September the Regia Aeronautica dive-bombed the aerodromes at Hal Far and Takali, with twenty to thirty planes carrying medium-weight bombs. Little damage was done either time, mainly because the Italian pilots were unskilled in dive-bombing techniques. In fact, these raids would hardly be worth mentioning were it not that the Italians were flying Junker 87s on loan from the Germans for training purposes. This marked the first appearance of the dreaded Stukas over the island. Within a few months they would return, this time in far greater numbers and with experts at the controls, bringing with them sorrowful days for Malta.[9]

But all this lay some distance in the future. Meanwhile, life on Malta gradually adjusted to the conditions of war. For some people the accommodation was more difficult than for others. Hundreds had lost their homes and virtually all of their belongings. An even greater number had been affected by the death of a loved one, for although there were relatively few fatalities from the early raids, the fact that Malta was a nation of closely knit extended families meant that each loss was deeply felt by dozens of relatives, as well as fellow villagers. Others among the islanders had experienced psychological shock. Many had become badly disoriented. During the days immediately following the outbreak of the war, public medical officers reported a steady stream of patients suffering from a variety of psychosomatic ailments, such as paralysis or loss of speech.[10] Several others had been scared literally out of their wits and would have starved to death, cringing in their cellars, had they not been removed by force. Don't worry, the fiercely pro-British *Times of Malta* advised its readers after the first few raids. "It takes nearly a week for human beings to get accustomed to this new life."[11]

For those thousands of Maltese who fled the target areas for the interior, the initial trauma of the bombings was compounded by the anguish and hardships of evacuation. It was no easy matter for a family to leave its home and village in order to live under someone else's roof and worship in a church with unfamiliar saints looking on. In most cases the refugees were received with great kindness, whether taken in by relatives, friends, or complete strangers, but their accommodations often left much to be desired. A Sliema businessman who had lived the good life, surrounded by comfort and cleanliness in his coastal villa, had left everything behind and fled with the others when the bombs began to fall. With his wife and two children he found refuge in the home of a poor farmer. Next door to his new quarters was a stable with a foul stench and a horse that kept kicking the wall. All this was a far cry from what he and his family had been used to, but he was thankful to the Blessed Virgin that they were all still alive and well.

The main problems of resettlement stemmed from overcrowded conditions, which could have been avoided or at least alleviated if the colonial authorities had done more to prepare for a well-ordered evacuation. On the day *after* the war began, the government announced that refugee centers would be set up in inland towns for the purpose of receiving evacuees and finding them places to stay. But by the time the centers were open, practically all of the refugees had made arrangements of their own, and most of them ended up living in not more than half a dozen towns just outside the main target areas. As a result, these communities mushroomed. Both Hamrun and Birkirkara, for instance, grew from their normal size of about 10,000 each to four times that number by the evening of the second day of the war. Densely settled even in ordinary times, these villages and others like them were now unbelievably congested. Often as many as thirty people lived under one roof—all using the same kitchen facilities and sharing a common cesspit. Amazingly, there were no epidemics, and, on the whole, the health of the people appeared totally unaffected. Still, it was an awkward and unpleasant experience for everyone concerned, especially for the refugees, who in addition to all their other hardships and inconveniences, were forced to live in an alien setting. And who could say when all this would end and they could go home again, if indeed they still had homes to go to?

As disturbing as the various physical effects of the enemy attacks were, they counted for little when compared with the awful spiritual anxieties suffered by the islanders. When the six Maltese artillerymen were killed at Fort St. Elmo during the first raid of the war, a priest rushed to the scene only to discover that the victims had died instantly in the blast. Their souls had obviously already departed from their bodies, and it was therefore too late to administer extreme unction. Word of this spread like a shock wave over the island. Among a people who had experienced little of violent death, or, for that matter, sudden death of any kind, the possibility of dying without first receiving last rites had never been a cause for much concern. In fact, the idea had probably never even crossed the minds of most of them. Dying was something a person did in bed, after having been properly confessed and annointed in order to prepare his soul for its journey into the hereafter. But now there was a very real possibility that the end might come at any moment without warning, and the soul would be sent on its way without having received the final sacrament of the church. What did this mean? Would it still be possible for a righteous man to enter heaven, or, deprived of extreme unction, would his soul wander indefinitely through the shades of purgatory?[12]

Church officials soon provided an answer that was somewhat, but not entirely, reassuring: While it was of course true that extreme unction should be received if at all possible, the sacrament was not absolutely essential for salvation. The important point was that a person be in a state of grace at the time his soul took flight, and, in the absence of last rites, this could be accomplished only by being pure of thought and deed at the time of, and prior to, the moment of death. Therefore, one must look inward and ask himself several times each day: If I should die before the hour is out, how would I appear in the eyes of the Almighty? Have I shown a helping hand and a generous heart to my neighbor? Have I praised the Lord and lived in such a way as to be worthy of His love? "Suddenly we became very well behaved," a Senglea schoolteacher would later recall. "We were trying to build up points while there was still time, you see."[13] Conscience money began to flow into the colonial treasury in unprecedented amounts to atone for past transgressions, real or imagined. Men abandoned their mistresses and went back to their wives. Illegitimate children were recognized and provided for. Backsliders returned to the faith. Good-for-nothing types who had previously idled their time away at the Marsa racetrack could now be seen sitting at home on their doorsteps, whittling likenesses of the Madonna. "Most of all, we were very kind to one another in those days, even in the little things, and every time a bomb fell and someone else's life was snuffed out before he could be attended to by a priest, we grew kinder still."[14]

But even Christian charity has its limits, and with the Maltese it certainly didn't extend to the enemy. When the bombs began to fall, the initial reaction of the civilian population was one of disbelief that the Italians could do such a thing. As the weeks passed and the raids continued, however, disbelief gave way to anger and then to that passionate sort of hatred usually reserved for perfidious friends or lovers. Pro-Italian sentiment, at one time so widespread, all but disappeared from the island, or went into deep hiding. So did the earlier notion that this war was none of Malta's business. By their deliberate and repeated attacks, the Italians had united the island almost solidly against them. "How different things might have been for everyone concerned if they had dropped only leaflets during those early weeks of the war," a Nationalist professor later lamented.[15] But they didn't. They dropped bombs instead—which, next to not taking Malta in the first place, was probably the Duce's second greatest mistake in his dealings with the pesky little island.

7 "*The Lord Has Spoken*"

How kind the gods were to have the Italians strike first, thereby giving Malta a grace period in which to prepare for worse days ahead, as well as the incentive to do so. Had there been no Italian raids to usher in the war, the government would probably have continued to do next to nothing in readying the island for its coming visitation from the Germans. As it was, during those six precious months of only light to moderate dusting from the Regia Aeronautica, the authorities took measures, which, although in many instances woefully inadequate, would nevertheless enable Malta to survive the awful ordeal to come.

First of all, the colonial government finally got around to organizing a more ambitious civil defense program, staffed almost entirely by native personnel. This was no easy matter. Among a people notably lacking in education and accustomed to being ruled by outsiders, there was a serious shortage of trained administrators. Also, for the most part the islanders suffered from a feeling of inferiority, a mark of their colonial status that left many of them ill suited for the exercise of authority—either because they were too reluctant or, in some cases, not reluctant enough to order others about. This lack of personnel who could be entrusted to take charge, even at the lowest level of responsibility, was a problem that would never be entirely resolved, although as time went on it became less serious. Recognizing the situation for what it was, the British responded by setting up parallel and often overlapping offices and procedures in the apparent hope that if one of them didn't get the job done, another would. This was probably a good idea, but the price was high in terms of jurisdictional squabbling, wounded egos, and chronic confusion. By the time the war with Italy was only a few weeks old, the islanders were taking orders from a bewildering array of new officials calling themselves district commissioners, protection officers, special constables, ARP wardens, and sanitation inspectors—many of whom often appeared to be working at cross-purposes with one another. "Sometimes it seemed to me that I was the only man on the whole island without an armband or whistle," a Maltese government worker later commented.[1]

Fortunately the problem was not so bad as it might have been because many of the civil defense workers held two or more positions concurrently. Emanuel Tonna of Floriana, for instance, was at one time a district commissioner, protection officer, and inspector of the Special Constabulary. He was also the town's head schoolteacher, which is not surprising, for the teachers were the mainstay of the island's civil defense effort. "Dear Albert," the colonial governor had written to Malta's director of education early in the war, "we're counting on you and your teachers to run things."[2] Albert was Dr. Albert Laferla, an unusually gifted Maltese administrator, who deserves to be listed among the real heroes of the siege. It was he more than any other person who, while somehow managing to keep the schools open during the war, also implemented and sustained the civil defense program by staffing its key positions with his most able teachers. He was, in effect, the program's czar, and, as befits a czar, he often dealt with a heavy hand. Because of his practice of volunteering their services for any position or chore he saw fit and otherwise ordering them about, his teachers denounced him bitterly as a tyrant. Still, they respected his ability to get things done and on the whole served him well—including young Elia Galea, who at the beginning of the war was teaching in the pleasant inland town of Rabat:

> Oh, yes, I remember Dr. Laferla very well. He was a hard man but very fair. When the war began, he assigned us to all sorts of jobs, such as special constables and ARPs. It was voluntary, you understand, but you'd better do it. All of the old and infirm teachers were transferred to safe areas inland, and the young ones were sent to Valletta and the Three Cities.
>
> When he told me I was being sent to Senglea, I asked him why the young were being so honored, and he told me: "Because you can run faster." So suddenly I found myself, even though I was very young for such a position, head schoolmaster of Senglea, replacing a jittery old man who was moved to a safe school.
>
> You see, the point was that the schoolteachers were going to be the shock troops of the civil defense effort, and it was necessary to have vigorous people in the target areas. As for running faster, at the time I thought Dr. Laferla was joking, but I found out differently the day the Germans came. I can tell you that![3]

Actually it made good sense to use the teachers wherever possible. They were the largest and most effectively organized group of government workers on the island as well as the best educated. They had the further advantage of being literate in both languages and through their teaching experience had received at least some practice in administration and the exercise of authority. For more than two years, often under conditions of almost unimaginable hardship, Malta's schoolmasters and schoolmistresses, in addition to carrying out their regular classroom duties, stood in the forefront of the island's civil defense effort. According to no less a judge than Francis Gerard, Britain's wartime director of information for the island and a man not given to easy praise:

> These men and women of the Education Department stood head and shoulders above the rest. They showed outstanding ability, initiative, and resource. They displayed tact, patience, and courage. They knew a firmer, quicker grasp of a situation than their fellows. They were uncomplaining and enduring. . . . More than any other section of the community in Malta, they came to the fore and proved their solid worth.[4]

In early January 1943, not long after the siege had been lifted, Dr. Laferla died, a thoroughly worn-out man. Shortly before his death in one of his final reports he congratulated his teachers on a job well done. "When the present hard times will merge into the past," he wrote in his usual, uneffusive way, "you will be able to look back with some satisfaction on your share in the war."[5]

During the summer and autumn of 1940 as the Regia Aeronautica continued to peck away at the little island, the various components of Malta's civil defense network fell more or less into place. Foremost among the program's hundreds of workers were the protection officers, of whom there was at least one in every village, with generally two or more assigned to the larger communities. Appointed by the lieutenant governor, usually on recommendation from the village elders, they were responsible for the welfare of the people within their jurisdiction in all war-related matters, save the spiritual. Was each family receiving its fair share of kerosene? Did the miller mix too much foreign substance with the flour? Was there room enough in the public shelters? Could accommodations be found in the area for additional evacuees? And more: In the early weeks of the war the little inland villages of Lija and Attard became so congested with refugees that a cesspit crisis developed: "Sir, since I now have more than twenty people living with me, the cesspit has to be cleaned out more than three times every month, which amounts to an extra expense of 18 shillings." Was it fair for the homeowner to have to bear this added cost? Why shouldn't the government pay for it? Furthermore, why should the cesspit cleaners be permitted to exploit the situation by charging such outrageously high prices? "Before Italy's entry into the war I was charged 3*s* for the cleaning of the cesspit of my house. This charge was then raised to 4*s*, followed by a further rise of two shillings to the abnormal price of 6*s*." In Lija the point was soon reached at which the cesspits were filling so rapidly that in order to keep down the cost of having them emptied the people were simply throwing their waste into the gutters—which, as one resident complained, was "not a very hygenic practice."[6] Surely the protection officer should be able to do something about such matters. And what of Tony Falzon and dozens of others like him who, even though their homes in the Grand Harbour area had been destroyed by bombs, were still having to pay rent to their landlords?

In time, as enemy bombs gutted some areas and overwhelmed others with refugees, the protection officers were forced to give more and more of their attention to the needs of the homeless. Still, much like the tribunes of ancient Rome, they continued to serve all of the people as best they could, and if at times they tended to be arbitrary, perhaps even a bit despotic, it should be remembered that their job was one of the most demanding on the island. In fact, virtually unique among civil defense assignments, it was eventually made into a full-time, salaried position.

Working closely with the protection officers were the inspectors of the Special Constabulary, one for each village (usually the head schoolmaster). Although a part-time volunteer worker, the inspector of the Special Constabulary was the most visible local official because of the wide variety of duties he and his men were called upon to perform. When first organized on the eve of Italy's entry into the war, the special constables were intended solely to handle the added burden of law enforcement brought about by the raids, such as seeing that blackout and curfew regulations were obeyed and that the people behaved in the shelters. But as the war progressed, the range of their activities increased, along with their numbers, until at times they appeared to have a hand in practically everything of importance that was happening. In late October 1940, for instance, on successive days the special constables were charged by the government with overseeing the collection of scrap iron in their village, conducting a census of goats, and escorting the kerosene wagon on its rounds to prevent the people from mobbing it. Later in the war they would be called upon to assist in doling out rations and even to help in the unloading of convoys. Meanwhile, in addition to all else, they were to keep a sharp lookout for quislings spreading defeatism or malignant rumors.[7]

To attend to all this required the services of 31 inspectors and 632 sergeants and constables, with teachers occupying most of the higher positions. On the whole the specials (as they were commonly called) were not well loved by those they watched over, especially during the early months of the war when many of them appear to have taken themselves too seriously:

Circular: Special Constabulary, July 12, 1940:

The good work of the Special Constabulary which has been praised by all sections in Malta, is running the risk of being spoiled owing to the manner in which many Special Constables go about their duty.

People are being subjected to an unnecessary amount of persecution with the result that in many cases the authority of the S.C. armband is losing much of its former prestige. Inspectors are requested to impress on all Specials that we must aim at co-operation more than intimidation. This should be particularly impressed on those extra zealous Specials who are found in every area. One example among many is the system by which three or four patrols of Special Constables in full view of each other, each stop an approaching car, in spite of the fact that the first had allowed it to proceed.[8]

Eventually, as the exercise of authority became more familiar to them, the specials grew less officious. But despite all their good works, performed entirely without compensation and often under conditions of extreme danger, they continued to be resented—probably to some extent because the people they were ordering about were their lifelong friends and neighbors. "They were necessary and helpful," an instructor at the university would later recall, "but they were also very obnoxious. They were forever throwing their weight around, as if that armband made them better than the rest of us."[9]

Of all the civil defense positions, that of air raid precaution worker was the worst, especially in the main target areas. Although the ARPs were responsible for helping the specials in such routine matters as enforcing the blackout and curfew and maintaining order in the public shelters, the most important part of their job began after the bombings. Immediately following the "raiders passed" signal, they would emerge from the shelters and search the surrounding area for unexploded bombs, booby traps, and other hazards, such as falling masonry. Not until they had declared the area safe was the "all clear" sounded. Only then were the people permitted to leave the shelters. That done, the ARPs rummaged through the ruins, collecting the bodies of the dead and dying, and in some cases digging out survivors who had been buried alive in their private cellar shelters. It was not a job for the weak of limb, or of stomach. Often it was possible to piece together bodies that had been blown apart. At other times, unidentifiable human parts were simply deposited into empty cement bags. With each ARP team there was at least one builder or mason, who knew where best to dig in order to prevent further collapse of damaged buildings. There was also a priest. Unlike the Special Constabulary the ARP was made up mainly of manual laborers, accustomed to strenuous work. Although classified as volunteers, they were recompensed at the rate of five shillings a day (about one American dollar) whenever their duties took them from their regular jobs. Not enough can be said about the courage and dedication of these men, who carried out what was a decidedly unpleasant and dangerous assignment. Not surprisingly, several of them would be cited for heroism, and many would be killed performing their grim tasks.

While these and other civil defense groups were being organized and eased into their duties during the first few months of the war with Italy, the military reinforcements so badly needed were slow in coming. As already mentioned, not until early September did the first meager shipment of matériel arrive, mainly antiaircraft guns and supporting equipment. A few weeks after that, however, help began to reach the island more or less regularly and in greater quantity. On the final day of September about 1200 troops came in on naval cruisers from Alexandria, followed in less than two weeks by a major convoy loaded with military stores of all kinds, including half a dozen light tanks that proved to be next to useless on the island's hilly, rocky terrain. About a month later, November 6–9, an ambitious and daring two-pronged operation was successfully carried out when a troopship with 2150 men reached Grand Harbour from England by way of Gibraltar, while at the same time a convoy of five merchantmen was brought in from Alexandria. A similar joint operation carrying several hundred troops and 20,000 tons of supplies arrived safely on November 26–27, followed in mid-December by four more heavily laden merchant ships from the East. In all, fifty-five merchant and naval escort vessels reached Malta during the final quarter of 1940, their passage contested only feebly by the enemy.*

In Berlin the reinforcement of the island was watched with growing concern by certain members of the German High Command, especially Hitler's naval chief, Adm. Erich Raeder. In early September, with the Battle of Britain already under way, Raeder presented the Führer with a plan for bringing the British to their knees without having to invade their home island. The plan called for sending German units to Libya to join the quarter of a million

*In order to avoid having to run the dangerous Sicilian narrows, most traffic to Malta at this time was sent by way of Capetown and the Suez Canal to Alexandria, an 11,000-mile route that added forty days to the trip.

Italian troops already there in an offensive against the British naval base at Alexandria and the Suez Canal. Once these had fallen, the British fleet would be forced to withdraw from the eastern Mediterranean, leaving the way clear for the Germans and Italians to continue their advance toward their ultimate objective: the rich oil fields of Iraq and Iran, which provided Britain with most of its military fuel. With their oil choked off at the source, what choice would the British have but to sue for peace? And as a bonus, the Axis would have Russia flanked on the south.

Raeder's plan had much to recommend it. With the surrender of France in late June, French contingents assigned to General Archibald Wavell's command in Egypt had been withdrawn, leaving the Army of the Nile in a precarious position. Not only was it outnumbered five to one by the Italians in Libya, but it was also critically short of field guns, tanks, and especially aircraft. A British defeat, in Raeder's estimation, was almost a foregone conclusion. And beyond the Nile there was nothing to oppose an Axis advance except a few underequipped battalions in Palestine and Iraq that could easily be ground to dust. In fact, according to Raeder, a popular uprising by the Iraqi could be engineered at any time against the British, who had ruled the country as a protectorate since World War I and were not widely loved. At most the entire operation would require only a few months and would cost very little in men and matériel. Of course, as a precaution Malta would have to be seized, thereby driving the British all the way back to Gibraltar and securing Axis shipping lanes to North Africa.

Hitler's rejection of Raeder's plan to capitalize on Britain's vulnerability in the Mediterranean theater may have cost him the war, for a German-backed offensive in North Africa and the Middle East at this time would probably have worked out much as the admiral had envisioned. At first the Führer expressed mild interest, but then backed off. The Mediterranean was, after all, the Duce's responsibility. Indeed, Mussolini himself had repeatedly insisted that each country wage its own separate war against the common enemy, with Germany fighting north of the Alps and Italy to the south. He referred to this arrangement as "parallel war," and considered the Mediterranean and North Africa the proper setting for Italian action. Within a few months the Duce's crumbling fortunes would cause him to change his mind and call upon Hitler for help, but up to that time he welcomed the Führer's assurance that "everything concerning the Mediterranean is an exclusively Italian affair." This was fine with Hitler, who had never had much interest in the Mediterranean anyway, or any other body of water. He was, as several of his advisers later pointed out, almost totally land-oriented, with little or no understanding of naval strategy. It is not surprising therefore that he re-

Malta cargo.

fused to act upon Raeder's advice. The admiral did not give up easily, however. From time to time over the next two years he continued to press his plan upon Hitler, and it may have been partly to placate Raeder that the Führer wrote to Mussolini in mid-November advising him to take more aggressive action to prevent British shipping from reaching Malta—advice that the Duce failed to follow, thereby giving the island two more months in which to strengthen itself for the big trouble ahead.

By the end of the year the number of British soldiers on Malta had almost doubled, and the two native regiments had been considerably strengthened, for a total troop presence of more than 10,000. This was not a very substantial force for defending the island against any serious assault, but it was a decided improvement over what it had been six months earlier, for in addition to being twice as large, it was better armed and equipped. The old Vickers guns, for instance, had been largely replaced by Brownings and Brens, and the presence of two new field batteries of twenty-five-pounders had given some muscle to the artillery. The most important gains, however, had been made in the island's antiaircraft defenses, which had been strengthened not only by more and better guns but also by the arrival of three crack batteries of gunners.

At the same time, Malta had acquired a modest air capability. According to official figures, on December 31 the following planes were based on the island's three airfields and at its flying-boat facilities in Marsaxlokk Bay:

One squadron (12) Swordfish torpedo bombers
One squadron (16, plus 4 reserves) Wellington bombers
One squadron (4, plus 2 reserves) Sunderland flying boats
One flight (4, plus 1 reserve) Glenn Martin Marylands
One squadron (16, plus 4 reserves) Hurricane fighters

In all, sixty-three aircraft, counting the reserves—a far cry from the lonely days of *Faith, Hope,* and *Charity*. Unfortunately, however, most of the planes were the wrong kind. The Swordfish and Wellingtons were both attack craft, while the Sunderlands and Glenn Martins were used primarily for reconnaissance. These were nice to have, but what the island needed mainly were fighter aircraft to reinforce its single squadron of Hurricanes. Without them Malta would continue to be highly vulnerable to enemy air attack, for although guns could be helpful, by far the more effective defense against bombers was fighter cover.[10]

But getting fighters to the island was no easy matter. Unlike the larger planes with their greater fuel capacity, the fighters lacked the range to fly in from Gibraltar or Alexandria. Unless brought in crated as ships' cargo, which could be done only in limited numbers, they would have to be flown in off a carrier. As already mentioned, this was done in early August when a squadron of Hurricanes reached the island safely from the deck of the *Argus,* and it would be done several more times during the next two years. But there were so many elements of danger involved that the undertaking was always a risky one. For one thing, the carrier dared not come too close to Malta for fear of enemy bombers, which could range 500 miles or more from their bases in Sicily, Sardinia, and North Africa. There was also the chance of being intercepted by enemy surface units or submarines, not to mention the whimsical Mediterranean weather, which could make both the takeoff and the flight itself extremely hazardous. Finally, there was always the possibility that the fighters, stripped of their guns and ammunition in order to increase their range, would be shot down like so many clay pigeons by waiting enemy aircraft as they approached the island for a landing. Still, it was a thing that had to be done if Malta were to survive, and generally it would be done without major mishap. Generally, but not always.

A few hours before dawn on November 15, 1940, the *Argus* again set out from Gibraltar with a dozen Hurricanes perched on its flight deck. Escorted by Vice Admiral Somerville's western Mediterranean fleet (Force H), including one battleship, a second carrier, and several cruisers and destroyers, the *Argus* hoped to repeat its successful "fly-off" of three months earlier. Code-named White, the operation called for the fighters to be flown into Malta from a point 400 miles to the west, roughly south of Sardinia. From almost the beginning, however, Operation White seemed star-crossed. Shortly before noon of the first day the convoy was spotted by a Spanish civilian airliner, which, the British assumed, meant that before long the Italians would know the size and location of Force H and would probably also have a pretty good idea of its destination. That evening the weather began to turn for the worse and by the following afternoon had become so foul that the escort carrier had no choice but to recall its reconnaissance and weather planes. At the same time Malta's Glenn Martins, which had been keeping watch on the Italian fleet, were forced to return to base, but not until they had reported sighting several enemy surface units, including one battleship and at least seven cruisers, standing north of Naples and seemingly up to something.

During the night the weather let up somewhat but remained uncertain. So did the intentions of the Italian fleet. Proceeding blindly eastward at better than fourteen knots toward who-could-say-what, Admiral Somerville came to a reasonable, although not very stout-hearted, decision:

> It seemed to me [he wrote in his official report] that (1) the Italians were probably aware of our departure from Gibraltar. (2) They might well consider engaging Force H with their superior forces. . . . In view of this I deemed it advisable to fly off the Hurricanes from a position as far to the west as weather would permit.

In other words, get rid of the planes as soon as possible and head for home. Early the following morning (November 17), with skies beginning to clear and brisk tail winds to help them along, the Hurricanes were flown off the *Argus* at a point some forty miles short of the designated takeoff area. Of the twelve, only four arrived at their destination. The others, their fuel exhausted, dropped into the sea before reaching the island. Only one of their pilots was rescued. "I guess we just ran out of air," he commented.[11]

At the official inquiry Admiral Somerville was absolved of all blame, and perhaps rightly so. His understandable concern for the safety of his fleet had caused him to release the Hurricanes sooner than he would have preferred, but at the time there was no reason to suppose that they would have any difficulty reaching their destination. After all, the flight was well within their maximum range. How could the admiral have known that shortly after their takeoff the wind would do a complete turnabout. Indeed, how could anyone, when forced to work with weather reports that were nineteen hours old because of the necessary recall of the fleet's weather planes the day before? Nevertheless, in some quarters the mention of Operation White still causes people to shake their heads sadly and say that the mission would never have ended so tragically if it had been handled by Admiral Cunningham, who, when faced with similar decisions, was seldom known to stop short of the mark. "It takes two years to build a ship," he once remarked after an especially bloody encounter, "but two hundred to build a tradition."[12] Back in London the prime minister was sorely distressed by the news, but made no attempt to fix the blame, except to say years later: "Never again would the margin be cut so thin."[13]

For Malta's colonial governor, Gen. William Dobbie, there was no need to wonder why the sparrows had fallen. He accepted the loss, like all things great and small, as the unfolding of God's inscrutable plan: Thy will be done! "The Almighty makes no mistakes. He knows what he wants and what is best." A member of the Plymouth Brethren, Governor Dobbie was a man of deep faith, simple ways, and unbending purpose—not unlike the Pilgrim fathers of early America after whom his sect was modeled. His obsessively pious nature, coupled as it was with his career as a professional soldier, caused many people to liken him to Chinese Gordon or Stonewall Jackson.

Churchill thought of him as "Cromwellian" and referred to him as "that extraordinary man." But the praise and honors of this world were wasted on William Dobbie, who held himself accountable only to the Lord.

For nearly forty years he had served the empire on three continents, until, upon turning sixty in the autumn of 1939, he went into mandatory retirement as a major general. But not for long. The war with Germany had just broken out, and Dobbie, still an alert and vigorous man, urged his superiors to return him to active duty in any capacity they saw fit. Throughout the winter he received little encouragement, but then one day in mid-April he was asked by the War Office if he would go to Malta as governor. He agreed at once. "It was a thing I had never dreamed of in my wildest flights of imagination, but that was what God had in mind for me." Later he admitted that he would have preferred some other assignment but "God does not always call us to walk in the path one would choose."[14] It is unlikely that he realized, then or ever, that like Malta itself he was considered expendable—a suitable captain for a ship that seemed almost certain to founder.

It is hard to imagine a better choice than Dobbie to take over as governor and commander in chief of Malta at this time. Not that he was an especially gifted administrator or military leader. He was, in fact, rather mediocre in both respects, as his record during his two-year tenure would bear out. Still, there was an undeniable element of greatness there—not in what he *did,* but in what he *was* and stood for. Someone called him "God's original honest man," which was high praise but didn't go far enough. He was also a righteous man, completely without guile or by-ends of his own, who insisted upon doing the proper thing, rather than the expedient. He never played favorites; he had no palace clique; and in the residency at San Anton he lived quietly and simply with his wife and spinster daughter, entertaining only when the occasion demanded and even then not very elegantly. "How we dreaded those awful dinners," the wife of a government official would recall many years later:

> There was absolutely nothing to drink, of course. Alcohol was never served in the governor's presence. Not even wine. The food was awful and the conversation deadly—what there was of it. The governor was not much given to small talk, as you might imagine. Sometimes he would just sit for long periods, saying nothing and staring into space as if he had gone into a trance. Perhaps he was talking with God. He did, you know.[15]

He was a stern and serious figure, a stickler for discipline and respect for authority. When he entered a room, even in the privacy of his home, his wife and daughter were expected to rise—not for Wiliam Dobbie, but for the governor and commander in chief of Malta. He was also hardworking, humorless, and intolerant of frivolity. And yet, those who had dealings with him and managed to survive the initial chill were invariably struck by his kindness and unfeigned concern for their welfare. It was as if he held himself personally responsible for everyone on the island. "He was a marvelous man," the wife of a British officer later exclaimed. "Absolutely marvelous. I don't know how we could have managed without him."[16]

The essence of his character was his intense spirituality, which kept him in constant communion with God and manifested itself most strikingly in his remarkable serenity. He was obviously a man at peace with himself, with neither fears nor doubts to cloud his vision. There was no problem too complex, no danger too great, or emergency too urgent to cause him to despair, for was not the Almighty Himself guiding his hand? Each night in his drawing room at San Anton he put aside a certain time to talk with the Lord, and each morning he would set out with new orders from above. And if unforeseen difficulties should arise during the day, the governor would frequently kneel in silent prayer wherever he happened to be and ask for divine guidance, after which he would rise, perhaps several minutes later, and proclaim: "The Lord has spoken, and so shall it be." Sometimes this could be hard on his associates. Melita Strickland, wife of the leader of the elected majority in the Council of Government, would remember one such occasion:

> Once early in 1942 during a meeting of the Council there was an especially fierce raid and Roger and the other members were half scared out of their wits. The palace was rattling; the chandeliers were swaying; and there was a general consensus, I think you might say, in favor of recessing the meeting and dashing to the shelter. But the governor went out onto the balcony and got down on his knees, with his hands clasped in front of him. After a little while he came back and announced: "The Lord has spoken, and so shall it be," and the meeting was continued. Just like that![17]

His appearance was striking. Over six feet, four inches tall and well proportioned, he dwarfed most of those about him, especially the Maltese, who are a small people. He was not what one would call a good-looking man. His head was too elliptical, his ears uncommonly large, as was his nose, and his complexion somewhat ashen. Still, there was something different, almost unique, about his face that commanded attention. Dostoevski would have called it "the pale, untroubled look of a religious nitwit." Others preferred to see it as an expression of beatitude. He spoke little, but when he did, his words were deep and resonant, and his message, which was often laced with the language of the Scriptures, was unmistakable. The people of the island regarded him with great reverence. More important, they had an almost intuitive faith in the strength and integrity of his leadership, particularly the Maltese, who stood in awe of his mysticism. It was almost as if he were another Saint Paul, this godly man from beyond the sea. As time passed, they came to look more and more to him for guidance and reassurance. Every week or so, and more frequently during the periods of heavy raids, he would speak to them over rediffusion radio, which was piped into the larger shelters, reminding them that God was still in control and that those who believed in Him need never be afraid. "He is the same today as He has always been. His hand is not shortened that it cannot save." Later, in his brief autobiography, a remarkable testament of faith, Dobbie noted with typical understatement: "It helped perhaps to turn the minds of the people away from their present difficulties and fears to the great God who alone could deliver."[18]

Meanwhile the governor went tirelessly about his duties as the island's chief civilian and military officer, oblivious to all danger and seemingly impervious to harm. "He really did appear to lead a charmed life," Melita Strickland said of him:

> He was forever popping up some place in the middle of a raid to check the damage and see how the people were faring. The bombs would be falling all around him, but he didn't pay the slightest attention to them, and as far as I know, he never once received so much as a scratch. It was really quite remarkable, and naturally this made a great impression on the people.
>
> Once while visiting the aerodrome at Takali, there was a terrible raid. The governor took no notice of it except to mutter something about the Lord having spoken and everything would be all right. Meanwhile his companions were pushing at one another in order to get as close to him as possible. My Roger was practically crawling up his sleeve.[19]

This was the man, with his simple, mystical ways, who would lead his people through the valley of the shadow—or at least all but the final mile of it. He would sometimes move in a mysterious manner, as will be seen, but like Tennyson's Galahad, his strength was as the strength of ten, because his heart was pure. Through seemingly endless days and nights of unspeakable horror he would hold the island together by his remarkable spiritual power over the people, which in time became almost messianic. Once, many years later, retired Maltese businessman George Zarb, who had worked under Dobbie during the war, reflected upon the governor and his place in Malta's history: "Churchill was right," he said, "in calling him 'that extraordinary man.' There was something very special about him, which I don't think anyone could put into words. All I can say is that we Maltese knew instinctively that he would see us through, and we followed him almost worshipfully." Of course, being a religious people the Maltese realized that in the end God's will would be done. "But," Zarb added, "few of us doubted that when the proper time came, God would fall in line with the governor."[20]

8 Counting Down

All things considered, it was not such a bad time, those early months of the war. The weather was exceptionally fine, even for Malta, and by and large the amenities remained undiminished. During the summer and early autumn, corridors were kept open through the barbed wire entanglements to allow access to most of the island's beaches, which were well attended by people of all ages. In the larger towns movie theaters continued to show first-run films brought in by mailplane from Gibraltar, although because of the curfew the last show now ended at 8:00 P.M. This left plenty of time for a leisurely pastry or soda at the nearby sweetshop before heading for home, where on those pleasant evenings a man might sit outside and chat with his next-door neighbors for an hour or so before going to bed—provided he didn't smoke, which would have been a serious blackout violation, or wander more than five yards from his doorstep. Late in the summer the curfew was relaxed to permit people to go where they liked, as long as they remained within their own village from dark to dawn. This was a decided improvement, but life was still hard for lovers unlucky enough to have sweethearts in other communities. Not surprisingly, the great majority of curfew violators reported by the special constables during those early months of the war were young men or boys, caught attempting to sneak to or from a girl friend in a neighboring village.

Gradually the refugees, prodded by homesickness and a growing dissatisfaction with life in the hinterland, drifted back to their own villages. Many were given added incentive for doing so by a number of official directives ordering all dockyard and other government employees back to work and threatening shopkeepers with loss of license unless they reopened for business. By the time school began in early September perhaps as many as three-quarters of the evacuees had returned to the Grand Harbour area, and life there, as elsewhere on the island, had resumed a more or less normal course.

As the bombing raids continued to diminish in size and frequency, they were taken more casually by most of the islanders, who soon came to consider them less a menace than a nuisance, or, in some cases, a welcome diversion. During the late summer and autumn a growing number of people took to disregarding regulations by hurrying not to shelter areas at the sound of the siren, but to their rooftops where, crouched behind the facing so as not to be spotted by the special constables, they watched the drama overhead. In September the Italians began coming mainly at night, and what a thrill it was to see the sky suddenly light up with the long, probing fingers of thirty or more 1,000,000-candle-power searchlights and the brilliant trajectories of tracer ammunition streaking through the darkness like skyrockets at *festa* time! Now and then a spectator would be shredded by some of the falling shell fragments that rained down for miles around during the raids, but this happened too rarely to discourage the people from their rooftop fun. And in those early months, when the excitement far outweighed the danger, the war *was* fun for many of the islanderes, including the children, who staged mock battles in the narrow streets of the villages and played "bomb ball" in the square in front of the local church.

The weather held sunny and unusually mild into early December, but despite the almost ideal bombing conditions, enemy raids dwindled to an average of only ten a month, or about one every three days. People and property continued to be destroyed, although the overall damage was light and tended to be concentrated in only half a dozen areas. When Governor Dobbie's daughter, Sybil, arrived on the island in mid-October to join her parents and take over as her father's confidential secretary, she was surprised to see so few signs of destruction. The dockyards had been largely repaired, the maintenance sheds at Hal Far and Luqa had been patched up, and much of the rubble had been removed from the Three Cities and other villages that had taken the brunt of the bombings during the first two weeks of the war when most of the damage was done. In fact, the entire scene was quite different from what she had expected. Spirits were generally high. Most foodstuffs and other everyday items were still available, and the island seemed to bustle with business as shopkeepers, hawkers, and whores found ways to separate the hundreds of newly arrived troops from their soldiers' pay. Had it not been for the abundance of military uniforms and an occasional intrusion by the Regia Aeronautica, the casual observer would have found it difficult to believe that there was a war going on. As the governor's daughter later remarked, "The Italians were really not very alarming opponents."

But there had been some changes. Almost from the beginning a few shortages had been felt. Nothing very serious. Sugar, for instance, could still be purchased over the counter, but in August, solely as a precautionary measure, the Office of Food and Commerce Control had ordered an end to the manufacture of all ice cream and soft drinks. Timber, glass, and certain other building materials had become scarce, mainly because of the heavy demand for them following the damage inflicted by the June raids. Also, reserves of animal feed had dipped below their normal level—so much so that the army agreed to plow up its parade ground and polo field at Marsa for the cultivation of maize and millet.

In early autumn rumors of impending shortages set off a frenzy of panic-buying among the islanders, and Malta's shops would probably have been stripped bare had not the government enacted a number of antihoarding measures. Even so, hoarding remained a problem, and as more and more goods went into hiding, prices rose sharply. The authorities responded by placing several of the more essential items under price control, but the controls were so loosely enforced that they were widely disregarded, and prices continued to climb. Meanwhile, wages failed to keep pace, and most families found themselves increasingly hard put to make ends meet. By the final week of October certain elected members of the Council of Government, appalled by the soaring cost of living, were calling for the introduction of rationing. But despite the fact that prices were by now rising at an annual rate of 45 percent and food items at more than 70 percent, the colonial administration dismissed the idea as "unwarranted." There were no shortages, the government insisted, except those created by the public imagination. Once the people returned to their senses, the situation would begin to right itself automatically in accordance with the basic laws of the marketplace. Then the hoarders and profiteers would be begging to sell their goods at break-even prices, and the people would see how foolish their fears had been.[1]

There was one item, however, that the administration was not willing to see trifled with. This was gasoline, which within a few weeks after Italy entered the war had become a tightly controlled government monopoly. On July 3 the authorities announced that all petrol on the island would be bought up by the government and that thereafter its private purchase or sale would be illegal. Effective ten days later, no privately owned motor vehicle, except those used for public transportation, would be allowed to operate without a special permit, which would ordinarily be issued only to doctors and certain government officials.[2] By mid-October taxis had been ordered off the road and buses reduced in number and in the frequency of their trips. Thus, within a few months after the first bombs had fallen, Malta's 4000 automobiles had virtually disappeared from sight—a not-altogether-grievous loss for the islanders once they got used to the change. Horse carriages, so popular in years gone by, reappeared in surprising number, including dozens of those graceful, elegantly appointed victorias (called *karrozins*) that had formerly served as Malta's taxis. "At certain hours of the day," a resident of Sliema wrote not long after the war, "it seemed as though the island had retrogressed a hundred years. Not a toot of an electronic horn, nor the purr of a motor engine. Only the clop-clop of horses' hoofs and the crunch of carriage wheels on the gravel."[3] Bicycles also became popular, so much so that the shops were soon sold out of them, and replacement parts, especially tires, began to be hoarded. Several years later Melita Strickland would recall riding with her husband to formal dinner dances at the fashionable Sliema Club on a bicycle-built-for-two:

> This sort of thing was common then. Even the governor rode a bicycle a good deal of the time. Losing our motorcars caused some inconvenience, of course, but nothing we couldn't put up with easily enough. Life went on, you know. Actually, I remember those days as being rather pleasant.[4]

Perhaps too pleasant. Lulled into a false sense of security by the slackening of enemy activity and, after September, by the sagging fortunes of Italian arms, the Maltese on the whole failed to make adequate preparations for their safety during the dangerous days to come. "The time has arrived to dig in," the governor had announced soon after the initial raids, and for the following few weeks there was a flurry of activity on all parts of the island as the people began to burrow their way into the soft coralline limestone. This was phase one of what the Information Office would label "the shelter offensive." Unfortunately, the effort wouldn't last long or progress very far toward its intended goal, which was to provide rock-shelter protection for every resident of the island.

From the outset the shelter program was meant to be a joint undertaking by the government and the people. Individual families were urged to see to their own safety by digging private chambers in the cellars of their homes or in the labyrinth of ditches and ramparts constructed throughout the Grand Harbour area by the Knights centuries earlier. Meanwhile the government was to prepare neighborhood shelters large enough to accommodate those persons who lacked the space or other wherewithal to provide for themselves. As expected, this group would include the great majority of the island's population.

During this initial phase of the shelter offensive the people acting on their own showed considerably more energy and enterprise than the government. Emanuel Aquilina of Pieta, for example, started his shelter soon after the dust of the first raids had settled and completed it within three weeks:

> Since our home was not suitable for a cellar chamber, I was given permission by the government to dig in the giant bastion near the Porte des Bombes between Pieta and Floriana. I hired a gang of laborers who worked all day long every day but Sunday and followed a general plan of construction that had been recommended by the government in the newspapers. The opening into the shelter was a corridor about six feet high and three feet wide that ran six feet straight into the base of the wall. At that point another corridor of the same size headed off at a right angle to protect us against blast. This led into a chamber which was about six feet by nine, although the size of the chamber varied from shelter to shelter according to how much a person could afford. This was our main living area. Ordinarily there would have been another corridor, again with a right-angle turn, to a second entrance in order to avoid getting trapped by falling rocks, but if I had dug this back door, I wouldn't have had money enough for such a large chamber. So, we put our trust in God and in our neighbors to dig us out if necessary. As it was, the shelter cost me £33 (about $132), and I had to haul away the cuttings. This took all my life's savings, but it turned out to be the best investment I ever made.[5]

The Magros of Battery Street, Valletta, and several neighboring families on the Grand Harbour waterfront got by more cheaply. Scarcely had they begun to dig in their cellars when they broke through into a network of underground chambers that had housed many of the 8000 Turkish slaves used by the Knights in building their golden city nearly 400 years before. Unfortunately, however, the Aquilinas and Magros were hardly typical of the population at large, who in the matter of shelter construction behaved more like the grasshopper than the ant. Of the thousands of individuals and family groups who began digging so enthusiastically during the early days of the war, all but a few had either quit entirely or slowed to a near standstill within a few weeks. Thus, when the time came for disaster to strike, most of these private shelters were only partially completed and, more often than not, quite unusable.

Meanwhile the government had accomplished even less. For all their talk about rock shelters, the authorities decided in late June to concentrate instead on the construction of slit trenches, which, in the words of a government spokesman, would afford "the best possible shelter for the most people in the shortest time."[6] They would also cost considerably less to dig. Usually no more than fifteen feet long by three feet wide and at the most eight feet deep, the slit trenches were meant to provide protection against blast only. At first they were left uncovered, but after several people had pitched headlong into them during the total darkness of the blackout, most were capped with a thin layer of cement supported by wooden ties. Within a few months after Italy's entry into the war, hundreds of these trenches had been dug in all parts of the island. However, except for those along the rural bus routes where there was no other cover, they were seldom used for the purpose intended. Because they offered so little in the way of overhead protection, the slit trenches (or "caterpillars" as they were commonly called) were shunned by most people as being even less safe than their cellars or stairway alcoves at home. Besides, the trenches were usually filthy as a result of their widespread use as latrines. What the people of the island really needed (or would need soon) were rock shelters, which is the direction the government had originally been headed when the shelter offensive began.

Finally in midautumn, after precious months had passed with little progress in the way of of shelter protection, the government again turned its attention to rock-shelter construction. Areas were staked out in the various villages, and digging was actually begun by crews of professional miners. How the work progessed is indicated by the following letters, typical of dozens received by the *Times of Malta* during the final few weeks of the year:

November 20, 1940

Sir: May I through the medium of your widely advertised paper bring to the notice of those concerned the deplorable methods that are being used in the building of an air raid shelter on St. Philip Street, Birgu [Vittoriosa]. This shelter, *when* finished, is intended, I believe, to hold a large number of people. At the present moment there is *one* laborer working on this shelter. Is this work really going to be done? If so, when? In this war or the next?

December 29, 1940

Sir: May I express my extreme gratitude to the Government for taking in hand so important a work as the construction of bomb-proof shelters at various points throughout the Island.

In every town and village, and practically in every street, underground shelters are being dug, but contrary to all expectations, these are either left in suspense when two or three feet down, or their progress is so slow that months are likely to elapse before any of them may be completed.

I do not in any way intend to interfere with the technical procedures of these shelters, but personally I believe that one *complete* is far more useful than any number of incomplete ones.

By the year's end, on the entire island there were only five dug shelters ready for public occupancy, and none of these could really be called finished: They lacked handrails on the stairs; there were no lights, except for an occasional hurricane lamp stuck in a niche carved out of the wall; and many of the steps still needed squaring to prevent people from stumbling down them. Still, with time rapidly running out, the government repeatedly issued assurances that the shelter program was going well. "Looking back on it all today," a Maltese writer would comment a few years later, "we hardly know whether to weep with rage or laugh at our ingenuousness when we confront those assurances."[7]

Actually, however, the public shelter situation was in better shape than it appeared. True, there were only five dug shelters ready when the bombs began to fall in earnest, but all five were in the Three Cities area where, along with Valletta, most of the civilian damage would occur. As for Valletta, far beneath the city were several large tunnels that had been dug by the Knights centuries before in expectation of a return visit by the Turks. Foremost among these was Lascaris, a high, spacious passageway that extended for a hundred yards or more under fifty feet of solid rock and had been taken over before the war as headquarters for Malta's military and air operations. During the summer of 1940, four smaller tunnels were unsealed and, after being outfitted with electric lights and ventilation shafts, were made available to the people for shelters. Even so, by the end of the year, after six full months of war with Italy, Valletta offered rock-shelter space for only 5300 people—barely a third of the city's prewar population. This was not a very comfortable ratio, and had it not been for the Knights, there would scarcely have been any ratio at all.

Fortunately, though, besides their own shelters Vallettans had access to the Old Railway Tunnel, which ran for about half a mile under neighboring Floriana and could be entered from the dry moat (the Great Fosse) that separated the two towns. The tunnel was left over from the days of the Malta Railroad that had run from Valletta to Rabat in the center of the island for nearly fifty years before succumbing to the competition of trolleys and buses in the early 1930s. From the first day of the raids until the bombings had all but ended two and a half years later, thousands of people from Floriana, Valletta, and neighboring towns would find refuge in this abandoned tunnel, so providentially placed. Prior to the war, though, the authorities had failed to prepare it in any way for possible use as a shelter. Thus, for several months after the bombings began the tunnel lacked adequate lighting and sanitary facilities, and its ventilation system was notably deficient. People who made use of it in those days remember it as a foul, stifling place filled with the stench of sweating bodies and human excrement and urine. Still, it was *there,* and with forty feet of rock overhead, it was *safe.* Maltese author Frank De Domenico recalls standing by the Great Fosse during one of the earliest raids and hearing the wail of the siren:

> People poured out of their homes and ran panic-stricken for the Railway Tunnel. At the entrance a woman stopped and began screaming after her child who had become lost in the stampede and carried along by it. Another woman was being carried unconscious into the tunnel. An old man was hustled along by being lifted under the arm-pits. One corner of his mouth sagged and was dripping saliva. The strain and excitement had been too much for him. He had suffered a stroke.[8]

The failure of the islanders, particularly the government, to do more in the way of shelter construction during these early months of the war was tragically shortsighted and irresponsible. It was also quite understandable, simply because the further the digging progressed, the less likely it appeared that rock shelters would be needed by the time they were completed. As summer gave way to autumn the fortunes of war had begun to turn against the Italians, and with each succeeding week the Duce's prospects seemed to grow bleaker. By mid-November he was in deep difficulty, with even worse trouble on the way.

The first setback had occurred in late June when Italian troops in North Africa mistakenly shot and killed their own theater commander. This not only postponed Mussolini's much-heralded offensive against Suez, but also deprived the Italians of a gifted officer who would be replaced by one of far lesser ability. When the offensive finally did get under way later that summer, the Italian army progressed only as far as Sidi Barrani, some seventy miles inside Egypt, before being brought to an inglorious halt by its own timidity and indecision.

But all this was only a prelude to the Duce's more serious trouble, which began in late October when, disappointed and embarrassed by the breakdown of his African campaign, he unleashed a senseless attack against Greece—without prior consultation with the Führer. "Hitler always faces me with a fait accompli," he complained to Count Ciano two weeks before the invasion. "This time I am going to pay him back in his own coin. He will find out from the papers that I have occupied Greece."[9] Later the Duce had second thoughts on the subject and wrote Hitler of his plans shortly before the attack was set to begin. Upon learning of his partner's intentions, the Führer left immediately for Florence to try to change his mind, but as Hitler's aide Gen. Alfred Jodl glumly noted: "We arrived a few hours too late."[10]

Hitler was furious ("He really slapped my fingers," Mussolini confided to Ciano).[11] And with good reason. With the Greeks now in the war, their bases would be available for use by British ships and planes. The ships were Mussolini's worry, but the planes presented a danger to Hitler himself. Germany's new ally Romania was within easy reach of Greek-based strategic bombers, and Romania was the home of the rich Ploiesti oil fields, Hitler's principal source of fuel for his war machine. Furthermore, although he had not yet informed Mussolini, the Führer had already decided upon an invasion of Russia that following May, and he had no desire to have the British hovering on his southern flank. Of course, if the Italians could successfully overrun the Greeks, then there would be no need for alarm. But by this time Hitler had come to expect little from the Duce's legions, and the upcoming Greek campaign would in no way change his opinion. After penetrating ten miles into Greece from their bases in Albania, the Italians were brought up short by the small but tough Greek army. From the diary of Count Ciano:

[November 16, 1940] We are putting up a strong resistance in Albania.

[November 18] I fear that we shall have to withdraw to a pre-established line.

[November 29] Our soldiers have fought but little, and badly. This is the real, fundamental cause of all that has happened.[12]

By December the Italian army, far from having overrun Greece, was in danger of being pushed back into the Adriatic.

Meanwhile, on the night of November 11 Mussolini suffered another rude shock when Swordfish torpedo planes from the British carrier *Illustrious* staged a surprise attaack on the Italian battle fleet, riding at anchor in Taranto harbor, and sank or seriously damaged three battleships. The operation did not, as Admiral Cunningham claimed in a rare instance of overstatement, "cripple half the Italian navy," but it did go a long way toward reducing the enemy's capital-ship advantage in the Mediterranean. The attack also dealt another cruel blow to the already sagging morale of the Italian people, who, despite all their government could do to prevent it, soon learned the truth about Taranto. For the Maltese the victory was especially sweet, for it had been made possible by aerial photographs taken by Malta-based reconnaissance planes and flown to the *Illustrious* on the day before the attack:

To: Air Commodore F. H. M. Maynard
Air Officer Commanding
Malta

My Dear Maynard:

I hasten to write you a line to thank you for the most valuable reconnaissance work carried out by your squadron, without which the successful attack on Taranto would have been impossible.

I well know what long monotonous flying time they have had to put in and I am very grateful to them.

The work over Taranto has been particularly valuable and gave us all we wanted to know.

Good luck and my grateful thanks again for your cooperation.

Yours Very Sincerely,
A. B. Cunningham[13]

At long last, after months on the receiving end, Malta had helped deliver a telling blow against its tormentors, and, having drawn blood, it had no intention of backing off now and resuming a passive role. During the following weeks the island's tiny air strike-force of sixteen Wellington bombers and twelve Swordfish torpedo planes took the war to the enemy by staging dozens of raids against targets in the harbor areas of Sicily and southern Italy, and, more important, against Italian shipping bound for Albania and North Africa. The results, while modest, were nonetheless gratifying—except to Governor Dobbie, who had serious misgivings about Malta's new role. Only a month before, he had sent a special message to the Home Government, urging that for the time being Malta not be used as a base for offensive operation. His reason: fear that the enemy might be provoked into a major retaliation against the island while it still remained dangerously vulnerable to attack. Wait until the following spring, the governor cautioned, when Malta's military capabilities would be stronger and the island would have a better chance to defend itself. As matters turned out, London would have done well to weigh the governor's advice carefully, but there is no indication that it did.[14]

December was a terrible month for the Duce. While his legions continued to give ground to the Greeks in Albania, even worse things were happening in North Africa. On December 8, while preparing to resume its offensive against Egypt, the Italian army at Sidi Barrani was suddenly attacked by a much smaller British force and sent reeling back toward Libya. "There is something wrong with our army," Count Ciano complained to his diary, "if five divisions allow themselves to be pulverized in two days."[15] By the middle of the month the Italians had been driven entirely out of Egypt and were still retreating westward, with the British in hot pursuit.

None of those developments was at all conducive to a happy holiday season for Mussolini, who had never liked "pagan festivals" anyway. The weather had turned unusually cold for Rome, and on the day before Christmas a light snow began to fall. At his office in the Palazzo Venezia the Duce sat staring out through the glass-paneled door that led to the balcony where only six months earlier he had stood before thousands of his cheering followers in the piazza below and taken his country into war. Now the piazza was all but empty, and silent. "This snow and cold are very good," he remarked to his son-in-law. "In this way our good-for-nothing Italians, this mediocre race, will be improved. One of the principal reasons I have desired the reforestation of the Apennines has been to make Italy colder and snowier."[16] This may or may not have made sense, but with the Duce's world rapidly crumbling about him, there was hardly time to wait for trees to grow in the mountains. What was needed was help in a hurry—which is why, after swallowing what was left of his pride, he had recently approached Hitler to ask for military assistance.

In Malta, after an exceptionally warm autumn, the weather had also grown cold and raw as the Christmas season approached. The wind came in sharply from the north, bringing pounding rain and, for the first time since 1904, snow in the higher elevations. Inside their little limestone houses, which soaked up moisture like a sponge, the people coughed and shivered before their kerosense heaters and, as was their way when anything went amiss, cursed the Turk. But not even the ugly weather could prevent their spirits from soaring. Enemy air activity over the island had virtually ceased, and the war news from abroad was getting better all the time. Italy appeared to be reeling. Its newspapers had become doleful and in some cases guardedly critical of the Duce. There were even rumors (discouraged by the Maltese authorities but widely repeatedly nonetheless) that Mussolini was about to be overthrown and that Italy would then sue for peace. On December 20 thousands of cheering islanders lined the embankments as Admiral Cunningham's flagship, *Warspite,* visited Grand Harbour for the first time since the beginning of the war. Its presence was considered a good sign—especially after the great ship had remained in port for nearly two days without the slightest enemy activity directed against it. Soon, no doubt, the *Warspite* would be coming back to stay, along with the rest of the fleet.

Admiral Cunningham was less sanguine, however. During his brief visit he inspected the harbor's gun emplacements and was not pleased by what he saw. The antiaircraft defenses, both heavy and light, were plainly understrength. This came as no surprise to the admiral, who since long before the war had chafed under the failure of the Home Government to do more to defend the island. Still, he was nevertheless disturbed—particularly in light of a secret report that had reached him within the past few days: According to British Intelligence, the Luftwaffe's battle-hardened 10th corps (Fliegerkorps X) had been ordered to report as soon as possible to Italian air bases in Sicily. This was the outfit that had bloodied British shipping so badly during the Norwegian campaign that past spring. Its specialty: low-level bombing.

9 The Day the Sky Fell In

Shortly after noon on Friday, January 10, 1941, Sybil Dobbie was playing tennis at the San Anton residency in Attard with her father and two of his aides. After weeks of almost unremitting rain the weather had cleared temporarily, and the pale winter sun shone weakly from an almost cloudless sky. The war news continued to be encouraging: Thus far there had been only one enemy raid of any significance during the new year; two Italian merchantmen had been sunk on their way to Albania; the harbors of Palermo and Naples had been successfully attacked by Luqa-based Wellingtons; and only a couple of days before, the cruisers *Gloucester* and *Southampton* had arrived unscathed in Grand Harbour with 500 more troop reinforcements. In North Africa the Duce's legions seemed about to disintegrate. Four days earlier, units of Britain's Army of the Nile had fallen upon a much larger Italian force a few miles inside the Libyan border and captured 40,000 prisoners, along with tons of matériel. "If I may debase a golden phrase," a jubilant Foreign Secretary Anthony Eden wrote to Churchill, "never before has so much been surrendered by so many to so few."[1] At San Anton the tennis match had barely begun when it was interrupted by a number of deep rumbling sounds from the west. The governor excused himself and went inside to phone Valletta. In a moment he was back: "I must leave for the Palace," he said. "There is a great battle going on at sea."[2]

That same evening, not long after dark, the merchantman *Essex* sailed safely into Grand Harbour, carrying 4000 tons of ammunition, 3000 tons of precious seed potatoes, and a deck cargo of sixteen crated Hurricanes. A few hours later what was left of the carrier *Illustrious,* smoking, listing, and steering on its engines only, cleared the breakwater and tied up at Parlatorio Wharf in French Creek, while, incongruously, the multitudes of people watching from the embankments cheered and the navy band played "Roll out the Barrel." There had indeed been a great battle going on at sea. While escorting the *Essex* and a merchant convoy bound for Greece, units of Admiral Cunningham's fleet had been intercepted by enemy planes sixty miles west of Malta. It was inevitable perhaps that the new supercarrier *Illustrious* would be singled out as the prize target and that its intended executioner would be Fliegerkorps X, which took this opportunity to announce its arrival in the Mediterranean theater.

Within six minutes a wave of forty or so Stuka dive bombers had scored half a dozen direct hits on the giant carrier, and on a later visit still another—all with armor-piercing bombs of between 500 and 1000 pounds. "There was no doubt that we were watching experts," Admiral Cunningham later wrote of the German attack. "Formed roughly in a large circle over the fleet, they peeled off one by one when they reached the attacking position. We could not but admire the skill and precision of it all. The attacks were pressed home to point-blank range."[3] What kept the big ship from sinking is a mystery, and how it was able to reach harbor an even greater one. Never before had a vessel taken such punishment and managed to stay afloat, to say nothing of proceeding to port under its own power, and with its steering mechanism totally inoperative. Prime Minister Churchill was visibly shaken by the news. "The effective arrival of German aviation in Sicily may be the beginning of evil developments in the Central Mediterranean," he wrote to his chief of staff.[4]

At its berth in French Creek the once-mighty *Illustrious* was a sad sight to behold. At first light on the morning after the carrier's arrival, hundreds of spectators gathered on Corradino Heights almost directly above Parlatorio Wharf and looked down at the battered ship in disbelief. During its brutal engagement at sea the carrier had been ripped from bow to stern. Its 300-ton rear lift had been completely upended and sent crashing down onto the hangar deck, flattening everything beneath it. The forward lift had been struck at an angle and was now protruding upright from the gutted hull like a triumphal arch. The final bomb had buckled the entire flight deck inward. During the battle, fire had swept through the lower levels destroying virtually everything aft of the wardroom. In places the heat was so intense that the heavy steel decks and bulkheads had become laminated. On the outside of its hull the *Illustrious* had been perforated by hundreds of bomb fragments from near misses. One hundred and twenty-six members of its crew were dead and ninety-one wounded. The latter were rushed to the island's two service hospitals at Imtarfa and Bighi. The dead, many of them charred beyond recognition, were loaded onto a minesweeper and taken a few miles outside the harbor for a traditional burial at sea—the largest ever. A few days later the Admiralty announced in an official communiqué from London that during a recent engagement with the enemy in the Mediterranean the *Illustrious* had "received some damage and casualties."[5]

At first the naval engineers at the dockyards despaired of saving the carrier. Even under the best of conditions, months (perhaps years) of work would be needed to restore it to its former condition, if indeed such a thing were possible. And, although most of the damage done to the dockyards by the early Italian raids had been repaired, facilities for tending to the *Illustrious* were far from ideal: Much of the heavy equipment needed for the job was lacking; so were many of the essential materials, such as heavy armor plate of the kind that had saved the ship's life; besides, there was no drydock big enough to accommodate the vessel, which meant that it couldn't be raised out of the water. There was also the unsettling fact that all work would have to be done under the watchful eye of Fliegerkorps X, now poised at full strength in nearby Sicily.

Still, there might be a way. An inspection of the ship's engines revealed no serious damage. This being the case, if the *Illustrious* were pumped out and made at least temporarily seaworthy and if certain makeshift repairs were done on its power systems and steering mechanism, it could again put out to sea. True, it would be little more than a hull and practically defenseless against any kind of attack, but at least it would be able to travel, and, ironically, once lightened by the removal of its thousands of tons of wreckage, the ship's top speed would be greater than before. In view of all this, the decision was soon made by the Admiralty to ready the *Illustrious* for a desperation run to Alexandria.

Time, of course, was the most critical factor, for, having come so close to destroying the carrier, German planes would surely try to finish the job, and it would not do to offer them a stationary target for longer than was absolutely necessary. Thus, within twenty-four hours repairs were begun. Stages, scaffolding, Jacob's ladders, pumps, and fire hoses soon festooned the ship, while a thousand or more Maltese workers—shipwrights, electricians, fitters, welders, riveters, and common laborers—swarmed over the vessel, removing the debris and patching up its vitals as best they could. Beneath the waterline hard-hat divers rounded out the jagged shrapnel wounds and plugged them with wooden pegs. Meanwhile the carrier had been given a quick spraying of yellow paint to match its limestone surroundings. And the harbor antiaircraft defenses had gone onto around-the-clock alert.

From their reconnaissance planes, which began to appear on the first morning, the Germans kept close track of what was going on, but, like Brer Fox, continued to lie low and do nothing. Perhaps they believed that the *Illustrious* was beyond saving and would eventually sink without further effort on their part, which would be all to the good since they had already lost ten or a dozen planes in their attacks against it and would prefer not to up the cost. Whatever the reason, for a period of nearly six days, much of it passable flying weather, they held their fire. This decision would prove to be a costly mistake for the Germans. Not only were the early (and most critical) repairs on the carrier permitted to proceed without interruption, but, more important, the island's defenders were given the time needed for setting up a box barrage, without which the *Illustrious* would almost certainly have ended up at the bottom of French Creek.

An aerial box barrage was nothing new. It had been tried several times before during the German blitz against England and had generally worked well. The idea was for each AA gun to direct its fire not against enemy aircraft but at a certain segment of the sky. In this way a blanket of shrapnel could be thrown up over a specified target area to inhibit low-level penetration by hostile raiders. The key to an effective barrage was pinpoint coordination, which could be achieved only through the most painstaking planning and preparation. In the underground combined-operations room at Lascaris, dozens of officers worked feverishly over maps and grid plots to orchestrate the more than one hundred guns that would figure in the barrage. Light antiaircraft batteries were hauled in from outlying areas to the Grand Harbour embankments, where they were positioned in support of those units already there. The heavies, too awkward to be repositioned on such short notice, remained in place with their barrels depressed in varying degrees toward the barrage area, which in many instances was several miles away. In the harbor itself the guns of the recently arrived cruiser *Perth* and what remained of those on the *Illustrious* stood ready, as did two banks of pom-poms on the tip of Senglea. All gunnery officers were checked and rechecked on their grid coordinates and fuse settings. It was essential that every shell go where it was supposed to and explode at the right time. It was also essential that the most rapid rate of fire possible be maintained, in order to keep the protected zone cluttered with flak. Naturally some of the raiders would manage to get through; then it would be up to the island's fighter planes to combat them as best they could. Shortly before one o'clock on

Thursday afternoon, January 16, a crisp, cloudless day, Lascaris notified the governor that the barrage was in place. Less than half an hour later some seventy German bombers took off from Sicily's Catania and Comiso airfields and, escorted by several dozen Italian fighters, headed south for Malta.

In the hilltop town of Mellieha near the northern extremity of the island, a twelve-year-old schoolboy heard the planes fly over shortly before two o'clock. He had long since grown accustomed to the sound of enemy aircraft on their way to Grand Harbour and normally would not even have bothered to look up. But these were flying much lower than usual, and from his window he could tell that they were different from any he had seen before. And there were many more of them. Rushing to the roof, he watched as they veered inland and approached Grand Harbour from the south. Then, suddenly, a most unexpected thing happened: "Papa! Come see," the boy shouted. "The planes are falling out of the sky!"[6]

In textbook fashion they came from out of the sun: first the no-nonsense twin-engine Ju 88s releasing their bombs from a low but still respectful 5000 feet; and then the rowdy, insolent Stukas, perhaps as many as fifty of them, each with a huge, armor-piercing bomb cradled between its front wheels. Spaced only a few seconds apart, they peeled off and aimed their yellow noses almost straight downward toward the wounded ship. Engines roaring, machine guns barking, and their notorious screamers reaching an almost ear-shattering climax, the Stukas came down upon the carrier with incredible fury. Finally, when they seemed bound to crash, they would release their bombs and pull out of their dives, sometimes so low that the faces of the pilots were clearly discernible from the ground. Even the *Times of Malta* was forced to concede that these were brave men, whose courage was worthy of a better cause.

Meanwhile the most intensive antiaircraft barrage ever witnessed had opened up. Never before had so much firepower been used to protect a single target. For the better part of five minutes the guns fired frantically, throwing up a heavy cover of shrapnel over the *Illustrious*. The effect was a continuous earth-shuddering, mind-shattering roar, punctuated by the explosion of the enemy's heavy bombs. Giant clouds of limestone powder drifted upward for hundreds of feet to mingle with the white and gray puffs of the bursting shells, whose carpet of flying steel should have been impossible to penetrate—but wasn't. The Stukas kept coming down like a wolf upon the fold. Just below the barrage, nearly hidden amid the smoke and dust and the towering geysers of water created by the bombs, half a dozen Hurricanes met the attackers and attempted to destroy them before they released their bombs, or at least throw them off target. It was all one incom-

Bofors crew guarding Grand Harbour.

prehensible, deafening inferno. Some of the ack-ack guns fired so rapidly that their barrels began to melt. When the pom-poms on Senglea Point grew red hot, a Maltese priest poured water over them as he urged the crew on and absolved them of their sins.

For over half a mile in every direction people in their makeshift "Italian-proof" shelters were bounced around like ping-pong balls. Scared half out of their senses, they vomited, emptied their bowels and bladders, and cried out to God for protection. In nearby Floriana, across the narrow foot of the harbor, teachers huddled with their students in the cellar of the school. As the building above them shook and began to crumble, the youngsters became hysterical. "It was during this terrible experience that we teachers prayed in full faith to our Lady of Sorrows for the safety of the children and made a solemn vow to commemorate Her feast day each year in a most befitting manner."[7] Later that same afternoon the Germans, having failed to finish off the *Illustrious,* staged a second raid of equal fury. It was indeed a day to remember. "If the future holds nothing more terrifying for us," a resident of Sliema noted, "this date will remain indelibly impressed on our minds until the day of our death." It was, he said, like a preview of the Last Judgment.[8]

Early the following morning a Maltese ordnance worker who went aboard the *Illustrious* to help change its gun barrels found it covered ankle-deep with limestone dust and rubble from Corradino heights. Human parts were strewn over the deck and superstructure—all that remained of two of the ship's gun crews and several Maltese workers who had failed to leave the vessel when the siren sounded. Although the morning was cool and a bit breezy, an awful stench had already settled over the carrier. Flies were everywhere. Looking for something to brush them away with, the ordnance worker picked up a dust-covered object from the deck. It was the lower jaw of a man. As for the ship itself, of the hundreds of bombs targeted for it, only one had found its mark: a direct hit on the rear lift-well which did so little damage that workers were able to repair it within twenty-four hours.

The survival of the *Illustrious* was due to many factors, including the artful orchestration of the box barrage by Lascaris; the raw courage and efficiency of the antiaircraft crews, who, bathed in sweat and oozing blood from their ears and noses, stood their ground as the Stukas came screaming down their gun barrels; and, of course, the derring-do of those pitifully few RAF fighter pilots who did their best to confound the enemy raiders, and in the process downed at least five of them. But the main hero of the piece was Corradino, the stark, uninhabited bluff that rises sharply out of French Creek to a height of a hundred feet or more. Berthed in the lee of Corradino, the *Illustrious* presented an extremely difficult target to hit, and the nature of the enemy's approach pattern made it even more so. As a Maltese gunner later described the attack:

> The Germans chose to come in from the southwest, directly over the Corradino heights, probably because this was the safest direction for pulling out of their dives. The result was that most of their bombs either fell short and hit the heights, or, as was more often the case, overshot the mark. In either event the ship itself was scarcely touched. It was like trying to kill a mouse in a corner.[9]

The surrounding area was not so fortunate, however. Valletta, Marsa, and Paola were all struck repeatedlly, sometimes at points a mile or more from the target. In nearby Floriana the King George V Hospital was partially destroyed by a direct hit on one of the wings, even as its patients were being wheeled frantically to half-completed shelters in the embankment behind the building. But the Three Cities, so close to the ship and more or less in direct line of fire, took most of the punishment. Senglea, scarcely two hundred yards across French Creek from the *Illustrious,* suffered the worst—so much so that by the end of the day's second raid the town lay in ruins. More than a generation later Father Victor Jaccorini, an eleven-year-old schoolboy in Senglea at the time of the attack, would remember vividly his own experiences on that terrifying afternoon:

> The warning signal sounded at about two o'clock, and we marched out of the school by classes in a double column. It was like a game almost. The older boys up front started singing a dirty song about Mussolini, and before long the singing had gone all down the line. For this our teachers scolded us, of course, but kept hurrying us along.
>
> The new rock shelter was very near the school, and I remember going down many steps. There were a lot of people there, and it was hard to see at first because the only light came in through the ventilator shafts. Pretty soon we could hear the screaming of the Stukas and the booming of the guns. When the bombs began to land the earth shook all around us, and dust came pouring down the ventilator shafts.
>
> There was much coughing and choking from the dust. My older brother Mario, who was thirteen, thought it was gas and became very frightened because by this time nobody bothered to carry his respirator anymore. He remembered the advice of our father, who was a doctor, that, if we were ever caught in gas without our respirators, we should put a wet cloth to our nose and mouth. Having no cloth or water, Mario tore off a piece of his shirt and peed on it, and that made us laugh a little, but not much because everyone was so scared. I don't remember any panic, though. The people were all very quiet. They seemed stunned. There had never been anything like this before.

Although the attack was soon over, the people kept to the shelter, waiting for an "all clear" signal that never came because the town's siren had been destroyed. After a while young Victor became bored and started wandering about. As he later remembered, the shelter was very long with damp walls and slime on the floor. At one point he came across a group of boys younger than he, all huddled together too terrified to move or even speak. Being a doctor's son, he could tell they were in a state of shock, and he slapped each of them in the face. From time to time he stopped and talked with grown-ups he knew, but they all seemed confused, not knowing what to do next. Many of them were shaking all over. By now Victor had been separated from his schoolmates for some time, and since it had been quiet outside for so long, he began to worry that they had returned to school without him. Making his way back to the entrance, he joined a group of grown-ups who were crowding up the stairs. Several had already left the shelter and Victor himself was on the top step when the planes returned and everybody rushed back down again.

Not long after the noise of the second raid had stopped, people in the shelter near Victor began to argue. Some said they had heard the "all clear." Others said: "No, there has been no signal. We must wait." But Victor decided to go out anyway. He had been in the shelter for nearly three hours, and now suddenly he wanted very much to go home. Once outside, he was confused for a time about where he was. With some buildings entirely leveled and others only partly standing, Senglea seemed unfamiliar to him. But he soon found his way to Victory Street, which he knew would lead him to his home near the end of the peninsula. As he looked down the street he was surprised to see that it was heaped high with rubble, and he wondered how he could get through. At first he tried to avoid the wreckage by going down side streets, but no matter which way he turned, he soon found his way blocked. Finally he realized that if he were ever to get home, he would have to claw and climb.

By now other people had begun to appear, most of them from out of their homes, where, expecting only another routine raid, they had taken refuge in their cellars. Practically all of them were heading in the opposite direction from Victor, on their way out of town, many with children in tow and loaded down with household possessions. A few were hysterical; others moved quietly and mechanically as if in a trance. Most of them were covered with yellow dust, in many cases streaked with blood. Splintered glass was everywhere, producing a strange, crackling sound underfoot. Here and there were the littered parts of dead animals—dogs, cats, donkeys, and rats—but, as far as Victor could see, no human remains. They would be found later in the cellars and stairwells of Senglea's devastated homes. Halfway down Victory Street, Victor spotted his mother and father with the younger children, picking their way slowly through the rubble in his direction. Hurrying to them as best he could, he grabbed hold of his mother and hugged her. And then, for the first time in a long while, he broke down and cried.[10]

Meanwhile, after the second raid had ended at about five o'clock, head schoolmaster Elia Galea, acting in his role of special constable, was busy trying to get the people out of the shelter. But many, frozen with fright, refused to budge. An old woman would remain cowering there for three days before being forcibly removed. Once outside, the people reacted in various ways to the devastation around them, including the damage done their beautiful Our Lady of Victory Church, constructed nearly four hundred years before by Grand Master La Valette to commemorate the Knights' great victory over the Turks. Some wept. Some simply stared in disbelief at what had happened to their town. Others fell to their knees and prayed to the Virgin or wailed as they saw their homes and all their possessions ruined. Everyone complained of the acrid odor of cordite, which caused severe headaches and coughing spasms. Several people felt an overpowering urge to eat.

By half past six that evening Elia Galea, once again the schoolmaster, had crossed over to Valletta to report to his boss, Dr. Laferla, whom he finally located in the reading room of the British Library:

> I was a very young man at the time, only twenty-three, and I was nervous about appearing before the director, who was a stern man and had a very commanding presence. The doorman stared at me strangely and then called him out of the reading room. When Dr. Laferla met me in the hall, he said: "Look at yourself, young man! What a sight you are! You're covered with dirt. Even your hair is filled with dust. Why did you come here like this? I expect my teachers to set an example." Dr. Laferla was not an unkind man. He had spent much of the afternoon in a shelter and didn't realize how badly Senglea had been damaged. When I tried to describe the destruction, he put his hand on my shoulder and said: "Now, young man, you are very excited. You must calm down and not exaggerate so." Then I told him that I had come to see him because I had ordered all the schools in Senglea closed until further notice. He was very upset with this news and said: "You have exceeded your authority. The schools must remain open." But after I had explained the situation to him more clearly, he agreed that I had done the right thing, and then, seeing that I was in a very agitated state, he gave me a ride home to Rabat in his official car and instructed me to bring my logbook to him on the following day.
>
> The next morning I returned to Senglea but couldn't get through the rubble. When I reported this to Dr. Laferla, he was again upset with me. He found it hard to

believe that I had been unable to find my logbook. "Dr. Laferla," I said, "not only can I not find my logbook; I can't find my school. I can't even find the street." Again he thought I was exaggerating and told me that, after teaching in Senglea for several months, I should certainly be able to find my way around. "But you don't understand," I replied. "There is no Senglea anymore."

Nearly forty years later Galea would still shudder at the memory of that brutal afternoon. "These days when I see the old newsreels of the bombing on the television, I turn to my wife and ask her, just to check on my sanity: 'Did I really live through all that? Did anyone?' "[11]

Next to Senglea, the heavily congested communities of Cospicua and Vittoriosa (the other two towns constituting the Three Cities) were the hardest hit. In Cospicua ambulances were prevented by the tangle of rubble from even entering the town. Stretcher-bearers had to struggle for blocks through the debris to bring out the dead and wounded. Wherever they went, they encountered people wandering aimlessly about, many of them inquiring after a child or an aged parent. Beside a huge crater near St. Michael Street lay a human head covered with yellow dust. A few feet away two dogs gnawed at a dismembered corpse. Vittoriosa, only 300 yards across Dockyard Creek from Senglea, was much the same: Scarcely a waterfront building was left standing, and where a few hours earlier shops and homes had stood, there were now only piles of shattered masonry, splintered wood, broken glass, and the scattered remains of dead animals.

Throughout the Three Cities and the other affected areas, digging-out operations began almost at once, but, typical of the island's civil defense program, they fell far short of what they should have been. Even the staunchly progovernment *Times of Malta* complained about the absence of any overall coordination and supervision: "Haphazard and slipshod," said the *Times,* "dawdling," "lacking in direction." The authorities had obviously failed to prepare for anything beyond the most modest rescue effort. Good enough perhaps for the pipsqueak raids the Italians had been conducting, but, asked the *Times,* had no one in the government foreseen the possibility of larger, more devastating attacks? "There can be little excuse for this lack of imagination after seven months of war."[12]

Still, with undermanned, undertrained units of the ARP serving tirelessly, and hundreds of soldiers and civilian volunteers helping out, scores of lives were saved: In Senglea, after two days of digging by more than two hundred troops and dockyard volunteers, the opening to a cellar shelter was cleared of rubble, and twelve men and women were brought out alive, amid the cheers of workers and onlookers. Elsewhere in the same town, rescue teams worked nonstop for three days, removing huge blocks of masonry and cutting through a rock layer four feet thick to save three elderly sisters and their dog. In Cospicua, ten people, including an old man and a six-month-old baby, were removed from a cellar after four days of nearly total darkness. All were still alive, thanks to a few canned goods and some homemade beer. Only a few blocks away a married couple remained trapped for three days under a stone arch in their basement. Fortunately the wife had prepared a few sandwiches and a small thermos of coffee for her husband, who had been about to leave for the dockyards at the time of the first raid. When finally rescued, they were so thirsty that they were licking the damp walls of their underground tomb. Nearby, rescue workers came across a dog in front of a pile of debris. When he refused to budge, the workers removed the debris and uncovered a cellar shelter where the dog's master, together with his wife and two children, were alive and unharmed. In the neighboring town of Paola soldiers and civilian volunteers raced the clock to reach twenty-one people in a private shelter that had been blocked by rubble and was slowly filling with water from a cracked well nearby. After two days all but three were removed alive.

And so it went: dozens of rescue teams ranging in size from three or four workers to more than two hundred, all digging against time and for the most part without equipment or supervision—men with their hands and arms bloody from clawing at the rough masonry, some of them standing knee-deep in the slime of broken sewer mains, with handkerchiefs around their faces to help filter out the awful stench. Every so often one of them would blow a whistle as a signal for everyone to pause and listen, in an attempt to determine what direction a moan or cry for help was coming from. And then the heaving and tugging would resume. Hardened dockyard workers cried as they pulled the mangled bodies of children (sometimes their own) from the ruins. In all, over two hundred trapped victims were rescued. But many others were not: In Vittoriosa, where only one rock shelter had been ready for occupancy, thirty-five people took refuge in the sacristy of St. Lawrence Parish Church only minutes before a direct hit buried them alive under tons of rubble. Their groans and screams could be heard for days, but rescue teams were unable to reach them in time.

The official casualty report released by the Information Office listed sixty civilians killed and seventy-three badly wounded on that devastating afternoon of January 16, but these figures were far too low. According to a later statement by the area's chief medical officer, the dead alone exceeded two hundred, while the number of wounded was several times that. And there is no way of telling how many wounds went unreported or how many people sustained emotional shock. Many suffered from internal disorders for weeks after the attack—unable to keep food down or control their bowels or bladders. Others, mainly those who had been buried alive, couldn't stop shaking or crying out involuntarily.

But bad as the carnage was, it could have been far worse, and would have been, save for an extraordinary bit of good luck: Only a few hundred yards from the *Illustrious* the merchantman *Essex,* although already six days in port, had yet to be unloaded when the Germans struck. With its 4000 tons of bombs, torpedoes, antiaircraft shells, and other high explosives, the ship was a floating powder keg of tremendous destructive force. Therefore, when an enemy bomb hit the *Essex* amidships, the entire harbor area should have been blown sky high. But, miraculously, instead of landing on the deck, the bomb dropped neatly down the ship's funnel all the way to the engine room, where the blast was contained by the heavy bulkheads. Why such a dangerous cargo had not been unloaded after so much time, especially when it was known that a major enemy raid was in the offing, is a question that has never been satisfactorily answered.

An even more perplexing mystery is why the Three Cities were not evacuated, or, failing this, why the authorities didn't at least warn the people that serious enemy action was imminent and it would be dangerous for them to remain there. Given the proximity of the *Illustrious,* the Three Cities were almost certain to come under heavy pounding. And yet not a word of forewarning was given by the government, save for a brief radio announcement barely an hour before the raid that in the event of an enemy air attack a "new type of defense" (the box barrage) would be used and the people should therefore be sure to take cover—presumably to protect themselves from falling shell fragments. The most charitable explanation that can be given for this almost total disregard for the safety of the civilian population is that the authorities were simply remiss, as they had been so often before in matters involving civil defense. They may have been guilty of something far worse, however. Again, the Maltese author Frank De Domenico:

> The British were concerned mainly about the *Illustrious.* It was necessary to get it seaworthy as soon as possible and get it away from Malta, where its days were certainly numbered. For this they needed workers around the clock, and they were afraid that if they ordered Cottonera [roughly the area contained in the Three Cities] abandoned they would lose their work force. They didn't even want to chance evacuating the women and children, because Maltese families are very close, and if the women and children were to leave, the men might go too. . . .
>
> Later some people would say that if the British had only known how fierce the raids would be they would have ordered the entire area cleared. But this is foolish-

> ness. During the Battle of Britain they had seen plenty of the German air force, and they had a good idea of what it could do. They knew all about the Stukas and the size of the bombs. . . . And they also knew that the Germans would go all out to destroy such a valuable prize as the *Illustrious,* especially since it was already badly damaged.
>
> So, in my opinion, and there are a lot of other people, mainly Maltese, who will tell you the same story, the people of Cottonera were deliberately sacrificed in order to save the *Illustrious*. It was as simple and cold-blooded as that. And then on the day after the raids, when the people were already scattered anyway, the government ordered evacuation. Imagine, on the day *after,* when it no longer made any difference except to make it appear that the British were really concerned about the people! If they had actually cared about the people, they would have evacuated the place as soon as the *Illustrious* reached Grand Harbour.

And finally, with unconcealed bitterness: "They might at least have warned them."[13]

On Sunday morning, three days after their initial visit, the Germans unleashed an even heavier attack against the carrier. As before, the enemy dive bombers cut through the barrage and pounded the Three Cities mercilessly, adding rubble to rubble, but this time there were few casualties, since most people had fled the area. Once again the *Illustrious* escaped major damage, despite being slammed violently against the wharf by a near miss. A dozen more enemy planes were lost in the fruitless attempt, but no one was deluded into thinking that this would discourage the Germans from trying again. During the next three days the weather was unsuited for air operations. On Thursday, however, conditions improved, and three reconnaissance planes came over at different times to study the situation and take pictures. Another raid against the carrier was considered imminent.

But it would never occur. That evening, soon after dark, the big ship slipped its moorings and, with its deck still cluttered with a tangle of staging and ladders, cleared the breakwater to begin its dramatic race for survival. Traveling at speeds of up to twenty-four knots throughout the long January night, the carrier was nearly 350 miles southeast of Malta by daybreak, safely out of range of German planes. Shortly after noon on the second day it arrived at Alexandria, from where, after being worked on for several weeks, it was moved by way of the Cape to the United States for further repairs before being reassigned to active service nearly a year later. Thus, after thirteen perilous days and nights in Grand Harbour under the very shadow of the Luftwaffe, the mighty *Illustrious* would live to fight another day—which came as no surprise to Governor Dobbie. "All will be well," he had assured his people amid the fury of the German attacks on the crippled carrier. "Just put your faith in God and carry on."[14]

10 The Fury of Fliegerkorps X

Thus a new and more deadly phase of the war had now arrived for Malta. Convinced that without German help North Africa would fall to the British and fearful of the effect this would have on Italian morale, Hitler had finally decided to make a serious military commitment to the Mediterranean theater. In early January he issued orders to Fliegerkorps X that (1) communication lines with Libya were to be protected, especially during the months of February and March when German army units would be sent to North Africa to help strengthen the Italians; (2) passage through the central Mediterranean was to be denied to all enemy shipping; and (3) Malta was to be neutralized to the point of no longer being able to serve as a base for British offensive operations. ("The complete destruction of the air and naval bases at Malta is indispensable," Hitler wrote to Mussolini in early February.) To carry out this assignment, Fliegerkorps X had approximately 180 bombers, nearly as many fighters and fighter bombers, and a small number of reconnaissance planes and other craft—all manned by seasoned crews. It could also call on the help of more than 300 Italian aircraft based in Sicily, Sardinia, and North Africa. By and large, however, the air action in the central Mediterranean during the early months of 1941 would be a German operation, with Italian planes being used sparingly and mainly in a supporting role.[1]

Although a man of God, Governor Dobbie would have been the first to acknowledge that the Almighty helps those who help themselves. Following their remarkable achievement in saving the *Illustrious,* however, the people and garrison of Malta would find few opportunities for self-help during those first months of 1941 when the Luftwaffe swarmed relentlessly over the little island, administering grim lessons in destruction. "By comparison the Italians had been cowards or gentlemen. We weren't sure which," a Maltese civilian would remark in reflecting on the earlier days of the war. "We only knew that the Germans were a different breed and that they were very much in earnest. One could hardly help but admire their boldness and efficiency."[2]

The only answer to the German raids, and indeed the key to ultimate victory in the Mediterranean theater, was fighter aircraft. But fighters were in such chronically short supply on Malta in those days that after the *Illustrious* raids until the end of May the RAF was seldom able to put more than six or eight in the air at one time. Occasionally a dozen Hurricanes would be flown in off a British carrier, but, being so heavily outnumbered, they were soon devoured by the enemy. "I have just seen the Air Vice Marshal who is here from Malta to report," Admiral Cunningham wrote from Alexandria to the first sea lord in mid-March:

> He tells me the Germans are right on top of them. He has only eight serviceable Hurricanes left, and the German fighters are coming over in droves. . . . He is being sent six from the shortage here; but that is no good. He ought to have two full squadrons and at once. I am really seriously concerned about Malta. . . . We must have large numbers of fighters rushed out to us if we are to make any headway, and, indeed, they are needed to save what may be a serious set-back.[3]

And again, a week later:

> The most drastic and early measures are needed to restore the situation at Malta, which alarms me seriously. Enemy air forces operate over the island just as they please.[4]

As late as the middle of May, although several dozen Hurricanes had been flown in since January, the situation remained desperate. According to Vice Admiral Wilbraham Ford, reporting from the island, Malta was still at the mercy of the Luftwaffe. Faced with only token fighter opposition, enemy planes were, in Ford's words, "having a heyday."[5]

Under the circumstances the Germans had little difficulty in carrying out their threefold mission to near perfection. By the end of March the central Mediterranean had been all but sealed off to British shipping. Meanwhile, under the protective umbrella of Fliegerkorps X, Gen. Erwin Rommel's Afrika Korps was able to cross from Italy to Libya with a loss of less than 3 percent of its personnel and equipment. As for Malta, the Germans outdid themselves in eliminating its usefulness as an offensive base—at least for the time being. For more than four months the Luftwaffe pounded the island mercilessly and, for long stretches at a time, almost constantly. In the four-week period beginning February 10, when the main body of the Afrika Korps was being transported to Libya, Malta experienced 105 alerts, all but a few of which resulted in actual bombing raids. From April 11 to May 10 there were 111! On February 10, ten separate raids were carried out against the island, the largest daily total of the war up to that point.

Most of the enemy's attention was directed against the harbor areas and the aerodromes, where Malta's meager offensive capabilities were concentrated. Wave after wave of Ju 88s, Heinkel 111s, and Stukas, sometimes in groups of forty or more, would range over the island, striking almost at will with their medium and heavy bombs. Often they would be followed by fighter sweeps, made up of dozens of low-flying Messerschmitt 109s and 110s, dropping smaller explosives and raking the target areas with machine-gun and light cannon fire. By all accounts the attacks were savage and highly destructive, but they were also very correct. Among the hundreds of German raids during this period, there were no known instances of attacks against anything but legitimate military targets. "They were quite good about that," an officer with the King's Own Malta Regiment would later confirm. "Of course, with everything in Malta so crowded together, there was bound to be a great deal of civilian damage, but in fairness one must admit that the Jerries obviously tried to stick to the rules. I must say that they were entirely proper."[6]

The island's antiaircraft batteries did their best, but they were more of a nuisance than a deterrent to the Germans, who, unlike the Italians with their neat, predictable flight patterns, came in on the targets from every direction and angle, continually altering their speed and altitude. "They were very good pilots, and very clever," a Maltese major would recall. "With them, we might as well have thrown away our predictors and fuse setters, for all the good they did us. We shot down a few of them, mind you, but not enough to make much difference. They kept coming on and did about as they chose."[7]

By April 1, a date the Admiralty had mentioned to Churchill only a few months before as a likely time for the return of the main fleet to Malta, conditions in Grand Harbour were far from inviting. The workshops were down to less than 50 percent of their normal efficiency; some were as low as 25 percent. The drydocks were operable only by hand, their heavy equipment having been almost totally destroyed. Piers and jetties had been badly damaged, and the harbor itself was thickly seeded with German mines. In Marsamxett Harbour, on the other side of Valletta, German air attacks were so fierce that the half a dozen submarines and four destroyers that had returned the previous autumn to operate out of Malta against enemy shipping were forced to sneak in and out of port under cover of darkness and spend as little time as possible tied up there. This made maintenance and repairs difficult and also lessened the efficiency of the crews by preventing them from getting shore leave.

The island's aerodromes were in even worse shape. From the diary of a British airman at Hal Far:

> [February 28] Heavy raids on the aerodrome by three formations of at least 110 aircraft. . . . Damage preliminary assessed as follows: Three Swordfish and one Gladiator burnt out. All other aircraft, including the last of the Hurricanes, rendered unserviceable. All barrack blocks unserviceable, two heavily damaged and one demolished. Water and power cut off. Two hangars gutted, others damaged. Airfield reduced unserviceable. . . . This was a heavy raid. Our forces were not strong enough to ward it off. If the air defence of Malta is to continue, more fighters are essential.[8]

Other diary entries, these from Luqa:

> [February 26] Big blitz by German Junker 87s [Stuka] dive bombers. . . . Lasted about 90 minutes. Great clouds of smoke rise from Luqa, five Wellingtons destroyed on ground. We also lost three Hurricanes and three pilots.
>
> [March 10] One week of big blitz, haven't time to look at my diary before now. Yesterday morning four Me 110s came across our drome and machine gunned the Hurricanes and runway crews. They set one kite [plane] on fire and burnt it out, bullets flying in all directions.
>
> [April 16] Just remembered that I haven't filled this in recently. Since March 27th we have lost seven pilots and nine kites. Last Friday German aircraft came over by moonlight and dropped bombs for 90 minutes. The same occurred Saturday, Sunday, and Monday nights.[9]

When Foreign Minister Anthony Eden visited the island briefly in late March, he was appalled by the extent of damage done the aerodromes: hangars, repair sheds, and barracks leveled; fuel dumps and pumping equipment demolished; runways pockmarked with deep craters. And, shoved back against the stone walls that separated the aerodromes from adjacent farmland, now green from the winter rains, were the charred remains of dozens of aircraft that had been destroyed on the ground—like so many sitting ducks.

Meanwhile, communities in and about the main target areas received extensive damage. The Three Cities continued to suffer the most, as the Germans hammered away at the dockyards. The village of Luqa, scarcely half a mile from the aerodrome, was badly battered by dozen of enemy bombs that fell long or short of their mark. Gzira and Sliema, both facing on Marsamxett Harbour, were severely damaged by recurring raids on the submarine and destroyer bases nearby. Valletta, with its government offices and military headquarters, was hit repeatedly, though never harder than during a night attack in late April when, amid the eerie white glow of enemy flares, tons of heavy bombs pulverized much of the city's shopping and business center. In nearby Floriana, where the island's main granaries were located, heavy German raids shook the town to its foundations. Emanuel Tonna, Floriana's head schoolteacher, would long remember one such visitation:

> Another alarm sounded at 1:45 a.m. We all went down to the shelter and tried to sleep but this was not to be. Bombs were dropping again on Floriana—where could it be this time? Someone from above called me up; I guessed the reason and I was right. Premises at 27 Granaries Square was hit—my house, no doubt! There was no one inside; they were all in the shelter and Mother was in the Old Railway Tunnel. When the news reached her, she took the loss very badly. It was a very sad experience to lose all one's belongings.[10]

As if the bombs weren't bad enough, in mid-February the Germans began seeding the island's main harbors with hundreds of mines—huge, round, sinister-looking objects that often drifted inland as they floated leisurely down on their aquamarine parachutes. On the very first drop one of them landed in Senglea and leveled an entire block. Some time later one descended on the little town of Zebbug, four miles from Grand Harbour, where it destroyed more than 150 homes. "They were monstrous devices," the Marchesa Zimmerman would recall:

> Sometimes one of them failed to explode, and the whole area for blocks around would have to be evacuated. One day one settled down on Pieta and caused quite a stir. The police cordoned it off, and we all stared at it from a respectful distance. Finally a dog went up to it, sniffed it, and peed on it. Strange how little things like that stick in one's mind."[11]

On a night in March, Francis Gerard of the Information Office stood on a roof with several of his friends in the little village of St. Julian's, three miles up the coast, watching the Germans as they dropped their parachute mines into Grand Harbour.

> Suddenly a great column of light and flame shot up, reaching high, high into the sky, a terrible pillar raised above Valletta that leaped and leaped in ever-ascending levels. The wave of the explosion, when it came, shook the house beneath us sickeningly. "Good God," someone whispered.[12]

The following morning revealed that an errant mine had almost totally excised an entire block of buildings from the once-proud city of the Knights. Hundreds of rats had deserted the sewers and were scurrying about the town in a frenzy of fear.

During the four months following its initial appearance over the island in early January 1941, the Luftwaffe dropped more than 2500 tons of high explosives on Malta. This was a mere trifle compared with what would come a year later, but it was many times what the Italians had dropped during the preceding seven months and resulted in vastly more property damage. According to official figures, more than 2000 civilian buildings were destroyed during this period of the first German blitz, as opposed to only 300 during the earlier, Italian phase. And yet, after that incomprehensible first day when the Three Cities were offered up to the Luftwaffe like a sacrificial lamb, casualties from the German raids were surprisingly light—scarcely more than those inflicted earlier by the Regia Aeronautica. The main reason: During the days and weeks immediately following the *Illustrious* raids most of the inhabitants of the island's prime target areas fled to safer surroundings. And this time, unlike before, they would stay there.

By May of that year nearly 60,000 people had left their homes and villages. The population of the Three Cities plus Floriana (normally more than 33,000) dropped to fewer than 9000, most of them dockyard workers and other essential personnel, along with their families. Paola, Marsa, Sliema, and Gzira lost over half their regular residents, while Valletta, with nearly two-thirds of its people gone (from 17,000 down to 6000), at times seemed all but deserted.[13] Meanwhile, such inland havens as Birkirkara, Rabat, and Mdina more than doubled in size. In the little town of Mellieha near the northern end of the island and about as far from the main target areas as it was possible to get, inspector of the Special Constabulary Joseph Wettinger noted in his report for early March that 800 evacuees had arrived since the *Illustrious* raids. As late as May 24, he wrote: "Evacuees are still on the increase, day by day, and week by week."[14]

Although the process of resettlement was eased considerably by the experience gained through the evacuation of the preceding June, it was still a bitter ordeal filled with great hardship and confusion for most of the refugees. A large number of them, perhaps the majority, had stampeded from the target areas within hours or days after the initial *Illustrious* raid, once more clogging the roads with overloaded donkey carts and hand-drawn wagons. As before, many would move in with relatives or friends, but others less lucky descended by the thousands upon reception centers that had been set up the previous summer in most of the interior villages. Here they were registered and assigned temporary refuge, usually in a school or church, until they could be processed and found regular quarters by the local protection officer. During the early days of the exodus, when the traffic was the heaviest, life was particularly hard for the evacuees, especially those arriving in what were considered the more desirable villages. In Rabat more than 300 refugees were received on a single day during the week following the first *Illustrious* raid. J. Borg Darmanio, then inspector of the Special Constabulary for Rabat, would later recall the occasion all too well:

> We were teeming with refugees. We had run out of all blankets and mattresses; cart loads of hay were procured and the floor of the school covered with it for the refugees to sleep on. The rooms housed an average of 20 persons each; both upper and lower corridors were full. There were so many people that there was not enough room for them all to lie down. We picked our way through the mass of humanity by the aid of torches [flashlights] until we arrived upstairs. Here we found a little family all huddled in a corner. All they possessed was an old thread-bare blanket and a pillow case full of baby clothes. The blanket was folded and on it slept three small children; on the pillow case slept, or rather wept, a baby, while the mother reclined on the bare floor. . . . The mother was in no condition to withstand this hardship—she had been without food for two days due to the fact that she had been trapped in a shelter in Senglea. Special Constable G. Mifsud went home and brought her some pudding and two bars of chocolate while Sister Loreta gave us a glass of milk. The poor mother distributed everything to her children, leaving nothing for herself; so we had to get some more food for her. She tried to thank us but all she could do was cry and sob.[15]

In the best of seasons this situation would have been bad enough, but January is an especially cold, wet, windy month on Malta, when the dampness seeps through the porous limestone buildings and blackens their interior walls and ceilings with ugly blotches of mold. And this January was worse than most. In dozens of refugee centers throughout the island thousands of uprooted people, many without blankets or adequate clothing, huddled together for warmth in cheerless, unheated, makeshift dormitories, awaiting the unknown—sometimes for as long as a week.

Although to the refugees themselves it must have seemed otherwise, their processing was begun as soon as possible. This usually involved only a cursory physical examination and sometimes minor medical treatment. Then came assignment to their new homes, which were chosen for them by the protection officer, presumably with an eye to the special needs of each refugee family. A master register, compiled months before during the early Italian raids, listed information such as the number of rooms, the amount of floor space, and toilet facilities in all private dwellings in the host villages. Most of the homeowners had supplied this information willingly. Some, however, fearful perhaps of what the government might have in mind, had been reluctant to cooperate. This prompted the governor's office to issue a blanket warrant authorizing the protection officer and certain public health officials to enter any house without notice for the purpose of inspecting the premises and estimating the number of persons that could be accommodated there.[16] Each refugee over seven years of age was to have at least forty square feet of floor space for himself and his belongings, while a child seven or under was entitled to thirty.[17] At first the homeowners were under no compulsion to accept the evacuees. Later, however, as the refugee situation worsened, they were required by law to admit as many as the protection officer assigned them. Either way, as during the evacuation of the previous June, the matter of compensation was to be worked out between the landlord and his new tenants. The government provided nothing, except the loan of a stencil with which the homeowner could, if he chose, paint a Maltese Cross on his door, for much the same reason that Americans had stuck Blue Eagles in their windows a few years earlier: "We Do Our Part."[18]

Almost from the beginning it was apparent that the government's method of resettling the refugees left much to be desired. As might be expected when total strangers suddenly find themselves living under the same roof, problems arose: competition for space, which was usually at a premium in the diminutive Maltese homes; squabbles over the use of the well and the toilet; bickering over the amount and schedule of rent payments; imagined (or sometimes not imagined) slights or insults; and, worst of all, understandable resentment over the loss of privacy. Even in the best of situations, where both landlord and tenant made a genuine effort to accommodate one another, tensions were bound to build up over a period of time. In others, where there was less understanding and tolerance, families often lived together for months without exchanging a single kind word. Occasionally, but not often, acts of physical violence resulted.

There was a way out, however. If a point were reached at which the landlord and the tenant could no longer abide one another's presence, the protection officer would usually provide them with new partners, who might or might not turn out to be an improvement. But what is most surprising is that changes of this sort were seldom requested. In fact, for all its nagging tensions and annoyances, over the long haul the island's resettlement program seems to have worked out well. While not offering the ultimate in gracious living, it did provide safe quarters for tens of thousands of refugees, and, as critics of the British are wont to point out, it cost the government practically nothing.

While all this was going on, Malta was digging in—this time in earnest. Activity extended not only to the target areas but throughout the rest of the island as well, for although until now the Luftwaffe had stuck to miliary targets, there was no guarantee it would continue to do so. The examples of Poland, the Low Countries, and more recently England itself left little doubt that the Germans would attack whatever and wherever they chose. No part of the island could be considered immune to the enemy's wrath. There was also the danger from jettisoning, which became more widespread as the number and intensity of the raids increased. Enemy planes that ran into trouble, such as flak damage or mechanical malfunction, could be expected to drop their bombs anywhere in order to lighten their load and improve their chances of reaching home safely. Many of these jettisoned bombs would fall harmlessly into the sea or fields, but over the course of the next two years many others would strike heavily congested villages miles away from any target area. A few landed in the least likely places, such as the quiet little town of Sannat on nearby Gozo, and resulted in some of the cruelest casualties of the long air war over Malta.

With the coming of the Germans the government seems to have awakened finally to the necessity of furnishing rock shelters for its people. With a special grant of a quarter-million pounds sterling from Whitehall, the authorities now set out to provide each community with several neighborhood shelters, usually spaced a few blocks apart, depending on the density of settlement. A limited number of these, all located in prime target areas, were of the deep-rock variety that reached down forty feet or more and were proof against direct hits from even the heaviest bombs. These deep shelters were expensive and slow to construct, however, and were judged unnecessary for the needs of most communities. In all but a few cases shelters were dug to a depth of no more than fifteen feet—enough to give adequate protection against blast and direct hits from light bombs.

By the beginning of May, according to official figures, there was public rock-shelter space on the island for 166,000 people, including room for 18,000 in the immediate vicinity of Grand Harbour—or about all who remained there after the exodus. At first glance these figures may seem impressive, but a closer look reveals that, while 166,000 people were protected, 75,000 (100,000 if Gozo is included) were not. In addition, this total number of shelter spaces comprised not only those shelters constructed by the government but also those inherited from the labor of others, such as the numerous burrowings of the Knights, the ancient catacombs beneath Rabat, and the Old Railway Tunnel, which in itself could accommodate over 9000 people. Finally, in the government's calculations a shelter space equaled only two square feet, or literally standing room only. Clearly, insofar as the extent of shelter construction was concerned, after nearly a year of war the authorities had little to be proud of.

The quality of the accommodations also fell short of what it should have been. In fact, in most of the public shelters conditions were appalling. Few had any lighting except that provided by the people themselves. Most had neither benches for sitting nor even rails to lean against, with the result that many people, especially the elderly and pregnant women, collapsed from exhaustion. Or from lack of proper ventilation. In the great majority of neighborhood shelters, which usually ran about thirty to forty feet long by six to eight feet wide, provisions for ventilation were virtually nonexistent. Apparently the entranceway was expected to furnish all the air needed. This would hardly have been the case, however, even if the entranceway could have been kept clear of people, which, given the crowded conditions of the shelters, was impossible: "The very narrow entrance is so blocked," a Maltese father from the inland town of Mosta complained, "that the air becomes extremely fouled, so much so that the light of a lamp which I provide fades out. . . . To stay in this refuge for prolonged periods . . . with a wife and seven children is an ordeal beyond description."[19]

During the months of February and April of that year, when the raids were heaviest and often came after dark, it was not uncommon for the people of the island to spend most of the night in these crowded, suffocating, little underground chambers, sometimes ankle-deep in rainwater that had run down from the street above. Young mothers stood for hours at a time, holding infants in their arms, while old people propped themselves against the wet walls and fell into a troubled sleep. "It was all so terribly wrong," writer Frank De Domenico would later remark. "To think that a year after the beginning of the war this is what the government had to offer us in the way of protection was enough to make a strong man weep."[20] Letters signed "workingman" or "patriot" or the name of some village or street poured into the *Times of Malta,* complaining of conditions in the public shelters and inquiring why the authorities weren't working to improve things. Why, asked one, didn't the government at least show that it cared: "The people are left to their own devices. Not a man in uniform goes to see how things are faring. Men, women, and children huddled together in a fetid, airless hole stand in coldness and in darkness with never a word of encouragement from any quarter."[21] In the Council of Government the Nationalist members warned the authorities to listen to the voice of the people and do something about the scandalous shelter situation.[22] But by and large the government remained unmoved. "No matter what the authorities decide upon there will always be a certain type to criticize that decision," reported the official *Information Service Bulletin:*

> In every walk of life there are a number of people who know better than the experts. Unfortunately these ignorant people are the ones who most frequently air their views and because they have the assurance of the ignorant and the misinformed they talk more loudly than those who really know what they are talking about.[23]

Nevertheless, the people had a right to expect better shelter protection, and, although seldom discussed openly, the reasons they didn't get it seemed only too clear to at least some of them: As so often during the war and the events leading up to it, the government was again demonstrating its lack of concern for the welfare of the Maltese people. Indeed, the islanders sometimes felt that the British were so occupied with protecting their precious aerodromes and dockyards that the safety and comfort of the people had become little more than an afterthought. How was it possible, for instance, that as late as May 15, after so many months of war and threatened war, there were on the entire island only ten pneumatic drills available for civilian use?[24] Virtually all shelter construction had to be done by hand chisel and axe, a painfully slow process that limited even the most experienced digger to no more than six or eight inches of progress a day in an average-sized chamber. And why had the government failed to assign paid attendants to the shelters to prevent their being used as toilets and to keep them supplied with such bare necessities as medical kits and fresh drinking water? Among family members and trusted friends and in anonymous letters to the *Times,* dozens of such questions were asked over and over again: Why was there no lighting? Why no fans? Why no drainage? Why no handrails to prevent slipping on the damp, slick stairways? And why no seating facilities (a narrow wooden plank would do) for the elderly and pregnant women? These were really such simple things. Would the installation of any of them, or all of them together, seriously tax the resources of the British Empire?

"There were two reasons for all this," a critic of the shelter program later explained:

> First, the government parceled out its shelter construction and related matters to three different departments instead of coordinating them all under one, preferably the Department of Public Works, which was the best equipped to do the job. This would have prevented a lot of confusion and have given the program greater efficiency. But of course this wasn't the British way of doing things. If they could muck something up, they would. In this case it was mainly the fault of the lieutenant governor, who was in overall charge of the program.
>
> But the main villain was parsimony, in which the British were specialists in their dealings with the Maltese. They were very lavish with their fancy-dress admiralty balls, you know, but when it came to spending a quid or two for our benefit, they weren't so keen on that. After all, how much would it have cost them to run an electric circuit into the shelters and provide them with lights and fans? Later in the war things got better, especially in the bigger shelters, but conditions were still not up to what they should have been, and the main reason was that the British were just too stingy to do the job right.[25]

This may or may not have been the case. Certainly the government's procurement of labor for its shelter program bespoke a high degree of frugality. Soon after the *Illustrious* raids the authorities preempted Malta's 2000 miners and stonemasons to work on public shelter construction for about nine shillings a day. Since many of them had been making four times that amount repairing bomb-damaged buildings and digging private shelters, they were understandably displeased—so much so that several hundred of them soon went on strike. "They were difficult people to handle," the governor's daughter later remarked. "They realized their skill, and some of them took advantage accordingly of the need."[26] Such conduct could not be tolerated, of course, and the governor himself immediately stepped in and ordered them back to work. Not wanting to appear defiant, the miners suggested a compromise wage based on volume dug rather than time spent, but Governor Dobbie would have none of it. The authority of the Crown was not to be bargained with. The miners would return to work for the specified wage or be drafted into the army. Faced with such a choice, the strikers were soon back on the job. The government had won. But the price would prove high. Angry and disappointed, the miners got their revenge by doing as little work as possible, while their supervisors, themselves miners, looked the other way. In late 1942 when the air war over Malta was all but ended, Roger Strickland, head of the pro-British Constitutional Party, admitted before the Council of Government that if the miners' request for "piece pay" had been granted, the island's public shelters could have been dug "at about one-third of the expense and in one-half the time."[27]

Under the circumstances it is hardly surprising that an increasing number of people decided to dig their own, private shelters. This was particularly true of those who remained in the principal target areas where it often seemed that as soon as one raid ended, another began. Rather than repair to a public shelter for several interminable hours a day (and night, which was worse), it made sense to arrange for accommodations where a person and his loved ones could be safe and more or less comfortable at the same time. There was also the matter of privacy, which meant a great deal to the family-oriented Maltese. Therefore, hundreds of families hollowed out bomb-proof chambers under their homes or at the bottom of their wells or, with the government's permission, in one of the many fortifications of the Knights, which stretched for miles on both sides of Grand Harbour. These shelters varied considerably in size and elegance, depending upon the means and enterprise of their owners. Generally they were crude, homemade affairs, sometimes not even high enough to stand up straight in, but otherwise sufficiently roomy to hold the entire family, along with the necessary number of beds or mattresses, stores of food and drink, a kerosene lamp, and a tiny shrine to the Virgin Mary and the patron saint of the village. Certainly not the best of conditions, but a great improvement over the public shelters, especially at night when, instead of having to spring out of bed and rush outside every time the siren sounded, a person could nestle down with his family for a decent night's sleep—unles he happened to be one of those timid souls who were forever worrying about being buried alive, which had been known to happen in home shelters. "We had a large, deep shelter under our villa in Lija," Melita Strickland would recall many years later, "but I simply couldn't bring myself to use it:

> I was terrified of being trapped down there and suffocating. Instead, when the raids came I would stay in the parlor, trembling and half-frightened to death. At times when I couldn't stand it any longer I would go up on the roof and stay up there, sometimes in the wind and rain. There were, oh, a great number of people just like me, who had this absolute horror of entombment and refused to enter an underground shelter. With bombs dropping all about, this was not very rational, I know, but there it was nonetheless.[28]

As the enemy blitz continued with unabated fury during the weeks and months following the *Illustrious* raids, Malta's military leaders became convinced that an invasion of the island was in the offing and responded accordingly. On February 19, by order of the governor, all able-bodied Maltese males between the ages of eighteen and forty-one, save for those holding essential jobs such as farming or mining, were declared eligible for military conscription. Five days later, twenty- and twenty-one-year-olds were called up for March 3. Early the next month those aged twenty-two and twenty-three were ordered to report, and in mid-May all those between twenty-four and twenty-eight. Eventually 14,600 Maltese, including several hundred volunteers, would enter the service—about one-sixth of the island's total work force. Most of them would serve in one of the two territorial units: the Royal Malta Artillery and the King's Own Malta Regiment. Four hundred and thirty-two would be killed as a direct result of enemy action.

Although the *Times* dutifully announced that conscription was "welcomed by the country as a whole," the truth is that from the beginning the Maltese were decidedly hostile to the whole idea, and as time passed they became even more so. Next to their religion these people held their family and village most dear, and to force a man to leave both of them against his will was considered downright cruel. Not even the threat of invasion could justify such extreme action. In fact, was it not indeed a sin to attack the sanctity of the Christian home in this manner? The church authorities said no, not under the circumstances. But this still didn't make it right. Here was a bit of British heavy-handedness that would not soon be forgotten, or forgiven. Over a generation later a prominent Maltese physician, who had been among the first to be drafted, remembered that although there was generally a good spirit between the Maltese and the British during the war, conscription struck a decidedly sour note:

> It was very hard for us to accept. We resented it. We resented it deeply, and still do. Do you know that Malta was the only place in the entire British Empire, outside of the home islands, that had conscription? The British found our attitude hard to comprehend and were offended by it. They thought we should consider it a duty and a privilege to help defend our homeland. Well, we did, you know, but we preferred to defend it from our own doorsteps[29]

As a rule the Maltese did not adjust well to military service. They were brave enough, and in combat situations they behaved creditably. Responsible for manning approximately a third of Malta's antiaircraft guns, they brought down their share of enemy raiders, and on the one occasion when the island's shore batteries were called into action, native gunners distin-

Children in a private shelter.

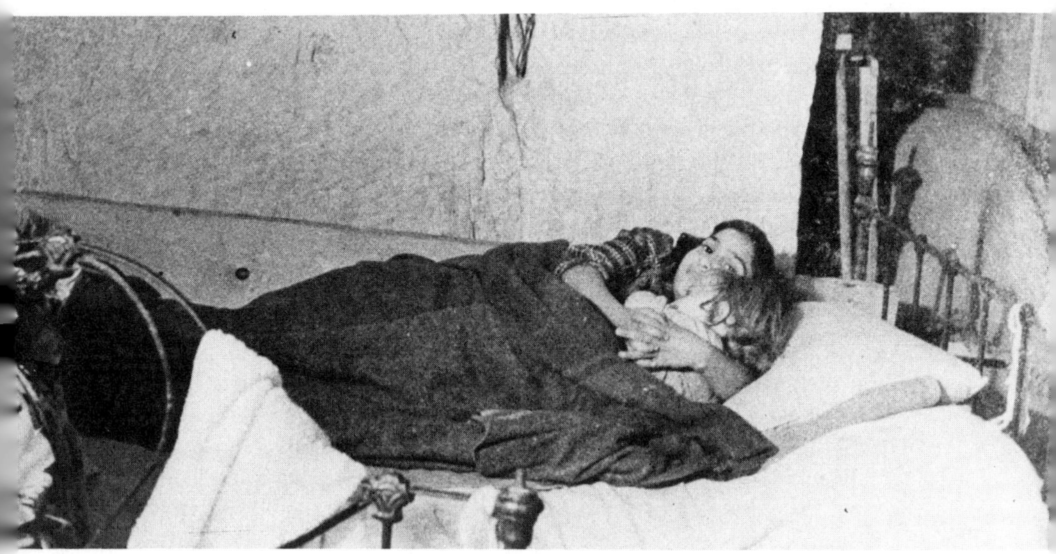

guished themselves by their readiness and their accuracy of fire.* But military discipline was alien to the easygoing nature of the Maltese. They found the routine of camp life, with its close-order drill, calisthenics, and kit inspections, hard to accept or even comprehend. Far better to stay at home with their families and, if the need should arise, shoot the enemy with their bird guns. Particularly galling to their superiors was what one of their training officers described as "a lack of the swaggering instinct." It was all but impossible to get these young conscripts to exercise authority over others. When offered promotions, they attempted to refuse them because, as they explained, they didn't want to boss their friends. "They didn't like giving orders any better than taking them," a British officer would later remark. "They preferred to talk things over with one another before making a move, which, of course, is not the military way."[30]

The draft would have been objectionable enough to the Maltese even if it had been handled properly—which it wasn't. In the first place, it would perhaps have been easier for the people to accept if it had come in the form of a legislative statute from the Council of Government rather than a decree from the royal governor, for although the Council labored under severe limitations, it was the nearest thing to a parliament the Maltese had. As such, its actions tended to be looked upon by the people as more or less representative of the popular will, or at least as having been influenced by the popular will. An imperial edict, on the other hand, was something hurled down willy-nilly from above without so much as a by-your-leave. It was unfortunate that the government chose this method of administering such a bitter pill—unfortunate and quite unnecessary because the Council had already indicated a willingness to pass such a measure if called upon. It was apparently the view of the government, however, that an imperial decree would speak with greater authority.[31]

The draft was rendered even more odious by the fact that the territorial regiments were paid considerably less at all levels than the British. This policy was not new. Traditionally the British had always paid their native troops less, but in the past these troops had been volunteers and therefore had presumably been free to accept or reject the conditions of their employment. Now, however, the situation was different. The conscripts, who had no choice in the matter, were being ordered to do the same work and take the same risks as the British troops on the island and yet received less pay. Considerable unhappiness resulted—not only among the conscripts themselves, who naturally felt cheated, but also among the Maltese community

*See below, pp. 125–28.

at large, who understood only too well the implications of this double standard. "Once again," one of them later remarked, "the British found a way to remind us of our inferior worth."[32]

Meanwhile, with invasion an almost foregone conclusion, the island was put on a full emergency footing. The various village contingents of the 3500-man home guard (*voluntieri*), made up largely of the too young and the too old, were issued recently captured Italian rifles and placed on standby alert; the island's curfew was extended from 5:30 to 6:30 A.M. in order to keep the roads clear during the early morning hours when the enemy would be most likely to come; and regular troop contingents were ordered into battle readiness. In early April the government decreed that upon the sounding of the invasion alarm all people, save those with official duties to perform, were to go inside their homes or shelters or risk being shot as quislings. The alarm was to be "15 seconds of warbling siren, followed by 30 seconds of silence, and then 15 seconds of steady siren, 30 more seconds of silence, and then 15 seconds of warble"—by the end of which, muttered the usual grumblers, the civilian population would be totally confused and the enemy halfway up the beach. Later the invasion signal was changed to the ringing of the island's church bells, which was generally considered an improvement, even though it meant suspending their regular use for the rest of the emergency.

In the high councils of the enemy, however, an invasion of Malta was not being seriously considered at this time. In early February a feasibility study by the German High Command (OKW) had produced a plan for a joint German-Italian airborne assault against the island. From his new post in North Africa, Rommel came out strongly in support of it and even offered to assume personal command. But Hitler rejected the idea and ordered it abandoned. Ordinarily this would have put an end to the matter, but a few weeks later Admiral Raeder made so bold as to bring it up again. Still convinced that the best way to beat Britain was to strike at its Middle East oil supplies through North Africa, Raeder once more attempted to impress upon the Führer the importance of seizing Malta:

> In English hands it threatens our transport of troops and . . . supplies to Africa. If it were in Axis hands our convoy traffic . . . would be facilitated considerably and the Italian naval forces which are being used as escorts would be available for operational purposes.[33]

Hitler remained unmoved, however. He had been assured by no less an authority than Air Marshal Hermann Goering himself that capturing Malta would prove difficult and expensive because of its uneven terrain and endless network of stone walls, which "would impede the employment of airborne troops." Besides, it was no longer necessary to seize the island, because it had ceased to have any military significance. Fliegerkorps X had bombed it into impotence, as demonstrated by the fact that during the first quarter of 1941, or roughly the period beginning with the arrival of the Luftwaffe in Sicily, a monthly average of less than 1 percent of all Axis shipping bound for North Africa was sunk by enemy action—well within the range of acceptable loss.[34] But most important in accounting for Hitler's lack of interest in seizing Malta at this time was his decision made sometime earlier to attack the Soviet Union, come spring. Specifically, the operation was set to begin in early May, and, as the Führer repeatedly impressed upon the OKW, nothing must be permitted to delay it.

Only, as the fortunes of war would have it, something did.

11 *Interlude*

A Balkan campaign was one of the last things Hitler wanted, especially in the spring of 1941 when he was getting prepared to strike at Russia. But he really had no choice. Mussolini's foolish decision to attack Greece that previous autumn had led to all sorts of difficulties, including another humiliation for the Italian army, and, more important, the arrival of British land, sea, and air contingents at key Greek bases, from where they could create considerable mischief. For the Führer this was a situation that must be remedied before he could comfortably turn his attention to the Russians. Thus in early April, German troops crossed into Greece and, in a skillfully conducted operation costing fewer than 5000 casualties, overran the country in seventeen days, forcing the Greek army to surrender and the British to withdraw their battered forces to the nearby island of Crete.

The question now arose as to whether or not to pursue the British and drive them from Crete. Hitler was inclined to think not. The campaign against Greece had accomplished everything he had hoped it would: It had relieved the Duce of further embarrassment from that quarter and it had effectively removed the enemy's threat to Hitler's southern flank. Clearly the British were no longer in a position to molest Romania's oil fields. In fact, with German bombers positioned in Greece only a hundred miles away, Crete would probably prove useless as an offensive base of any kind. Therefore, why not let the island go, especially since there was still time to regroup and launch the attack against Russia more or less on schedule.

At this point, however, the Führer was approached by Gen. Kurt Student, commander of the crack Fliegerkorps XI, an airborne assault unit made up mainly of parachute and glider troops. Speaking not only for himself but for other senior Luftwaffe officers as well, Student argued that the possession of Crete would give Germany an important strategic advantage in the eastern Mediterranean. For instance, seizing the island would bring Suez within range of Germany's medium bombers and enable the Luftwaffe to seal off that end of Britain's lifeline.* It would also deal a severe blow to the morale of an enemy whose sea power was supposed to prevent such things from happening. Furthermore, the Germans would stand a good chance of bagging the more than 30,000 British troops on the island. And this could all be done so easily, Student asserted as he explained his plan for the largest airborne operation ever attempted up to that time. "It sounds all right," Hitler agreed, "but I don't think it's practicable." Still, in the end he went along with the idea.[1]

The conquest of Crete was brilliantly conceived and bravely executed. Within little more than a week after their initial landing in the early morning of May 20, General Student's 22,000 airborne troops had overpowered a combined British-Greek force of nearly twice that number and had completely secured the island. For the British this was merely the final blow in a series of military misadventures stemming from Churchill's questionable decision in late February to go to the aid of the Greeks. Of the more than 60,000 British and Commonwealth troops who had subsequently been sent to Greece, well over half were killed, wounded, or left behind on the beaches—either on the mainland or on Crete. The loss of equipment was almost total. Another Dunkirk on a smaller scale. Without question, this was one of the darkest moments of the war for the British. In addition to all else, they had sustained heavy naval losses and, perhaps worst of all, had seriously weakened General Wavell's Army of the Nile by detaching some of his finest troops and matériel for the Greek expedition. Quick to take advantage of the situation, Rommel counterattacked in late March and within three months had pushed Wavell's forces back 400 miles. On June 21, while the pitiful remnants of the Greek disaster were still licking their wounds in rest camps outside Cairo and Alexandria, Rommel's Afrika Korps reached the Egyptian border.

And yet, although the British would have found this hard to believe at the

*The Germans had no long-range bombers, a situation arising from a prewar decision to channel their resources into the production of medium and light tactical bombers.

time, their intervention in Greece was actually a strategic victory of considerable long-range significance: Had it not been for Britain's military presence in Greece, Hitler might not have invaded the country at all. Surely he would not have bothered with Crete—and Crete would cost him dearly in both time and striking power. It is probably too much to say that Hitler's thousand-year Reich began to crumble with the decision to attack the island. There can be little doubt, though, that the Crete campaign gave rise to certain conditions, and to attitudes on the part of the Führer himself, that would lessen Germany's chances of winning the war. Not the least of these was the damage done Hitler's military timetable. Unquestionably, the attack on Crete figured heavily in his six-week postponement of Germany's massive assault against the Soviet Union, originally set for early May. Six weeks of lost springtime—and while it's true that weather and ground conditions were poor that spring along much of the Russian front, it still seems more than likely that, given an additional month and a half before running into the Russian winter, the German offensive would have forced the Soviet Union out of the war.

Of more direct concern to Malta were the heavy losses sustained by Fliegerkorps XI in the airborne invasion of Crete. According to unofficial Luftwaffe sources, 271 Ju-52 transport planes were destroyed, plus "a large number" of gliders.[2] Far more important were the troop casualties, which ran much higher than anyone had anticipated. Out of the total force of 22,000 that seized the island, 4000 were killed and another 2000 wounded—not just ordinary troops either, but among the best the fatherland had to offer. They had fought superbly against superior forces in entrenched positions, and by the narrowest of margins they had won. But a casualty rate of nearly 30 percent was hardly acceptable. Fliegerkorps XI, one of the finest units in the entire German military machine and high on Hitler's list of favorites, had been badly crippled. Germany had indeed, as the eminent military historian Liddell Hart later stated, "sprained its wrist in Crete."[3]

When the casualty report reached him, Hitler was visibly shaken. Naturally he had expected the invasion force to be bloodied a bit, but by no means this severely. In a letter to the Duce he described the tremendous difficulties of communication and supply, which had caused success in the operation to "hang by a silk thread," and he complained bitterly of the heavy losses in men and equipment. Without saying so in as many words, he acknowledged that the invasion had been a mistake. In fact, its outcome had left him convinced that the very concept of an airdrop behind enemy lines was faulty, unless supported by the element of surprise, which, according to the Führer, was now "worn out." There would be no more such undertakings, he assured Mussolini. "A repetition of these tactics is impossible." And for once the Führer would live up to his word. Never again did he permit German troops to be dropped behind enemy lines—a decision that would have considerable bearing on the future course of the war, and, especially, on the fortunes of Malta.[4]

Meanwhile, as the attack on Crete was being prepared and carried out, the quality of life in Malta took a decided turn for the better. In early May there seemed to be a slackening of enemy air activity over the island. By the middle of the month the number and intensity of the raids had diminished dramatically. At about that time a happy rumor began to spread among the islanders. Where it had originated, no one seemed to know, but it was widely believed and, unlike most rumors in the Malta of those days, would turn out to be true: The Regia Aeronautica had recently given a huge farewell party to their Luftwaffe comrades. Fliegerkorps X was leaving Sicily, and although its destination was unknown, as far as the Maltese were concerned, the farther away it went, the better.[5] One day toward the end of the month the rumor was confirmed when, for the first time since early January, the Italians came over alone. The *maccu* (little fish, or small fry) were back. The islanders breathed a deep sigh of relief and gave joyful thanks to the Virgin, but they were in no hurry to rehang their curtains or restore the bric-a-brac to its shelves—nor would they throng back to the target areas as they had before.

There were, in fact, some more anxious weeks in store for the islanders after the bad news from Crete became known. It wasn't as if the idea of an invasion were new to them. After all, for months they had been poised in readiness for one. Still, as Sybil Dobbie later recalled, the apparent ease with which Crete was seized had a decidedly chilling effect on the people. The question, seldom asked but in the back of everyone's mind, was: If Crete could be taken with so little effort, why not Malta, which was smaller and in a much more vulnerable position, with the enemy on all sides and its nearest friends 900 miles away? Governor Dobbie obviously shared this apprehension. To London he sent assurances that with God's help Malta would repel any Axis attack. Still, he would like more antitank guns as soon as possible, along with some heavy and light antiaircraft artillery.[6]

In late June the tension eased considerably when news of Hitler's assault against Russia reached the island, and as the summer wore on, the invasion jitters largely disappeared. Germany was now busy elsewhere, and the Italians were unlikely to mount an invasion by themselves. Once again, in fact, they were proving to be very halfhearted adversaries. As in the days before the Germans had appeared, Italian bombers, ranging in number from a single plane to groups of ten or twelve, flew over the island at altitudes in excess of 12,000 feet, dropped their undersized bombs, and then scurried for home. During the summer months slightly more than a hundred air attacks were made against Malta, most of them at night when there was less danger from the island's guns and fighters. Save for the unnecessary death of some fifty civilians who failed to take cover (many of them rooftop spectators), damage to persons and property was negligible. The raids did succeed, however, in keeping the islanders on edge by repeatedly interrupting their sleep and driving them into the shelters. "They didn't hurt us much," a district medical officer later remarked, "but they certainly proved wearing on the nerves."[7] Letters to the *Times* bespoke a growing weariness among the people: "We are all beginning to feel a bit run down," said one.[8] Still, as a British antiaircraft officer stated at the time—all things considered, the Italians were "a delightful enemy."

As ineffective as Italy's air force was that summer, its navy was even worse. Despite a vigorous letter from Hitler in late June, reminding the Duce of the necessity of "holding Malta down" and urging him to use his fleet to prevent supplies from reaching the island, Italian naval units, especially the heavier ships, seldom ventured beyond home waters. Part of the problem was lack of fuel. In June the Duce grumbled to Count Ciano that the oil and other supplies promised by Hitler were arriving in such small quantities that Italy would soon be forced to fight "an ersatz war." A few months later he complained that the Germans had delivered almost nothing of what they had promised: "Among the cemeteries, I shall someday build the most important of all, one in which to bury German promises."[9]

But it was not entirely for lack of oil that the Italian fleet held back when it should have been harassing Malta's sea-lanes: In late March at the Battle of Matapan off southern Greece, the Italian navy had lost three heavy cruisers and two destroyers at the cost of one enemy plane. The reason for this one-sided result was that the British now had radar-controlled gunnery, which enabled them to engage at long range with deadly accuracy, even at night. Cunningham's flagship *Warspite,* for example, scored five out of six hits from the first salvo of its fifteen-inch guns, fired in almost total darkness, whereas throughout the entire exchange the Italian battleship *Vittorio Veneto* expended more than ninety rounds in broad daylight without hitting anything. Mussolini was stunned—not so much by the loss of a few ships, because his fleet still maintained a comfortable numerical superiority over that of the enemy. But what good were numbers when, as Matapan had so shockingly demonstrated, the British could blow his vessels out of the sea practically at will?

Convinced that the Italian navy was no match for the British, the Duce would henceforth be even less willing than before to dispatch it into dangerous waters. Thus, much to the disgust of his German allies, throughout the summer and most of the autumn of 1941 British shipping passed practically unmolested through the central Mediterranean on its way from Gibraltar to Malta,* thereby allowing the island to replenish its reserve stores, which had been substantially reduced by the recent efforts of Fliegerkorps X. During this period thirty-two out of thirty-four merchant ships arrived safely from the west with their cargoes virtually intact. In addition, light surface units of the Royal Navy brought in several hundred tons of stores and close to 2000 troop reinforcements, also from Gibraltar. Meanwhile, from Alexandria five freighter submarines, laden with nearly 200 tons each of medical stores, dry milk, aviation fuel, and mail from home, made repeated shuttle runs in what would soon become known affectionately among the islanders as "the magic carpet service." What the submarines brought didn't amount to more than a tiny fraction of Malta's overall supply needs—really only a trickle—but the time would come when this trickle would look considerably larger than it did during that fair and easy summer of 1941. By autumn the overall supply situation on the island was described by military authorities as "excellent." It was estimated that, with the exception of coal, fodder, and kerosene, essential civilian stores should last until the following May. For most military items there was now a reserve supply of between eight and fifteen months, provided the enemy didn't destroy any of the island's storage depots—which, come the winter and spring of 1942, would not be the way of things at all.[10]

From time to time that summer and autumn, single, unescorted merchantmen, often specially outfitted for a speedy dash through enemy waters, would enter Grand Harbour and tie up at one of the buoys to be unloaded. Such an event was always the cause of interest and rejoicing among the islanders, who understood full well that their survival depended upon seaborne supplies from the outside world. It was the convoys, however, that set the island astir with excitement and celebration, and none more so than

*But not westward from Alexandria. During the early months of the war the Alexandria route had been considered the safer approach to Malta and was the one more frequently used. However, with the occupation of both Crete and Cyrenaica (eastern Libya) by the Germans in the spring of 1941, the narrow sea-lane between the two had become extremely dangerous to negotiate because of its exposure to German land-based aircraft. Thus, during the summer and autumn of 1941, with ships getting through to Malta more or less uncontested from Gibraltar, the Alexandria route was used sparingly by merchant shipping, in spite of the fact that thousands of tons of Malta-bound supplies, shipped weeks earlier from Great Britain around the cape, were glutting Alexandria warehouses.

Operation Substance, which reached Grand Harbour under heavy naval escort in late July. The first of three such expeditions to arrive during that summer and early autumn, Substance was made up of six merchant ships laden with more than 65,000 tons of military and civilian stores. Since it was the largest convoy ever to have reached Malta up to that time, and the first major reprovisioning of the island for nearly five months, it was a particularly welcome sight to the islanders, who lined the battlements on both sides of the harbor and cheered the vessels to their moorings in the middle of the bay. From there they would be unloaded by lighters and returned in ballast to Gibraltar. Or perhaps not!

During the night of July 25–26, only thirty-six hours after the arrival of Substance, the Italians staged a daring raid designed to penetrate the defenses of Grand Harbour and destroy the convoy. From the beginning everything went wrong: Shortly before midnight an Italian tender and two large torpedo launches (E-boats) arrived at a point twenty miles northeast of Malta. Here they held a stationary position for more than an hour while the tender unloaded several small craft that were supposed to make their way undetected to a checkpoint a thousand meters from the tip of Valletta. Unfortunately for the Italians, however, the tender was picked up by Malta's radar, and although the British didn't know what to make of this strange speck, their suspicions were sufficiently aroused to alert the coastal gun batteries. Thus, at its very outset the operation lost its most valuable ally—the element of surprise.

The Italian plan was almost as ingenious as it was bold. Between Fort St. Elmo on the tip of Valletta and the beginninag of the breakwater was a narrow channel not more than fifty yards wide. This had formerly been used by small boats going in and out of the harbor, but since the start of the war it had been closed off by a heavy metal net hanging from an overhead footbridge that spanned the opening. The fact that the bridge was in two sections, laid end-to-end and supported in the middle by a sturdy steel piling, would have a considerable bearing on the outcome of the raid.

It was through this narrow opening that the Italians intended to pass into Grand Harbour and attack the convoy with half a dozen outboard motorboats called MTMs, or *barchini,* each of which carried 300 kilograms of high explosives in its bow. The MTM had been specially designed by the Italian navy for just such an operation. Only sixteen feet long and capable of speeds in excess of twenty-six knots, it was highly maneuverable and, because of its low silhouette, difficult to spot at a distance or under conditions of limited visibility. Upon hitting the target the boat's bow would be blown loose by a light preliminary charge and then sink to a predetermined depth before ex-

The breakwater footbridge after the Italian raid.

ploding. Meanwhile, a few seconds before impact the pilot, by the simple pull of a lever, would have ejected himself and a section of the stern, which was designed to serve as a life raft until he was captured. That the *barchini* were not to be taken lightly had been demonstrated in the spring of that year when they surprised the British cruiser *York* in Greek waters and damaged it so badly that it had to be beached.

But before anything could be accomplished in Grand Harbour, the steel netting would have to be breached. This was the job of the SLC, or "pig," which in effect was a human torpedo operated by two pilots in scuba equipment a few feet beneath the surface. Two of these pigs, one to attack the net by Fort St. Elmo and the other to breach the boom guarding the entrance to Marsamxett Harbour, had been carried to the checkpoint in a small launch powered by a silent electric motor. Shortly before first light the two torpedoes set out for their respective destinations, with the MTMs waiting to follow at spaced intervals—six for Grand Harbour and three for the destroyer and submarine pens in Marsamxett. Almost immediately, however, the pig bound for Marsamxett developed a serious list and was unable to proceed with its mission. Ultimately it would be run aground and scuttled by its pilots, who then gave themselves up.

The attempt to break into Grand Harbour met with even worse luck. There are several different versions of what went wrong, but the most likely one is that the pig, its pilots having locked the rudder and jumped clear, hit the net as intended but stuck in the mesh without detonating. At about this time Italian planes began a diversionary raid on Luqa aerodrome, and, apparently mistaking the sound of one of their bombs for the explosion of the pig, the pilot of the lead MTM set out from the check point to enter the harbor and attack the convoy. At exactly 4:45 (summer time), just as darkness was beginning to lift, he slammed into the still-intact net at full throttle, detonating the charge in his bow and the unexploded torpedo as well. The resulting blast was more than the Italians had counted on. Not only did it destroy the net, but it also brought down the outer span of the overhead footbridge, which fell in such a way as to block the newly created opening. At the sound of the explosion the coastal guns, which had been waiting in readiness since the radar sightings hours before, went into action. From stations at Fort St. Elmo and Ricasoli Point across the narrow mouth of the bay, searchlights were soon flooding the approaches to Grand Harbour, where by now the remaining *barchini* were racing about in total confusion. For most of them the end was mercifully brief. Within five minutes all but two had been blown out of the water by the Royal Malta Artillery's six-pounders. The remaining two, both damaged, limped out to sea where, with the coming of daylight, one was sunk by Hurricanes and the other captured. At the same time, the two E-boats that had accompanied the tender and had been hovering some distance offshore for possible backup action were spotted by British fighters and disposed of by strafing. Of the fifteen attack and support craft that had been involved in the Italian raid, only the tender and a small auxiliary launch returned to Sicily. Twenty enemy sailors were killed and eighteen taken prisoner. The Tenth Light Flotilla of the Italian navy had been virtually obliterated, a sad end to a gallant attempt by uncommonly brave men. But the operation was not a total loss for the enemy. Lessons were learned that would prove useful when, as will be seen, a few months later in a similar attempt at Alexandria the Italians would succeed beyond their wildest expectations. The British also learned something from the experience. After this a picketboat would be kept on constant nighttime patrol at the breakwater, firing flares and dropping occasional depth charges to ward off uninvited guests.[11]

The Maltese were exultant. Aside from some mopping up by the RAF, the battle of Grand Harbour had been fought and won entirely by the coastal gunners and searchlight crews of the Royal Malta Artillery, an all-Maltese regiment. The victory was particularly sweet for the gunners, who, after sitting idly by for over a year watching the antiaircraft defenses duel with the enemy, had finally been given their first taste of battle. They had responded well and deserved considerable credit. But they had hardly covered themselves with glory. Their action had not, as the War Office in London announced, "excited universal admiration." It was, in fact, more on the order of a routine target practice than an actual battle. Indeed, the gun batteries would have been hard put to bungle the job, since the enemy craft were within easy range and had no way to escape or fight back. And the fact that the gunners had been alerted and were, in effect, lying in ambush certainly made their task easier. Even so, the story might have ended less happily for the islanders, had it not been for the Italians' extraordinary bit of bad luck with the footbridge. Except for that, gunners and searchlights notwithstanding, at least a few of the *barchini* would probably have been able to enter the harbor and press their attack against the convoy with some success.

Still, it was an especially proud day for the Maltese. They had suffered much from the enemy, and now finally they had been able to deliver a telling blow in return. Such a victory would have been sweet at any time, but coming so soon after Crete and the British retreat in North Africa, it was doubly welcome. Here, for a change, was something to cheer about, and the fact that it had been accomplished by the Maltese themselves (not the British) made it all the more gratifying. As Sybil Dobbie later remarked, the victory gave their morale a tremendous boost. For days thereafter they could talk of little else, and as the story grew more heroic with each retelling, the spirits of the people soared accordingly. Just the sort of tonic they needed—and deserved—after so many months of unrelieved adversity.

Aside from the Battle of Grand Harbour, the summer passed without much high drama for the little island, and despite the annoyance and fatigue caused by the Italian raids, it was not an altogether unpleasant time. As during the summer before, footpaths were opened through the barbed-wire entanglements to give people access to the swimming areas, except along the northern coast where the lovely sand beaches were heavily seeded with antipersonnel devices. Although there was some concern over floating mines, sailing conditions were the best they had been in years. The yacht club held races twice a week and had an exceptionally good season. Polo was no longer possible, of course, since the Marsa playing field had been taken over for growing fodder. The racetrack had met a similar fate, but the Maltese held their beloved sulky races just the same, on improvised courses laid out along the island's country roads.

The movies that summer, brought in regularly by ship and sometimes by bombers on their way to Egypt, included such up-to-date fare as Louis Hayward in *The Man in the Iron Mask,* Deanna Durbin in *A Hundred Men and a Girl,* and Gary Cooper in *The Adventures of Marco Polo*. Oddly enough, however, the newsreels that arrived were all at least five months old. As a result they were likely to be not only inappropriate but also bad for morale. Scenes depicting Wavell's great victories in the desert, when everyone knew that Rommel had long since pushed the British back to Egypt and Wavell had in effect been fired—or camera coverage of the Greeks mauling the Italians in Albania, shown several months after Germany had knocked Greece out of the war—were bound to have a depressing effect. It was no secret that the war was not going well, but why remind everyone?

For entertainment there were also musicals and cultural readings at the British Institute in Valletta, usually before a packed house. Garden clubs staged benefit exhibitions for the refugee fund. Military band concerts were held in the various villages, and from time to time there were even formal regimental reviews. Almost like the old days. Night life was still available, but the curfew and the blackout caused certain problems. Melita Strickland would later recall the weekly Saturday night dinner dances at the Sliema Club, which were resumed in early June after the Germans had left:

> By the time we had finished eating, it was nearly dark and the blackout curtains had to be drawn. This meant, of course, that the place soon became beastly hot, and the

activity of all the dancing turned the hall into a large steam chamber. The men, most of them in their dress military uniforms, dripped with perspiration, and all the young ladies in their formal white gowns looked like wilted flowers. Every so often when the heat became unbearable, we darkened the hall and opened the curtains to let some air in. And then, after a time, back to the dancing. . . .

Getting home on our tandem bicycle could be difficult, and, when there was no moonlight, we often had to get off and walk. And, of course, it was a violation of the curfew to go from one town to another. It was all very exciting. I was rather hoping that some night we would be challenged by the specials [constables]. But we never were. That summer the authorities tended to be rather lax about the curfew, especially on Saturday nights. Occasionally we would run into an air raid, and then we would really pedal as if our lives depended on it—which, I suppose, they may well have.[12]

For the island's children, especially the younger ones, the summer of 1941 was great fun, at least until school began in early September. Although not supposed to, they would poke through the ruins of bombed-out homes in search of shattered scraps of wood and bits of cloth for making model planes and miniature parachutes. By now the children had become authorities on aerial warfare. Most of them could identify the different types of British and enemy planes by sound, without even looking up. Some had become expert at imitating the wail of the air raid siren or a whistling bomb. For hours on end they played at being gunners, battling fiercely against make-believe Stukas and Italian SM 79s. Parades and military reviews were common among these barefoot brigades. Since the departure of the Germans the Italians had begun bedeviling the main target areas with large numbers of antipersonnel bombs, which looked a good deal like tin cans. A favorite game of the children was to find an empty can, sneak up behind a group of grown-ups, and roll it at them while racing off in the opposite direction, screaming: "Personnel bomb! Personnel bomb!" Killing rats was also a great sport, and in the devastated areas of Grand Harbour there were surely enough to choose from. Thousands scurried about the debris, some as big as cats, and almost as insolent. "Rattus! Rattus!" someone would shout, and the youngsters would drop what they were doing and join in an exciting chase with rocks and clubs and whatever other weapons might come to hand. The authorities encouraged the children in this constructive play and eventually would give them a bounty of a penny for every fifty rats they killed. But that was at a later time, after the people had begun eating the cats.

Thus the days passed during the summer and much of the autumn of 1941–not the best of times, to be sure, but on the whole not so bad either. Most of the Maltese knew little real suffering and even less danger. There were, however, unmistakable signs that leaner times were upon them. Although stores of various kinds had reached the island in sizable quantities that summer and early fall, and the supply situation was on the whole very favorable, the list of scarce items was considerably longer than it had been during the previous summer, and it seemed to be growing by the day. Beef, for instance, had all but disappeared from the market. Whereas each year before the war between 15,000 and 20,000 head of beef cattle had been imported on the hoof, now there were none. In July only 10 percent of the normal amount of beef was available, all of it canned or frozen.[13] An increase in native pork production helped somewhat, but it fell far short of making up for the loss in beef. In late summer the government ordered the islanders to refrain from eating meat for two days every week. Given that Friday was not one of the two specified, the prescription really amounted to three days, for although the church had granted dispensation from dietary restrictions during the war, the tradition-bound Maltese generally continued to avoid all meat on Friday. No matter. For most of the islanders a shortage of meat posed no great hardship anyway. Meat had never been a great favorite with the average Maltese, for whom a typical meal would consist of a hollowed-out loaf of bread stuffed with tomatoes and cheese and bits of onions, all saturated with olive oil. What was most important for the island's food consumption, then, was the availability of wheat and edible oil, and both of these were in abundant supply.

But many other items were not. In addition to beef, supplies of fish, butter, coffee, sugar, and canned milk were all growing very scarce. Except for potatoes, tomatoes, and onions, fresh vegetables were also becoming increasingly difficult to come by, and egg vendors often had to have police protection to keep from being mobbed. Among nonedibles, kerosene, coal and coke, soap, and matches were in especially short supply. It was during this time, the summer of 1941, that the Maltese housewife began to emerge as one of the heroes of the Battle of Malta. After her night's sleep had been ruined by a 2:00 A.M. dash to the neighborhood shelter, often with a child in her arms and others tugging at her skirt, she would be up at daybreak waiting in line at the local marketplace, shoving and being shoved for the sake of a cauliflower or a jar of jam. Good practice for the bleaker days ahead.

What underlay the whole problem, of course, was Malta's almost complete inability to provide for its own needs. As mentioned earlier, nearly everything but rock, water, and salt had to be imported, including all but a small fraction of the island's food supply. At the outbreak of the war Malta had some 24,000 acres under cultivation, about half of it on the little island of Gozo.[14] Of this tiny amount (less than one-tenth of an acre per person) roughly a third was in wheat and barley and practically all the rest in vegetables, grapes, and citrus fruits. A list of those crops that were produced, many of them harvested twice a year, is impressive for its variety: virtually everything imaginable from eggplant and American sweet corn to figs and even bananas. Aside from grains, potatoes, and onions, however, the quantities were negligible. The 1940–41 green bean harvest, for instance, amounted to about two pounds per person. All told, during the first year of the war Malta (including Gozo) produced considerably less than a third of its total food needs. And as time went on, the situation would worsen, for a number of reasons. Among them: the loss of hundreds of acres of arable land to military installations, especially airstrips and dispersal pens for the planes; the increasing difficulty in obtaining adequate supplies of fertilizer, most of which had been shipped in from Italy before the war; and, the sharp growth in the island's population brought about by the arrival of several thousand additional troops. Beginning early in the war, widespread distribution of free seeds, together with other efforts by the authorities to promote the raising of victory gardens, brought a positive response from the people. Many even went so far as to dig up their precious flower beds to make room for various kinds of high-yield edibles. But the results of all this were inconsequential: less than 1 percent added to the island's overall harvest.[15]

The only food produced on Malta that came close to meeting the island's year-round needs was fresh milk from its herd of 35,000 goats, and even this had to be supplemented by imported canned and dry milk—increasingly so as the war progressed. The goats were well suited to the marginal grazing conditions on Malta, and their milk and cheese made up an important part of the Maltese diet. They also constituted a reserve meat supply. But the idea of actually slaughtering the herd was unthinkable. It would mean sacrificing the island's fresh milk production in return for, at best, a few pounds of meat per person. At the time few people, if any, could imagine that the island would ever be reduced to such desperate straits.

For those on Malta at the time, the summer of 1941 would be remembered less for its encroaching shortages than for its remarkable potato glut. If it is true that for everything there is a season, then clearly this was the season for the potato. Blessed with an unusually bountiful crop (more than 24,000 tons), the island literally had more potatoes than it knew what to do with. Before the war potatoes had been Malta's principal (and virtually only) export, averaging in excess of 10,000 tons a year. But now, with merchant shipping no longer available for such low-priority traffic, they had no place to go. Nor could they be stored for any length of time in the heat of the Mediterranean summer. They would have to be consumed on the island, and, if they were not to rot first, they would have to be consumed in a hurry.

But how? It was estimated that every man, woman, and child would have to eat nearly two pounds of them a day for ten weeks or more in order to cope with the glut. Rising to the challenge, the *Times* ran a series of articles on the joys of potato soup, potato puree, potato casserole, etc., and suggested starting a potato chip industry on the island.

Meanwhile, the government launched a campaign to improve the potato's image. Diabetes, formerly attributed to too much potato, was now blamed on bread and pasta, and before long the potato was being presented as a health food of almost miraculous properties. Soon the ideal answer was found to this embarrassment of riches. In July the authorities ordered that until further notice all bread must contain between 20 and 30 percent potato.[16] In this way more than a thousand tons of flour could be saved for future use. For the most part the Maltese didn't care much for this new "wheatato" bread, as it came to be called, but they put up with it as just one more indignity brought on by the war. Not for long, however. Within three months wheatato and the potato itself disappeared from the scene. The great potato binge had run its course, and it would be a long time before the islanders would again have to worry about having too much of anything to eat.

During that summer, rationing became a prominent feature of life on Malta. Given the island's almost total dependence on imports and the vulnerability of its supply lines, the program had been a long time coming. Too long, according to some critics who maintained that a broad-based system of rationing should have been introduced at the very outset of the war, both as a precautionary move against future shortages and as a way of discouraging hoarding and price gouging. For several months the authorities had openly opposed rationing as unnecessary and likely to cause more problems than it would solve, but in early 1941 during the German blitz they announced that because of changing conditions it was now "highly desirable" to ration certain items.

Beginning in early April with sugar, coffee, matches, and soap, the number of rationed goods grew to a dozen by the end of the summer. Issued twice a month, all of the items on the ration list except kerosene were made available through the island's more than 1500 grocery shops—but not just any one of them a person might happen to choose. At the start of the program the head of each household was directed to register for himself and his family at his regular neighborhood grocer's, and thereafter he would be expected to draw his rations from that particular shop, unless of course it were bombed out, in which case another would be assigned. Kerosene, which alone of the rationed items was distributed weekly, was handled in much the same way, except by wagons instead of shops. On the whole this system of neighborhood distribution worked well, partly because it involved people who were known to one another and therefore less likely to cheat or play favorites. But credit must also be given to the Office of Food Distribution in Valletta, which engineered the entire operation and did an excellent job of seeing that the neighborhood outlets received their rationed items on time and in the proper amounts.[17]

The fact that an item was not rationed did not necessarily mean that it was in abundant supply, like, say, bread or pasta. More likely it was left off the list for the opposite reason: There was simply too little of it to go around. Such imported goods as chocolate, jam, and frozen meat fell into this category. So did virtually all foodstuffs grown on the island. To attempt to divide such paltry amounts among a quarter of a million people would have been downright foolish. At first the government even dismissed the idea of price controls for these items, in the belief that the distribution of such scarce commodities was "too much a question of supply and demand."[18] But soaring costs and the resultant public outcry eventually brought about an official change of mind. By autumn 1941 the price control list (which, it may be remembered, had been introduced to a modest extent early in the war) contained not only rationed items but also virtually all other goods and services on the island.

None of this was very successful in holding down the cost spiral, however. The consumer price index, which had already risen 80 percent since the beginning of the war, continued to climb, as the authorities were forced time and time again to make upward adjustments to keep from driving nonrationed goods completely underground. From July 31 to October 31, for example, the official cost-of-living index rose from 238 to 257 (8 percent), while food alone jumped from 261 to 292 (12 percent).[19] And it should be noted that these increases cited by the government were unrealistically low, for they failed to take into account the large volume of goods being sold on the black market at prices well above the legal limits.

Not the least of the colonial government's shortcomings during the war was its failure to cope more effectively with this problem of runaway inflation. Either for reasons of incompetency or lack of resolve, its attempts to hold down prices were feeble at best. What can be said, for instance, of a regime that permitted bus fares to triple at the same time service was being reduced by two-thirds? Not until September 12, 1941, fifteen months after the start of the war, did the government finally set up an official price control board to oversee the cost of the island's goods and services. It was never a great success, and perhaps was not meant to be. But more about that later.*

The result of the government's failure to hold down prices was a decidedly uneven distribution of goods and services between those who could afford to buy (legally or through the black market), and those who couldn't. And most people couldn't. Ordinarily wages would have tended to rise along with costs, but whereas the government's price control program had failed to hold the line, its wage controls, also begun early in the war, had managed to keep most wages close to their peacetime level. True, a few thousand workers in dangerous jobs, mainly at the dockyards and aerodromes, had been given substantial raises. Even so, by midsummer of 1941 the average dockyard wage of ten shillings a day could buy only two rabbits, whereas a year before it could have bought five. The lower grades of unskilled workers, many of them frozen to their jobs by wartime manpower regulations, were in a particularly bad bind. With their wages pegged at twenty-four to twenty-seven shillings a week (about five dollars), and the cost of living continuing to soar, several of them saw no choice but to swallow their pride and go on public relief, even though they kept working full-time. Some of their neighbors found a different way to make ends meet:

> It has come to the knowledge of His Grace the Archbishop . . . that some people are looting goods from houses which have been wrecked or laid open by enemy action. This is really a grave sin, and those who allow themselves to commit such a sin show that they have forgotten entirely the law of God, Who commands us not to steal others' property, and that we should not oppress those who are already stricken by adversity. . . .
>
> Confessors must remember that when such persons, who are guilty of looting, go to them, they must receive them with great charity, explain to them the gravity of that sin, and let them know that no absolution could be granted unless they are prepared to return the things they have stolen.[20]

Despite the shortages and high prices, however, conditions on Malta that summer could hardly be called desperate. Nobody starved or even went hungry. No one could deny that times were lean, but the basic items of the Maltese diet, such as bread, milk, and pasta, were still plentiful and, thanks in part to a succession of imperial subsidies, continued to be available at moderate prices. Grumbling may have increased a bit, but for the most part morale remained high as the islanders took their privations pretty much in stride. There was even a new note of optimism in the air. Although the

*See pp. 222–225.

Italians continued to pick away at the island, it was obvious that the battle for the Mediterranean was taking on a more favorable complexion and that Malta was very much involved in the process. Once again the little island, so recently left for dead by the Luftwaffe, had gone on the offensive.

12 *Teasing the Animals*

In May of 1941 Hugh Pughe Lloyd arrived on the island to take over as air-officer-commanding.* Here was a clear sign that the Home Government had finally awakened to the importance of Malta-based aircraft in the battle for control of the central Mediterranean. Not only was Lloyd a vice-marshal (no mere commodore like his predecessor Maynard), but he was also one of Britain's ablest and most experienced airmen. His days with the RAF dated back to France in 1917 when, after being wounded three times as a sapper, he decided that life would be more pleasant aloft and joined what was at that time the Royal Flying Corps. In the nearly quarter of a century since then he had grown and prospered with the young service, and by the time he arrived on Malta, he had gained a reputation for being an industrious, enterprising, and aggressive leader—a man who made things happen. "As I had expected, Malta was a lonely place," he later wrote:

> It was 900 miles to the nearest aerodrome to the east and 1100 to Gibraltar. There was not a friend at any point of the compass—there was hostility everywhere—and I dare say that had we decided not to tease the animals in the Axis zoo they would have left us to starve at our leisure.[1]

*Although Governor Dobbie was titular commander-in-chief of Malta, his direct military authority extended only to the army garrison. Both the naval and air commandants on the island operated independently of him and were responsible solely to their superior officers in their respective services, although as a courtesy they generally acted in consultation with the governor.

But Lloyd had never intended *not* to tease the animals. Indeed, he had been sent to Malta for precisely that purpose, and he refused to be discouraged by the fact that he had been given so little to work with. Upon moving into his underground headquarters in Lascaris tunnel, he hung a homemade sign near his desk: "Less depends on the size of the dog in the fight than on the size of the fight in the dog."[2]

Within a few hours after his arrival Lloyd made an inspection tour of the aerodromes and the main workshops at Kalafrana. What he saw was even worse than he had expected. With the recent slackening of German air activity, the number of planes on the island had increased somewhat, but still totaled fewer than sixty of all types. As for maintenance, absolutely no new replacement parts were available. Spares had to be obtained by sifting through the ruins of burned-out planes or by cannibalizing healthy ones. Furthermore, the fields were too small; there was no heavy equipment to work with; and even the commonest sort of tools, such as hammers and wrenches, were all but impossible to find. At none of the aerodromes was there anything even resembling a gasoline pump. All refueling had to be done by hand from individual cans. Worse yet was the awful vulnerability of what few facilities there were. The shelter for men, equipment, and valuable stores, including gasoline, was totally inadequate. Most of the planes were clustered together on the open runways, presenting tempting targets for enemy strafing operations. At Kalafrana, Lloyd was stunned by what he saw. All of its buildings were concentrated in a small area and were wholly aboveground. Its engine-repair facility, the only one on Malta, was just a few feet away from the island's only test benches, where engines were checked out after a repair or overhaul. As Lloyd himself later stated, "A few bombs on Kalafrana in the summer of 1941 would have ruined any hope of Malta ever operating an air force."[3]

Ordinarily it would have made sense to wait until the island could offer better protection before bringing in more planes and equipment, and certainly before stirring the enemy's wrath by mounting an offensive against him. But these were not ordinary times. With Rommel breathing hard on Alexandria and Suez, the British must somehow spike his guns, and what better way to do this than to attack his supply lines—often and soon? Since Malta lay directly astride the main Axis shipping lanes to North Africa, it was the most logical place from which to conduct these attacks. The little island was, in fact, the *only* place from which British bombers and torpedo planes could range far enough to do the job. And this was an important point, for throughout the summer and early autumn of 1941 the British relied mainly upon Lloyd's aircraft, along with a small flotilla of Malta-based submarines, to harass Rommel's supply lines. Not until mid-autumn would surface units, which had abandoned the island during the Crete campaign, return to resume their raiding operations out of Marsamxett. Meanwhile, it was sad indeed for Admiral Ford, naval commandant at Malta, to stand atop the battlements in Floriana and survey the surroundings without spotting a single naval vessel in either Grand Harbour or Marsamxett. "Not even a destroyer for my old age," he complained to Cunningham.

From June through September nearly 150,000 tons of Axis shipping was destroyed on its way to or from North Africa, almost all of it by air and underwater units operating out of Malta. According to Admiral Cunningham's figures for approximately the same period, one-third of Rommel's supply ships were either sunk or damaged. In June only one convoy got through to Tripoli unbloodied. The new U-class submarines, especially designed for the clear waters of the Mediterranean, were devastating—but no more so than "Lloyd's Legions," which in the first half of July alone carried out 122 bomber sorties against enemy ships and harbor facilities in Sicily and North Africa. During the summer Malta's air strength was increased to more than sixty bombers and twice as many Hurricanes. Sizable quantities of spare parts, tools, and equipment were also brought in, mainly by cargo submarines and Operation Substance. "Malta's sword was now a long one," Lloyd later wrote.[4]

But it was also a costly one to wield. Since conventional high-altitude bombing against such small targets was ineffective, Lloyd's most common method of attacking enemy shipping was to send in Blenheim bombers and Swordfish torpedo planes at masthead level. On the whole this got good results, but by midsummer, after the Italians finally armed their merchant ships with antiaircraft guns, British losses on these raids had soared to an average of 12 percent. Planes and crews were being shot down at the rate of six a week. The cost was almost as high for the Wellingtons, which were used mainly against the enemy's harbors and, because of the distances involved, often had to go in without fighter protection. Each enemy ship sunk, whether in port or at sea, earned the deserving airmen a bottle of Plymouth gin from Lloyd's private stock, which he kept stashed under his bed at Lascaris. For such hazardous work the tour of duty seldom ran for more than a month, but even this was too long for most. According to Lloyd: "Everyone realized that the chances of surviving a tour on Malta were very remote indeed."[5]

Meanwhile Lloyd was working feverishly to provide as much protection as possible, as soon as possible, for his aircraft and support facilities. Realizing full well that the Germans would eventually return to punish Malta for its insolence, he strove to take full advantage of those relatively tranquil days when there was nothing more fearsome to contend with than the Regia Aeronautica. During that summer and autumn he concentrated his efforts on moving his repair and maintenance facilities underground and on increasing the dispersal area and number of pens for his aircraft. Going underground was easier than Lloyd had expected. At Takali several hangars, spacious enough to accommodate fuel, equipment, and even a few fighters, were dug into the soft sides of the Mdina cliffs that conveniently abutted the aerodrome on the southwest. At nearby Luqa many of the machine shops formerly located at Kalafrana were moved into a magnificent natural cavern that seemed to have been put there specifically for that purpose. With few pneumatic drills or other power tools to work with, preparing these new accommodations was often a slow, tedious process, even when nature had already done much of the work. In the cavern at Luqa, for instance, it was necessary to cut ventilation shafts three feet square down through ninety-five feet of rock. To do this, Maltese miners dangled by ropes and chipped away with hand chisels while bellows forced fresh air down the holes for them to breathe.

Expanding the dispersal areas was mainly a matter of building taxi strips angling off in all directions from the main runways. This additional space would permit the island's planes to be kept far enough apart to minimize the effect of enemy attacks. By late autumn nearly thirty miles of these strips had been completed, roughly a ninefold increase over the previous spring. Unfortunately, in order to do this it was necessary to sequester hundreds of acres of farmland, much of it around Takali, where some of the richest soil on the island was found. At various points along the dispersal strips and a few feet off to the side, pens were built to serve as shelters for individual aircraft. These pens were usually square, corral-like structures with one open end. At first they were made out of sandbags, but these proved too cumbersome and were soon abandoned in favor of discarded gasoline cans, of which there was a seemingly endless supply on the island. Filled with dirt, crushed stone, and even sand from the beaches, these two-gallon cans would be the main building blocks for the dispersal pens. However, putting them all properly in place was a mammoth undertaking. A pen for a Wellington bomber, for instance, was ninety feet square and fourteen feet high, with each side tapered from a thickness of twelve cans at its base to two cans at the top. Conservatively, this amounted to more than 3500 tons of earth, hand-poured into some 60,000 individual cans, which were tied together by nearly three miles of wire. All this for a single pen.

Making the island's aerodromes less exposed to enemy raids involved a major commitment of manpower. For months thousands of Maltese laborers worked with shovels, hoes, and pony carts, building dispersal strips that could have been finished in a fraction of the time had there been even a single tractor available. To construct a bomber pen required the labor of 200 men working nine hours a day for twenty-one days, and the excavation of underground hangars took an enormous number of man-hours. But like so much else on Malta those days, labor had become a scarce commodity. Several thousand Maltese workers had been conscripted into the military, while thousands of others had been hired by the government to clear the streets of rubble left over from the German blitz, repair broken sewers and water mains, and demolish partially destroyed buildings whose weakened walls posed a threat to passersby.[6] For the first time that anyone could recall, there was no unemployment in Malta. According to Lloyd, finding workers had become "an exercise in sheer opportunism." Eventually he was able to borrow 3000 infantry troops to help out full-time. Regular aerodrome personnel, including clerks, wireless operators, and even flight crews, also chipped in whenever possible, and on a given day as many as a hundred civilians would show up at lunchtime to volunteer an hour's labor before returning to their regular jobs. It was a heartening display of cooperation, but it was not enough. There was simply too much to be done and too few people to do it in the time allotted. Despite all that Lloyd was able to accomplish (and it was considerable, given what he had to work with), when the Germans returned in December, the aerodromes would still present inviting targets.

The navy was also busy preparing for the inevitable return of the Luftwaffe. At the shipyards several of the principal repair shops were moved underground, while improved shelters, some of them with sleeping accommodations, were provided for the dock workers. The navy's major project at this time was a rock shelter for its submarines, to be cut out of the side of Mount Sciberras under Valletta. This was an ambitious undertaking. Too ambitious, as it turned out. Plagued like the aerodromes by a shortage of tools and labor, the digging had progressed no more than ten feet into the face of the cliff by the time the Germans reappeared and made further work impossible. This shallow, shadowed indentation, still clearly visible from the Marsamxett side of Valletta, remains as it was when abandoned more than a generation ago: an elongated arch rising fifteen feet or so above the water level, looking for all the world like a cavity at the gum line.

The final quarter of the year was a disaster for Axis shipping in the central Mediterranean. Besides Malta's aircraft and submarines the enemy now had to contend with Force K, which arrived at the island fortress in late October on orders from Churchill himself, who felt that, despite the damage being inflicted on Rommel's supply lines, too much matériel was still getting through. Composed of two cruisers (*Penelope* and *Aurora*) and two destroyers (*Lance* and *Lively*), all well appointed and capable of speeds in excess of twenty-eight knots, Force K provided Malta with another powerful dimension for its offensive arsenal, namely, surface raiders able to range far enough and fast enough to intercept enemy ships that might otherwise reach their destination by eluding the island's bombers and outrunning its submarines. Working together, Malta's planes, submarines, and surface craft made a shambles of Rommel's shipping during the final months of 1941. In October 63 percent of the total Axis tonnage dispatched to North Africa was sunk en route, virtually all of it by Malta-based attacks. During the following month the percentage rose to an incredible 77 percent.[7] In six weeks' time Force K alone accounted for eleven cargo ships and two tankers. Its greatest single triumph occurred on the night of November 8, when it attacked a heavily protected convoy off the toe of Italy. In his diary Count Ciano gives a more or less accurate account of what happened:

> Tonight we tried it again; Libya needs material, arms, fuel, more and more every day. And a convoy of seven ships left, accompanied by two ten-thousand-ton cruisers and ten destroyers. . . . An engagement occurred, the results of which are inexplicable. All, I mean *all,* our ships were sunk, and one or maybe two or three destroyers. The British returned to their ports after having slaughtered us. . . . This morning Mussolini was depressed and indignant. This will undoubtedly have profound repercussions in Italy, Germany, and, above all, in Libya.[8]

In all, some 60,000 tons of stores and an undetermined number of troop reinforcements were lost that night in a few minutes' time, without so much as a scratch being suffered by the attacking force.* Earlier that very day

*The principal reason for this one-sided result was that Force K had radar and the Italians didn't, which meant that the latter were fighting blind. It should also be noted, however, that in this instance and in many others involving attempts by enemy convoys to reach North Africa, British raiders had the added advantage of being in the right place at the right time because of "the Ultra secret"—a breach in the security of the enemy's high-level cipher. Thus, the sending out of reconnaissance planes from Malta to spot (and be spotted by) enemy ships was often merely a subterfuge. By intercepting and deciphering messages to and from Rommel, the British frequently knew well in advance the size of a given convoy, when it intended to leave port, what route it would follow, and in some cases, even what cargo it contained. For the story of "Ultra" see Ronald Lewin, *Ultra Goes to War* (New York, 1978); also, F. W. Winterbotham, *The Ultra Secret* (New York, 1975).

Rommel had complained bitterly to his superiors in Berlin that he was being starved for supplies and men. And now this!

But there was worse to come for Rommel. On November 18 the Army of the Nile (now the Eighth Army) under Wavell's successor, Gen. Claude Auchinleck, opened its long-expected desert offensive. Weakened by serious shortages of manpower and matériel, Axis forces were pushed back all along the line. As he had done so often during recent months, Rommel again sent out an urgent call for reinforcements. The results were much the same as before. From Ciano's diary:

[December 1] Out of the whole convoy two ships arrived; one was forced to beach at Suda Bay, and two were sunk. The result is not brilliant. But it might have been worse.

[December 2] Another of our ships has been sunk almost at the entrance to the port of Tripoli. It was the *Mantovani* loaded with seven thousand tons of petrol. It cannot be denied that this is a hard blow.[9]

Malta again! Always Malta!

Meanwhile the island's bomber force, augmente‹. by new arrivals from Gibraltar, had stepped up attacks against both ends of the enemy's supply lines, dropping more than a million pounds of bombs in less than four weeks on harbors, storage depots, and rail centers in Italy and North Africa. By the end of November, Rommel's situation had become extremely serious. Obviously something would have to be done, and soon, or all of North Africa would be lost. For months Hitler had been repeatedly warned by his military advisers of the deteriorating conditions in the central Mediterranean. In early September, Adm. Karl Doenitz estimated that Axis shipping in the Mediterranean was being destroyed at such an alarming rate that very soon none would be left. "Even if we invaded France and seized more ships, even by increasing the building of ships appreciably, we could not keep our forces in North Africa on a war footing for one year. Malta must be annihilated."[10] Later that same month Grand Admiral Raeder informed the Führer in a written statement that the Axis position in the Mediterranean had become desperate and urged that steps be taken to counter enemy action there. Having been rebuffed by Hitler several times before on the subject, he made no mention of seizing Malta, but the implication was clear enough. A few weeks later Raeder again wrote to Hitler, this time stating flatly: "Today the enemy has absolute sea and air control over the crossing routes of German transports, and operates completely unhindered in all parts of the Mediterranean."[11]

With winter weather having brought operations on the Russian front to a standstill, the Führer finally agreed to take action against Malta, but not to invade it. In early December he directed that those units of the Luftwaffe no longer required in the east be transferred to Sicily and southern Italy in order to "establish a focus of Axis strength in the Central Mediterranean." Field Marshal Kesselring was ordered from his winter headquarters in front of Moscow to take charge of these forces and others that might be added to the command. His assignment: "to secure mastery of the air and sea in the area between Southern Italy and North Africa in order to secure communications with Libya . . ., and in particular to keep Malta in subjugation."[12] When the Duce learned of these plans, he was privately outraged. He resented Hitler's uninvited interference in the Italian theater. It was clearly a violation of the parallel war concept and, worse than that, "an offense to the soldierly honor of the Italians." But what could he do? In light of the way things had been going, it was obvious that Italy needed help getting the convoys through. Thus, he accepted the Führer's assistance and pretended not to feel the sting. As Count Ciano wrote in his diary: "Under the circumstances we have no right to complain."[13]

Meanwhile, as autumn wore on, the people of Malta were feeling more and more the effects of what the poet Matthew Arnold once called "the gradual furnace" of events. Life was not exactly hard, and it certainly wasn't dangerous for those who had sense enough to take cover when the siren sounded. But it had become increasingly wearing, and at times downright depressing. The weather had turned cold and rainy in November and had settled like a shroud over the people's spirits. And the Italian raids, although not very formidable, seemed interminable. Week after week the Regia Aeronautica continued to pick away, driving the people into the shelters and steadily adding to the island's distress. Since most of the raids were conducted at night, the bombings were erratic and often struck nonmilitary targets. There was no one great night of destruction, no special *noche triste*. At most only a few buildings were hit and a few families made homeless by a single visitation. But after several months the cumulative damage was substantial. By the end of November the number of private dwellings destroyed or severely damaged since the beginning of the war had risen to nearly 2500.

To make a bad situation worse, there was the recent decision by the government as to who would foot the bill when the time finally came to rebuild: That summer the Council of Government had levied a special tax on all Maltese property holders. The purpose of this tax was to create a general fund that would be used for the eventual restoration of private property destroyed or damaged by enemy action. In other words, the people of the island themselves were apparently going to have to pay for rebuilding their ravaged homes and places of business. This decision struck many of the Maltese as unfair, to say the least. As one of them remarked several years later:

> We were aware that the British government had promised to compensate their own people back home for their losses, and we couldn't understand why they weren't willing to do the same for us. After all, we were old friends, fighting shoulder-to-shoulder with them. . . . Our feelings were hurt, and, to tell the truth, there was some bitterness and resentment. More than one person would say (but only among family and friends): "Why should I have to pay for having my home destroyed fighting England's war?"[14]

As if the withholding of compensation weren't bad enough, the colonial government continued to collect full real-estate taxes on property that had been partially or even completely destroyed. Furthermore, the authorities failed to make any adjustments in the inheritance tax, with the result that a person inheriting property had to pay according to its regular prewar evaluation, even when the property in question had been reduced to rubble. Under the circumstances it is not surprising that many people refused to come forward and claim what was rightfully theirs.[15] "It was difficult, and still is, to understand many of the things the government did and failed to do in those days," a Maltese professor would later comment. "The answer is, I suppose, that the British were not always very sensitive to our needs and feelings."[16] By the time the war entered its second winter, the only financial provision the government had made for those who had sustained loss through enemy action was a Personal Injuries Act, passed in the summer of 1941. Under its terms compensation was to be given to all persons injured as a result of the war (provided they could prove need), and to dependent survivors of those killed. Here at least was a move in the right direction. However, benefits of the act were so niggardly as to be insulting. For example, the wife of Louis Chetcuti, a dockyard worker killed during the attack on the *Illustrious,* was awarded a widow's pension of ten pence a day (roughly seventeen cents), while each of his three dependent children was given a flat-sum settlement of seven pounds sterling, or just over twenty-eight dollars. Not a very high price for a husband and a father.[17]

In mid-November the Italians began to step up the tempo of their air attacks against the island by coming over not only at night but also occasionally during the day. This meant more frequent trips to the shelters for the people, more fatigue, and greater all-round crankiness. Throughout the

The Old Railway Tunnel.

summer and autumn, work on the shelters had continued, after a fashion, and in late November the governor was able to announce that there would soon be enough of them, public and private, to accommodate the entire population.[18] However, as the governor admitted, little progress had been made in upgrading the conditions inside the shelters, which generally remained as crude and uncomfortable as they had been months before. The great majority continued to be without electricity, and many lacked lighting of any kind. In Sliema, for instance, residents had been trying for six months to obtain a single hurricane lamp for their neighborhood shelter. Furthermore, little had been done to provide the shelters with proper drainage, and despite the government's recent appropriation of 11,000 pounds to clean them up, most of them remained as filthy as ever. One thing the authorities did do, for which the islanders were deeply grateful: In midsummer they set up delousing centers to rid the people of "verminous objects," which were practically impossible to avoid in the tightly packed shelters.[19] Several years later Prof. J. Aquilina, one of Malta's most distinguished scholars and the father of its first dictionary, would recall an occasion when, as a young instructor on his way to the university, he was forced to take refuge in a small shelter on St. Paul Street in Valletta:

> It wasn't for more than twenty minutes at the most, but we were crowded together shoulder-to-shoulder, and when I came out I was bemedaled with fleas—hundreds of them—moving about on my white shirt. It was impossible, of course, to get them all off before reaching the university. They proved an interesting diversion for my students, who gave me far greater attention that day than they ever had before.[20]

In only a very few of the shelters, mainly the large prewar tunnels in the immediate vicinity of Grand Harbour, had the government made serious attempts to provide any of the amenities. Actually, these tunnels were more dormitories than shelters: Since the beginning of the war they had served as home to hundreds and later thousands of Grand Harbour residents who refused to evacuate the area even though their dwellings had been destroyed. The Old Railway Tunnel was by far the most important of these because it accommodated such a large number of people—perhaps as many as 9000 during the worst months. By late 1941 the tunnel had been provided with multitiered bunks, electric lights, rediffusion radio, freshwater taps, and ablution blocks that were connected to the regular sewer system. District medical officers conducted periodic inspections to check on the condition of the shelter and the people themselves, and from time to time bedding and other personal belongings were ordered outside for a sunning, while the entire tunnel was sprayed with disinfectant. By all accounts, the Old Railway

Tunnel, and a few lesser tunnels that housed another 3000 or so, were safe and reasonably comfortable. And if they were lacking in privacy, they at least offered the luxury of a decent night's sleep—which is more than could be said for the small neighborhood shelters.

December was a bad month for the British in the Mediterranean. Just when events had been going so well, a sudden and dramatic shift in naval power occurred. Actually it had begun in mid-November when one of twenty or more German submarines that had managed to slip through the Straits of Gibraltar sank the carrier *Ark Royal* shortly after it had flown off fighter reinforcements to Malta. Two weeks later the British battleship *Barham* was struck by three German torpedoes and sank like a stone. Soon after that the cruiser *Galatea* was sunk on its way back to Alexandria, again by a German submarine. But the most damaging blow was delivered by the Italians, who, in one of the most daring naval actions of the war, went a long way toward squaring the score with their old nemesis Admiral Cunningham: On the night of December 18, three small underwater scooters, similar to those used the summer before in the attempt against Grand Harbour, were launched by an Italian submarine a few miles off Alexandria. Entering the harbor when the boom was opened for an incoming destroyer, Italian frogmen attached a number of timed demolition charges to the hulls of the battleships *Queen Elizabeth* and *Valiant*. Early the following morning, amid a series of tremendous explosions, the two giant ships settled at even keel on the bottom of the harbor. That same day, while stalking enemy shipping off the coast of Libya, Force K ran into a newly laid mine field and was badly crippled. Incredibly enough, within barely a month's time the Mediterranean fleet had lost its entire top echelon, and then some. All that remained of Cunningham's once proud command were three cruisers and a "handful" of destroyers and submarines. The Mediterranean fleet had become, in Churchill's words, "nonexistent."

All this boded ill for Malta. Those easy days of the past several months, when friendly shipping could come in from the west pretty much unmolested, were obviously at an end. With German submarines prowling the Mediterranean and the Italian surface fleet now virtually unopposed, getting supplies and equipment through to the island from any quarter would be extremely difficult—and this included fighter aircraft. However, a more imminent danger than that now threatened Malta: With no longer anything to fear from the British fleet, what was to prevent the enemy from invading the island, or, failing that, standing a few miles offshore and pulverizing it with their fifteen-inch naval guns? It was not a happy time for the islanders, nor a hopeful one. Coming after months of war, this sudden reversal of military fortunes in the Mediterranean caused their mood to grow dreary—like the winter wind—and it was not improved by rumors reaching them a week or so before Christmas that German air units had returned to Sicily.

But something else happened that December that would have a far greater bearing upon Malta's future, and although at the time its full significance may have been missed by many of the islanders, it was clear enough to Prime Minister Churchill. Early on a Sunday morning, half a world away, the Japanese launched a devastating attack against American military and naval installations. For the United States it was an occasion for great sorrow and outrage, but as Churchill himself later admitted, he could scarcely conceal his joy. Finally, after two years of testing the water, America, with its awesome power, had been thrust into the war as a full-fledged partner of the British Empire. "So we had won after all," the great man wrote. "Being saturated and satiated with emotion, I went to bed and slept the sleep of the saved and the thankful."[21]

13 The Winter of Their Discontent

From Vice-Admiral Wilbraham Ford, Commanding, Malta, to Admiral Andrew Cunningham, Commander in Chief, Mediterranean Fleet, Alexandria, January 3, 1942:

I've given up counting the number of air raids we are getting. At the time of writing, 4 pm, we have had exactly seven bombing raids since 9 am. . . . The enemy is definitely trying to neutralize Malta's effort, and, I hate to say, is gradually doing so. They've bust a sad number of our bombers and fighters, etc., and must continue to do so. . . . I consider that Malta must be made stiff with *modern* fighters. . . . The powers at home must give up safety first and send out the latest if they want to hold Malta and use it as a base. . . . Minesweeping is now difficult, and they appear to be laying them everywhere. Poor *Abingdon,* the only sweeper, and in the daylight she got machine-gunned. . . . I am trying to sweep during the dark hours. . . . Work at the [dock]yard is naturally very much slowed up at present as a result of the constant raids. . . . As I write, another bombing raid is just over and at least two more of ours [planes] burnt out. Damnable to be so useless. Something must be done at once.[1]

From the *Times of Malta,* January 5, 1942:

In the ebb and flow of war one must recognize that there are alternative periods during which one side or the other holds a temporary advantage and it would seem to the uninitiated that at the moment the Luftwaffe has things all its own way.[2]

From the Office of Information's Situation Report, January 20, 1942:

During the night five alerts were sounded for a number of enemy aircraft which approached the island and were engaged by Anti-Aircraft Artillery, resulting in only a few bombs being dropped which caused neither damage nor casualties.

During the day four alerts have been sounded for a number of enemy bombers, escorted by fighters, which dropped bombs. The enemy were heavily engaged by Anti-Aircraft Artillery. Our fighters chased some of the enemy bombers but they escaped in a cloud

A raid is in progress at the moment of issuing this report and for this and other daylight raids full details are not yet available, but will be given in tomorrow's situation report. The total alerts sounded during the last 24 hours are 11.[3]

To nobody's great surprise, Field Marshal Kesselring had wasted little time making his presence felt. Beginning in the latter half of December, Malta's aerodromes were subjected to almost incessant bombing and strafing, intended to destroy their planes, demoralize the ground crews, and demolish the runways and maintenance facilities. Ships and naval installations in the harbors, especially the submarine base in Marsamxett, were attacked repeatedly, and the harbors themselves kept heavily seeded with mines. At night single bombers were sent over the island several times between dusk and dawn, discouraging cleanup operations and, if possible, adding further damage. In January there were 263 raids; in February slightly fewer, although half again as many bombs were dropped. On February 7 there were 16 raids, lasting a total of thirteen hours and six minutes—a new world's record for a twenty-four-hour period. Not until February 19, when weather conditions were extremely bad, did Malta experience its first raid-free day of the new year.[4]

As time went on, the field marshal gradually upped the intensity of attack. When his raids against the island first began, he generally sent over no more than three bombers at a time. By the end of January the average number had risen to five, and in February groups of between seven and twelve were the norm. At the same time the length of the raids also increased. The purpose of all this was to keep pounding away at the island with whatever amount of force was needed to "neutralize" it—that is, to eliminate its capacity to conduct offensive operations of any kind—and, to the extent that Malta's defenses stood in the way, destroy them as well, especially the island's fighters, without which it would be all but helpless.

In their attacks upon the island the Axis bombers came well protected by fighters, mainly Me 109s, which, besides battling the Hurricanes, would strafe the aerodromes and harbor areas with their machine guns and cannons. Sometimes additional 109s or 110s trailed the main body of raiders by several minutes, waiting for the British fighters to use up their fuel or ammunition and then swooping down on them while they were being reserviced on the runways. Often the Messerschmitts came over alone to taunt the Hurricanes into uneven combat. When the defenders refused to take the bait, the Germans would attack them on the ground from rooftop level.

The night raids had an eerie beauty about them. As the enemy aircraft neared the island, the sky would come alive with searchlights and the orange trajectories of tracer shells. Soon, several Messerschmitts would arrive, slightly in advance of a single Dornier or Heinkel bomber, and drop a dozen or so flares, flooding the entire target area with an intense brightness that all but drowned out the searchlights and tracers. For several seconds the flares would drift slowly downward on their little parachutes, disintegrating after a time into thousands of tiny phosphorescent particles, like sky rockets at *festa* time. Then came the bombs, exploding with a fiery fury that lit up the sky for miles around. For some reason the biggest raids, both day and night, came on Sunday, perhaps because Kesselring understood that for such a devout people as the Maltese, this was when they would hurt the most.

With only a few exceptions, most notably a savage attack on the Luqa aerodrome in mid-February, no single one of the enemy raids did a great deal of damage, but their cumulative effect was awesome. As a base for military operations Malta was being gradually reduced to a cipher, and the island's defenders could do little to prevent it except hold on and hope for reinforcements—which now seemed unlikely in view of the enemy's tight control over the air and sea approaches to the island. By March the Hurricanes, like the days in the song, had "dwindled down to a precious few" (twenty-one, to be exact), most of them patched up and running on cannibalized parts and the skill and daring of their pilots. This was not a very potent force with which to battle Kesselring's Luftflotte II, with its several hundred first-line aircraft. But it would have to do.

With so few fighters to protect the island, Malta's offensive capability was soon reduced to insignificance. On March 5 Air Marshal Lloyd informed Cairo that, his dispersal pens notwithstanding, he had only seventeen Wellingtons left—all of them damaged. During daylight they would be bombed or strafed on the ground, and then, after being patched up at night, would be battered again the following morning. Each day their condition grew worse. Lloyd advised, "with regret," that they be taken off the island while they could still fly.[5] As for the navy, the few surface raiders that had been in Maltese waters when the Germans reappeared in December had either left or been put out of action, like the destroyer *Maori,* which was sunk by German bombs in Grand Harbour early in February. Only the submarines of Flotilla X remained gamely in place, despite heavy damage to their shore installations on Manoel Island and the necessity of staying submerged throughout the daylight hours.

With the humbling of Malta's strike force, supplies began to flow more freely from Italy to North Africa. According to Kesselring, Axis shipping losses for January and February were between 20 and 30 percent—a marked contrast to the 70 to 80 percent of the previous autumn.[6] Toward the end of December, matériel and troop reinforcements began reaching Tripoli more or less regularly, which helps explain why on January 21, after having retreated nearly 300 miles in two months, Rommel was able to turn on his pursuers and send them reeling back toward Egypt in disarray. Within ten days, in a series of bold and sometimes brilliant moves, Rommel's forces advanced more than 200 miles, seizing vast quantities of British stores and recapturing most of Cyrenaica, including the strategic port city of Benghazi. "We have a very daring and skillful opponent," Churchill explained to a stunned House of Commons in late January, "and, may I say across the havoc of war, a great general."[7]

All this, of course, gave a decidedly different face to the military situation in North Africa and came as especially bad news to Malta. As long as the hump of Cyrenaica had remained in British hands, ships bound for Malta from the East had been able to receive fighter cover all the way. It was primarily for this reason that a small convoy from Alexandria had managed to reach Grand Harbour in mid-January, only a few days before Rommel launched his counteroffensive. However, with the British driven from the hump, their fighters no longer had the necessary range to provide this protection. Even worse, by moving back into this area, enemy aircraft again dominated both sides of the narrows south of Crete, through which all Malta-bound traffic from the eastern Mediterranean had to pass. In other words, the sudden reversal of British military fortunes in the desert promised to add even further to Malta's already worrisome isolation.

Even with the shadow of defeat once again lifted from the Axis forces in North Africa, Field Marshal Kesselring seemed determined to maintain the initiative. In February he visited the Führer at his headquarters to urge that Malta be seized; otherwise, like before, it would reacquire its offensive capabilities once the bombings let up. In this, the field marshal had the support of Rommel and the irrepressible Raeder, who advised Hitler that if the island were not taken, German air attacks against it would have to be continued at the same level of intensity for an indefinite period of time. "Tempers ran high," Kesselring later wrote. "Hitler ended the interview by grasping me by the arm and telling me in his Austrian dialect: 'Keep your shirt on, Field Marshal Kesselring. I'm going to do it!' "[8] But he didn't say when.

Given the mounting fury of the enemy's air attacks, however, the Maltese authorities were convinced that an invasion was imminent. The island's defense forces were again put on full alert; civilians were reinstructed to take cover at the ringing of the church bells; and, in the name of domestic security, an "unfortunate but necessary" step was taken by the government—one that the British would later have good cause to regret. This was the deportation of several of those pro-Italian Maltese who had been rounded up and detained during the early days of the war.

For over a year and a half the detainees had been held in close confinement at internment centers, first in Corradino, near the Three Cities, and then inland at St. Agatha's monastery in Rabat. As far as is known, they had caused no trouble and gave no indication of doing so. Before the return of the Luftwaffe in December of 1941 it had seemed unlikely that any further action would be taken against them. Around Christmas, though, the rumor began to circulate that a deportation order had recently arrived from the Colonial Office in London. Disturbed by this, Malta's staunchly pro-British Archbishop Don Maurus Caruana visited Governor Dobbie to check on the truth of the report. He was assured by Dobbie that the government had no intention of deporting anyone. Just to be on the safe side, however, the detainees took the matter of deportation to court, where a decision against the legality of such action was handed down on February 7, 1942. Four days later the government obtained a reversal of this decision, and the case was then sent to the Court of Appeals, the island's highest tribunal, which on May 4 declared deportation to be inconsistent with the law of the land. Too late, however. The authorities had decided not to wait.

On February 9, while the case was still being argued in the lower court, the colonial administration presented a bill for deportation before an emergency session of the Council of Government. Both Nationalist members of the Council denounced the measure bitterly. Sir Ugo Mifsud, the senior of the two and one of Malta's most respected public figures, had obviously seen the issue coming and was prepared to meet it head on. In an impassioned argument he took the government to task for its callous disregard of legality in its treatment of the detainees.[9] It was bad enough to have imprisoned them without a trial or even any formal charges against them, but now it was proposed to exile them from their native land. This not only went against civilized tradition but also was in direct violation of British law, which specifically prohibited the expulsion of any British subject from his own country. In fact, Mifsud pointed out, only a few days before the war when the Chamberlain government framed the Emergency Powers Act of 1939, which dealt with the arrest and detention of suspected security risks, a clause authorizing deportation was deliberately deleted because of Parliamentary opposition. Not even a national emergency warranted sending a British subject into exile.[10]

Yet, Mifsud continued, this was exactly what the colonial government now proposed to do, with neither proof nor even accusation of any wrongdoing against its intended victims. And, as a special touch of irony, the authorization being put forward by the colonial administration for this atrocity was that very same Emergency Powers Act of 1939. At this point Sir Ugo suddenly paused and glanced strangely about the chamber. "I feel ill," he said softly and crumpled to the floor. Two days later he died of heart failure, a martyr, some would later say, to the cause of Maltese freedom. Meanwhile, the deportation bill passed the Council, seventeen to one,* but not until after the government, apparently somewhat unnerved by Mifsud's arguments, had attached a last-minute addendum to the measure, asserting that subsequent court decisions would not be permitted to interfere in any way with the deportation proceedings.[11] This open defiance of the courts was not only high-handed, it was also illegal—a naked and indefensible bit of usurpation. Here was proof, if any more were needed, that one way or another the British would do what they pleased with the Maltese. Or so it seemed to those few islanders who gave much thought to the matter.

In fairness, however, it is hard to say how much of all this was the fault of the British. Certainly, some of the blame belonged to leading elements of the Constitutional Party, whose hostility toward their pro-Italian countrymen went back a long way and whose support of the government's internment policy had been vocal and unremitting. Indeed, there are indications that the British approached the entire matter of deportation reluctantly. It is known, for instance, that Governor Dobbie sat on the deportation warrant from London for nearly two months before seeking approval for its use from the Council of Government, and it is hard to believe that a man of his character would have deliberately lied when he told the archbishop that he had no plans to deport anyone. But this had been in December. Since then the enemy attacks had greatly intensified, and, along with them, the likelihood of invasion. There is no question that the leaders of the pro-British

*The dissenting vote was cast by the sole remaining Nationalist member, Dr. Giorgio Borg Olivier, who as prime minister some twenty years later would lead Malta out of what remained of the British Empire.

Constitutional Party had begun to weigh their future with some concern. Melita Strickland, whose husband, Roger, it may be remembered, headed the Constitutional Party and served as its main spokesman in the Council of Government, was plainly worried:

> We were absolutely convinced that if the enemy invaded Malta and gained control of the island the quislings [detainees] would be put in charge of the new government and that those of us Maltese who had opposed them would all be killed. This is one reason why Roger pushed so hard for deportation when the invasion seemed imminent. We simply didn't want those people around if the enemy took over.[12]

Regardless of who actually instigated the deportations, the authorities lost little time in carrying them out. On February 13, 1942, only four days after the matter had been introduced before the Council, forty-three of the sixty or so detainees were transported in military lorries from Rabat to Grand Harbour, where they were loaded onto the fast cargo carrier *Breconshire,* bound for Alexandria. Although the timing of the operation was supposed to have been kept secret, somehow word leaked out, and a large crowd gathered near the dockyards to jeer and hiss at the "quislings" and shout at them not to come back. "It was so unfair," a close relative of one of the detainees later complained, "and so unnecessary. They had done nothing wrong, and aside from their continuing enthusiasm for Italian opera, there was no reason whatever to doubt their loyalty."[13] As the deposed chief justice, Sir Arturo Mercieca, remarked at the time, he and his fellow detainees were being sent into exile because of "unestablished suspicion."

At the time, however, the move was favored by a solid majority of the Maltese people, who, temporarily at least, had lost whatever affection they had once had for the Italians and had come to look upon the detainees as Italian agents—the enemy within. It wasn't until some years later, after the smoke of battle had cleared, that the Maltese rethought the matter of the deportations and, conveniently forgetting their own complicity (or at least willing acquiescence), took the British to task for treating the detainees so badly. "Abhorrent" became a favorite word for what the British had done, but back in February of 1942, when the bombs were falling round the clock and an invasion was expected at any time, it hadn't seemed that way at all. In fact, to most of the islanders, deportation had seemed like a good idea.

Not that the British were free from sin on this issue. It was, after all, their decision. Furthermore, they could have softened the cruelty of the deportations by providing for the families of those who were sent away or later by compensating the deportees themselves. They did neither. With the exception of Chief Justice Mercieca, who continued to receive his crown pension, none of the deportees, or those detainees who remained behind, ever received so much as a farthing for their distress, or even an apology—a fact that would have some bearing on the postwar relationship between Great Britain and Malta when the Nationalists once again became politically dominant on the island. As one Maltese historian would later state. "The political and ideological harm done by British policy in wartime to intern and exile Maltese citizens was incalculable."[14]

By way of epilogue: After a brief stopover in Alexandria, the deportees were moved on to Uganda, where they sat out the rest of the war in loose confinement. By all accounts they were treated considerately by their jailer-hosts, and it could be argued that the British actually did them a favor by removing them from Malta before the awful terror of the April blitz and the long, hungry months that followed. At least, they all survived, which almost certainly would not have been the case if they had stayed at Rabat, where soon after their departure German bombs fell on St. Agatha's monastery, killing or maiming several of those detainees who had been left behind. But if the deportees were at all grateful to their British captors for providing them with this prolonged vacation from danger, they did a good job of concealing the fact. "It was a cruelty we would never forget, or entirely forgive," one of them remarked many years later. "Never."[15]

Meanwhile, Kesselring continued to step up the intensity and tempo of his air attacks against Malta, and there was nothing its defenders could do to stop him, or even give him pause. Now and then during March small numbers of British fighter reinforcements reached the island, but most of them were soon destroyed or otherwise put out of action by the enemy's overwhelming superiority. Those that survived had to be used sparingly because of a lack of replacement parts and a growing shortage of gasoline. To conserve fuel, the regular dawn patrol was discontinued, and fighters were allowed only limited time aloft. No one can deny that during those brutal days, which the Maltese refer to as their "Black Winter," Lloyd's pilots fought courageously and well. However, by mid-March the island's fighter force had become largely symbolic, or, more accurately perhaps, sacrificial. Practically unchallenged in the skies above Malta, German and Italian aircraft kept coming on relentlessly, pounding the battered little island at will.

Throughout this period the enemy raiders, as during the year before with Fliegerkorps X, were very correct in attacking military targets only, which helps explain why, amid such devastation, civilian casualties were so light. But mistakes were known to happen: February 15th was a gray, chilly day. It was Carnival Sunday. Ordinarily flowered floats and bands and masked revelers would have been parading joyously through the villages to celebrate the coming of Lent. But the war had put a stop to all that, as it had to so many other things. Since half past seven that morning there had been one alert after another, but no planes appeared, probably because of the heavy, unbroken clouds that hung low over the island. By early afternoon the people had become bored. Ignoring the alerts, many of them strolled along the streets, thankful for their unexpected reprieve from the shelters. Some went to the movies. Other sat in the Upper Barracca and chatted with servicemen from nearby gun emplacements. About midafternoon another alert sounded, but this one was not to be disregarded. Hearing the drone of approaching planes, most people rushed to the safety of the nearest shelter. In the Regent Picture House in Valletta, however, the planes were not audible, and the theater was packed with people when an enemy bomb scored a direct hit on the building. Untold numbers of civilians and servicemen were blown to bits; others were crushed under tons of falling stone or stampeded to death by the frantic survivors. With so many human fragments to piece together (and so many missing), the total casualty count could only be guessed at. Official sources placed the dead at twenty-five. Others would swear that the toll was nearly ten times that.[16]

It was not an easy time for the little island, but somehow, through those long months of torment and privation, life went on. Somehow, through the torrential rains and near-freezing cold of that Black Winter, through the growing shortages of food and fuel and matches and soap, the pushing, shoving, and waiting in line, and the bone-deep fatigue and filth of a hundred days and nights in the shelters—somehow through all this and the deadly visitations of a determined enemy, the people not only endured but managed to carry on with the business at hand. Men, worn down with weariness and worry, reported to work each day on time. Children continued to attend school regularly, often in bomb-gutted buildings or makeshift classrooms, such as abandoned houses. And at home the women, forced to make do with less and less under conditions of mounting duress, routinely performed their daily miracles:

To the Editor, *Times of Malta:*

Sir—When the history of the war is written and Malta's part in the victory assessed, a tribute will undoubtedly be paid to the women of Malta, to the mothers and wives, who have kept the Home Front intact.

I would like to take this opportunity to pay a tribute to my wife, who although spending night after night in a shelter for the past several weeks, manages to keep the family routine going, keeping my three children clean and warm and well-fed, sending them to school, and, raid or no raid, serving up hot lunches and dinners. With this backing on the Home Front, no man can help doing his bit and carrying on whatever task may have been assigned to him in Malta's war effort. Malta's women are marvellous.[17]

And yet, how hard life had become. And at times so soul-searing. On Easter Sunday, the holiest day of the year, mass had to be held in the shelters because of the nearly continuous raids. How inappropriate to celebrate the Resurrection of the Savior in such a place. Or to give birth to a child, as sometimes happened. Or to die, as many did from fear or exertion. The raids were especially hard on the elderly—like Emanuel Tonna's aged mother, who had never recovered from the shock of losing her home in Floriana during the enemy attacks of the year before. Soon after that her health began to fail. Within a few months she could no longer move about much, so her family found her a bunk in the safety of the Old Railway Tunnel. But the congestion and noise and the lack of sunlight upset her nerves, while the crude sanitary facilities offended and embarrassed her. In time she was moved to a hospital, but soon had to be evacuated because of the stepped-up bombings. By now her son had completed a private shelter for her in one of the giant bastions not far from her former home. It was a tidy little place, with its floor and walls covered by wooden boards taken from the ruins of nearby buildings, and a tunnel leading to an adjoining shelter occupied by an elderly cousin. The mother was pleased to have her own quarters again, but her condition rapidly worsened until she was no longer able to care for herself and had to be moved to the basement of her sister's house. There, indifferent now to the bombs and all else, she died during a day of heavy enemy action in February 1942. On the following afternoon the burial took place. No sooner had the funeral party reached the graveside than the Germans came over and scattered the mourners. Only the priest and a few others remained for the hurried ceremony. "It was a great relief," her son later commented, "when Mother's remains were buried and the grave sealed in the presence of the few who had defied the raid and remained by the tomb paying their last respects."[18]

As if bombs and foul weather were not bad enough, by early March the island found itself faced for the first time with a supply situation that, if not yet critical, was certainly approaching that point. Three months earlier the colonial authorities had estimated that the island's flour would last until May, its coal to the end of March, benzine and kerosene to the end of April, and aviation fuel well into the summer. These estimates had been based on the then current level of depletion, but following the return of the Luftwaffe the estimates obviously no longer pertained. In the course of the winter raids, hundreds of tons of stores were destroyed by enemy bombs. Also, the increased presence of enemy planes over Malta meant more work for the

Easter mass in a neighborhood shelter.

island's fighters and guns, thereby placing a greater strain than anticipated on its reserves of aviation fuel and antiaircraft ammunition.

As mentioned earlier, a small convoy managed to thread its way from Alexandria to Grand Harbour in mid-January, and, despite repeated attacks from Axis aircraft, unloaded its 21,000 tons of cargo without loss. This represented the first substantial reinforcement to reach Malta since Operation Halberd arrived with 50,000 tons the previous September, and although it brightened the overall supply situation somewhat, the island's reserves still fell far short of a comfortable level. According to Governor Dobbie, an absolute minimum of 15,000 tons of military and civilian stores would have to be received each month just to keep abreast of Malta's needs. Anything less than that would require dipping into supplies on hand, which, in Dobbie's judgment, were already unacceptably low. When in mid-February a convoy from Alexandria was forced to turn back because of enemy action, the governor immediately put the island on "siege-level issues" (short rations). In this way, it was projected, the reserves could be made to last through June.[19]

This was a wise precaution, but perhaps unnecessary, for reassurances were soon received from Alexandria that another, larger convoy would be sent out within the month. And this time the British, fully aware of the worsening supply situation on Malta, meant to see that there was no turning back. With overcast weather predicted for the following several days, four merchantmen set out from Alexandria on Friday, March 20, laden with 26,000 tons of supplies and escorted by four cruisers and ten destroyers. Some distance ahead six other destroyers swept for enemy submarines. By dawn of the following Monday the four cargo ships had all but reached their destination when, despite low cloud cover, they were attacked by German aircraft from Sicily. One of the four vessels, the *Clan Campbell,* was sunk ninety miles southeast of the island; a second, the *Breconshire* (recently used to transport the deportees), was hit and totally disabled only eight miles offshore. Shortly after 9:00 A.M. on what Admiral Cunningham called "that thick and lowering day," the other two merchantmen, the *Pampas* and the Norwegian freighter *Talabot,* appeared out of the mist and cleared the breakwater into Grand Harbour. And there they would remain, with very little effort made to unload them until they had been gutted by enemy bombs more than seventy-two hours later. "To some who watched the course of events at that time," a British officer on the spot would later write, "it seemed that there was a certain amount of lethargy and lack of urgency in getting the cargoes out. It was as though the 16,418 tons tightly packed in two merchantmen in Grand Harbour were considered to be in the larder and entirely safe."[20]

What happened to the remains of the March convoy after arriving at Malta is not a subject that either the Maltese or the British like to dwell on. In fact, most of the accounts of the war written from the British point of view, including Churchill's multivolume work and I. S. O. Playfair's more or less official history of operations in the Mediterranean, tend to skim over the affair. Those sources that do allude to it in greater detail usually seem more intent upon providing excuses than answers. The truth is that a priceless cargo that had been transported at considerable cost and peril over a thousand miles to a beleaguered people was largely lost because of a deadly combination of cowardice and lack of proper planning. The blame for this disaster must be shared by the Maltese stevedores responsible for off-loading the cargo and General Dobbie, who, as governor of the island, was in overall charge of the operation.

For three days German bombers, coming over in flights of thirty or more, attempted to sink the two ships, and for three days they were prevented from doing so by the feeble heroics of Lloyd's few remaining fighters and by a ferocious antiaircraft barrage that made the *Illustrious* defense of the year before seem puny by comparison. During this period the island's guns, now numbering close to 300, put up as many as 13,000 rounds a day over Grand Harbour—the heaviest prolonged concentration of antiaircraft fire ever.[21] But the Luftwaffe was not to be denied. On Thursday, Malta received its most intensive raid of the war up to that point. For nearly six hours massive waves of enemy aircraft dropped hundreds of tons of bombs on the harbor area, showering it with destruction, until finally by midafternoon both the *Pampas* and the *Talabot* were ablaze and foundering in their own oil. A resident of Sliema, on the far side of Marsamxett, noted in his diary that evening:

> From where I am writing . . . I can see the sky above Valletta condensed with black thick smoke, rising fanlike from the harbour. It has been a bad day for Malta. Between dawn and dusk Junkers 88 and Stukas have swept in three times in mass formation to attack the harbour. The destruction they have left behind is appalling.[22]

Later that night in order to prevent the fire from reaching the sizable quantity of ammunition stored in its forward holds, the *Talabot* was scuttled by Royal Navy personnel—but not entirely: For more than two weeks thereafter the stern of the vessel would remain tilted sharply upward out of the water and continue to smolder, sending forth giant clouds of black smoke that spread for miles inland. Meanwhile the *Pampas,* with four of its six holds flooded, sank slowly to the bottom of the harbor.

Of the more than 16,000 tons of cargo carried by the two ships, less than 5000 was unloaded, the greater part of it by British infantrymen who were called in to salvage what they could after the vessels had been hit and started to settle. For several days and nights the troops, most of them from the crack Cheshire Regiment, worked around the clock in shifts, racing against time to save another case of food or ammunition or one more can of gasoline. There wasn't much they could do on the *Talabot,* which was simply too hot to handle. Only a few tons were retrieved from it. But on the *Pampas,* which managed to stay afloat for the better part of a week after being hit, there was still a chance, and the Cheshires made the most of it. Refusing to slow down even for enemy raids (as many as eight a day), the men exerted themselves to the limit under extremely difficult and dangerous conditions. Working in cramped, dark quarters, where a sudden settling movement of the vessel might crush them beneath tons of the unstable cargo, they often stood for hours at a time up to their waists in seawater made vile not only with heavy black fuel oil but also condensed milk, catsup, and the contents of thousands of other cans and jars that had been blown apart by the bombs. In the end they managed to salvage 3300 tons, or about one-fifth of the total amount to reach the harbor—not very much, but at least something. For this courageous and inspiring piece of work the Cheshires would be awarded the George Cross for valor. The question remains, however, as to why the offloading was so late in coming.

"Well, there's not much mystery to it," explained a British major years afterward. "I was there and saw for myself: The truth is that the Maltese stevedores turned white-livered and knocked off work when the planes came. Instead of unloading the ships, they ran like scared rabbits to the rock shelters and wouldn't budge."[23] Other eyewitness accounts agree, some with considerable bitterness, that the behavior of the stevedores was less than heroic. Later an RAF publication stated simply that the Maltese dockworkers were "inhibited" by the heavy bombings.[24] Air Marshal Lloyd, after seeing his desperately needed spares end up on the bottom of the harbor, was less restrained. Although not saying as much, he was clearly disgusted with the stevedores. It was understandable, if not excusable, that they should refuse to unload the ships during the daytime when there was indeed a considerable element of danger. But:

> For three whole nights two fully loaded merchant ships lay in Grand Harbour and not one bomb had been thrown there during that time; in fact, on two of the nights, because of low clouds, such an event seemed highly improbable. Yet—and this is my point—only 807 tons were unloaded.[25]

While it does seem that, given the high stakes involved, the stevedores might have shown more courage, it should be borne in mind that they were civilians, not soldiers. Chances are that most men, lacking military training and discipline, would have behaved much the same way under such terrifying conditions. As an old soldier, Governor Dobbie should have understood this, and yet he failed to take proper precautions. "He should have sent the troops in right away," an officer of the West Kents declared:

> The governor was dead to blame for the loss of those cargoes. Everyone said what a wonderful man he was. An inspiration, they called him. Well, I say he was a bloody fool. He spent so much time on his knees praying that he couldn't see what was going on all around him. He kept saying: "Don't worry. God will take care of everything." Well, God didn't unload those bloody ships, did he?[26]

Besides not sending in troops earlier, the governor should perhaps be faulted on another count. Smoke, well laid down, could have made a considerable difference by concealing the ships' whereabouts from enemy planes. Given this added protection, the dockworkers might have been persuaded to leave the shelters and return to work. Perhaps not. At any rate, the vessels would probably have had a longer life and therefore been made to yield up more of their cargo. But no smoke was used, except for a few hand canisters, which had only a negligible effect over so large an area. What was needed was a heavy blanket over the entire inner harbor—the sort that could be provided only by pots. Years after the event Admiral Mackenzie, who had been in charge of the dockyards, stated that smoke would have been of inestimable help in unloading the two ships. At the same time he was careful to explain that Governor Dobbie was not to blame for failing to use it, because there was none available then on the island. What the admiral did *not* explain, however, was why not. Smoke pots had often been used effectively at the London docks. They were also in position around the harbor at Alexandria, and it would have been a relatively simple matter to transport a few dozen of them to Malta by submarine, or by Wellingtons en route from Gibraltar to the Middle East. None had been brought in, however, nor would any reach the island until May of that year, soon after Dobbie's departure. Nobody knows why. All that anyone can say for certain is that it was the governor's responsibility to defend Malta as best he could, and in the case of the March convoy, his best was none too good.

While the *Pampas* and the *Talabot* were being pounded by enemy planes in Grand Harbour, another, lesser slaughter was taking place a short distance down the coast. After being mortally wounded only a few miles offshore, the *Breconshire* was towed by tug to Marsaxlokk, where, following four days of almost continual bombing, it rolled over onto its side and sank. Its passing was an especially sad event for Malta, for the *Breconshire* was an old and valued friend that had served the island well. Although listed as a naval supply ship, it was outfitted as a modern merchantman, so fast and well armed that it was used primarily as a blockade-runner. In this capacity it had made at least twenty trips from Alexandria to Malta since the start of the war, arriving at odd intervals with cargoes of fuel, food items, ammunition, aviation parts, and whatever else the island happened to be particularly short of at the time. Usually it had come alone, often when no other surface ship could get through, and there is grim irony in the fact that, after so many safe solo voyages, the *Breconshire* should meet its end while running with the pack.

Thus ended the March convoy—sadly, and some would say ignobly, at the bottom of the sea. Even in the best of times the loss would have been a serious blow, but, coming as it did when Malta's reserves had already dipped to an ominously low level, it bordered on the disastrous. There was no question now that the island was in grave danger of being squeezed into submission. At the most it could hold out for another three months. Beyond that, as the governor himself stated in a report to the War Office: "It is obvious that the very worst must happen."[27] A sobering prospect, and yet what could be done about it? The February convoy had been bloodied and forced to turn back, and its March successor destroyed. Only the most foolish optimist could deny that, with the enemy continuing to tighten his control over the central Mediterranean, it would be exceedingly difficult, if not impossible, to reprovision Malta. With the islanders all but cut off from the outside world and rapidly nearing the end of their reserve supplies, it seemed that Kesselring need only bide his time, and, before long, the little fortress would drop into his well-manicured hands like a ripe plum.

But the field marshal was not a patient man.

14 The Cruelest Month

Beginning in late March 1942, at about the time of the convoy, Field Marshal Kesselring unleashed the full fury of Luftflotte II against Malta and for five straight weeks subjected it to the heaviest sustained bombing in history. Coming over in waves of thirty to a hundred bombers accompanied by several dozen fighters, enemy aircraft swarmed almost continually above the little island, pounding it at will. By April 1, only a week or so into this ferocious onslaught, the main target areas had become unbelievably wasted. A British correspondent for United Press estimated that 70 percent of all buildings in the once-populous Grand Harbour area had been destroyed or damaged and about the same percentage in the heavily congested village of Luqa, adjacent to the aerodrome. This came to roughly 15,500 separate structures. Most of them were private homes. But not all. Within a radius of seven miles of Valletta, fanning out in a ninety-degree arc to Marsaxlokk Bay and the fighter bases at Hal Far and Takali, seventy churches, eighteen convents and nunneries, twenty-two schools, eight hospitals, ten theaters, eight hotels, five banks, and forty-eight other public buildings had been completely or partially destroyed.[1] In the words of the Maltese poet M. Mizzi:

Whole quarters were ruined, beauty was slain. . . .
And a great kingdom of terror was set up.

But the worst was yet to come, for April would indeed be the cruelest month.

"The bombs dropped on Malta last month totaled a greater weight than during the 1940 blitz on England," the BBC informed its listeners in mid-May. The average daily number of enemy planes to attack the island during April was 190; the total for the month, 5715; the high for one week, 1638. In all, enemy aircraft were over Malta for 373 hours, the equivalent of fifteen-plus days and nights. During that period 6728 tons of bombs were dropped—thirteen times the amount that fell on Coventry, England, in the Luftwaffe's saturation raid of November 1940. Or, to put it another way, over an unbroken period of thirty days Malta received an attack the equivalent of Coventry's every 55 hours, and most of the bombs fell in only four target areas that together covered no more than five square miles. Besides the buildings, all but one of the island's reservoirs were destroyed; precious stores of food, including the underground granaries in Floriana, were blasted; fuel dumps could be seen blazing from as far away as Sicily. By the end of the month Malta's electric, gas, and water mains had sustained seventy-six direct hits. On the entire island only one power crane remained in operation.

For several days, beginning on April 3, saturation bombing was carried out against Valletta in an apparent attempt to wipe out the seat of government. The damage to the city and nearby Floriana was staggering. Almost nothing remained whole. The auberges of the Knights, the churches, the palace, and the magnificent opera house were all hit, some repeatedly. Irreplaceable old buildings were leveled or reduced to empty shells. In less than a week centuries of history were turned into rubble. Finally on April 7, a day when the Luftwaffe dumped 280 tons of bombs on the tiny peninsula, the government evacuated Valletta in favor of Hamrun, a couple of miles inland.

Across the harbor the Three Cities fared even worse. During the month of April almost as much tonnage was dropped on them as on all the other target areas combined. As early as April 5 a special constable reported that life there had virtually come to a standstill, except in the navy's underground workshops.[2] Streets were so blocked with rubble that supplies had to be ferried in from across the harbor. Every day dozens of dghajsa boats came over from Valletta and Floriana, carrying food and kerosene and returning with dead bodies to be taken to the cemeteries for proper burial. All phones and power lines were out, the rediffusion radio cable had been cut, and whole neighborhoods were awash with thousands of gallons of water pour-

Street scene, April 1942.

ing out of broken mains. Even the sirens had been destroyed. By the end of the month a three- or four-inch layer of limestone powder lay like a pale yellow blanket over the entire area. On a day when more than two hundred bombers came over in continuous waves, a young British corporal at a gun emplacement in Vittoriosa went mad and blew out his brains with his service pistol.[3]

Later the charge would be made that during the April blitz Kesselring purposely attacked the civilian population in order to break their will to resist. In his *Memoirs,* written not long after the war, the field marshal stoutly maintained otherwise, and on balance he was probably right. Most of his attacks were confined to the harbors and aerodromes. Those that weren't were usually directed against storage depots, gun emplacements, radar installations, and other legitimate objectives elsewhere on the island. Targets of no military importance, including most of the outlying villages, were generally left unmolested. Naturally, there were some ugly exceptions. Without question some enemy pilots, almost certainly acting on their own, committed atrocities against the civilian population. "With my own eyes I saw a Messerschmitt pilot machine-gun two boys in the fields tending goats," a Maltese woman recounted years later. "Why should he do such a thing?"[4]

Also, in their selection of targets the enemy occasionally made honest mistakes, some quite understandable. For example, there is no doubt that German planes deliberately marked the beautiful Church of St. Publius in Floriana for destruction. Indeed, they made several runs at it before finally succeeding in gutting it. However, one need only read Emanuel Tonna's *Floriana in Wartime* to conclude that the Germans believed themselves justified in doing so. According to Tonna, after Valletta had been so badly ravaged in early April and its streets left obstructed with debris, civilian and military authorities fell into the practice of parking their official vehicles alongside the church and walking the quarter of a mile into Valletta. When these vehicles, including military command cars and even lorries, began appearing regularly on German reconnaissance photos, what could the enemy deduce but that St. Publius was being used for some military or governmental purpose? Acting in his capacity as inspector of the Special Constabulary for Floriana, Emanuel Tonna wrote to the lieutenant governor expressing his concern and asking that the vehicles be parked elsewhere. The letter went unacknowledged, and on April 25 the Luftwaffe saw to it that there would be no need to write another.

But it is idle and even irrelevant to speculate on the intentions of the enemy. They may or may not have meant to hit civilian targets. The point is that they *did,* and, given the intensity of the raids and the compactness of settlement in those areas where most of the bombs were dropped, they could hardly have avoided doing so, even if they had wanted to. The Germans have frequently been faulted, for instance, for bombing the hospital at St. Andrew's. But it should be noted that the army's main electrical repair shops were only a few yards away. "The problem was," a British colonel remembers, "that in certain parts of the island practically everything was either a military target or next-door to one."[5] Another point worth mentioning is that, whereas the year before Fliegerkorps X had gone in heavily for low-level dive-bombing, Kesselring used this technique sparingly, preferring more conservative tactics. Approaching the target area at 12,000 to 14,000 feet, his raiders would suddenly drop down in a semidive to about 6000 feet before unloading and leveling off. This method of attack, known as glide-bombing, was considerably safer to execute than either conventional dive-bombing or the high-altitude lockstep type of precision bombing the Italians favored—so safe, in fact, that, of the thousands of Axis planes over Malta during the April blitz, only thirty-seven of all types were lost.[6] However, it was a far less exact sort of operation and often resulted in the destruction of people and property as much as several hundred yards from the intended targets. This perhaps explains why such unoffending villages as Mosta and Attard were so frequently hit by enemy bombs: They had the misfortune of being too close to the Takali aerodrome.

In early May, Kesselring's senior air chief reported to Berlin that "in the course of the period from 20th March till 28th April 1942, Malta has been completely eliminated as a base of the enemy's navy and air force."[7] At the time he could scarcely have been accused of exaggerating. As one historian of the war later described the situation: "By the end of the month the Germans hardly knew where to drop their bombs. So far as could be judged from the air, every military target had either been destroyed or badly damaged."[8] The dockyard area was a shambles. Only one of the drydocks was still fit for use. With virtually nothing for them to do and with bombs raining down almost continually, most of the laborers had been furloughed or assigned to other duty elsewhere on the island. Only in the underground repair shops did work continue—but a different kind of work now. With few if any ships to tend to, the shops turned to repairing certain types of military equipment, mainly antiaircraft ordnance and small arms, and to making pots and pans and other utensils for Malta's rapidly growing network of communal kitchens. In Grand Harbour itself nothing of consequence remained afloat, save for one wounded minesweeper and a few small tugs. Of the four naval vessels that had been in the harbor on April 1 awaiting repairs after being damaged escorting the March convoy, two had been sunk by enemy bombs and two had managed to limp away—one of them, the cruiser *Penelope,* so perforated by shrapnel that it was known ever after as HMS *Pepperpot.*

On the other side of Valletta in Marsamxett Harbour, the enemy's attention centered on Lazaretto Creek, the home of Malta's submarine force. Despite the heavy pounding of their facilities during the winter months, the submarines of Flotilla X had stubbornly refused to abandon the island and had even ventured forth to inflict occasional damage on Rommel's shipping. But with the all-out bombing of the April blitz and the clogging of the channels with mines, conditions in the harbor became impossible. Within a few weeks, six submarines were destroyed in or about Marsamxett. For the others to stay on would have been suicidal. Thus, toward the end of April what remained of Flotilla X (only five serviceable submarines) left the island for Alexandria. "It was a lonely feeling, knowing that they were gone," one of the islanders later commented. "Another strand in our ties with the outside world has been severed."[9]

By May 1 Air Marshal Lloyd could claim six hundred dispersal pens, forty-three miles of taxi track, and practically no planes.[10] Throughout April the Axis kept up a ferocious attack against the island's three aerodromes and the flying-boat base at Kalafrana. For weeks enemy bombers, mainly German, hammered the airstrips with 500-kilogram bombs that left the runways looking like a lunar landscape. Meanwhile, waves of fifty or more Me 109s and 110s conducted frequent fighter sweeps over the bases, shooting everything in sight with their machine guns and 20-millimeter cannons. From time to time a trickle of British fighters (now Spitfires) would be flown in from the carriers *Eagle* and *Argus* out of Gibraltar, but invariably they would be knocked out of action soon after their arrival, usually on the ground. At one point during the month Lloyd's situation was so desperate that not a single fighter was able to leave the ground for eleven straight days! During this period a young British pilot, stationed at Takali, wrote in his diary:

> People at home may think that two Ju 88s . . . was a heavy price for the enemy to pay to destroy a petrol bowser and putting splinters through a couple of Spitfires. The bowser, however, was our last one, and this means that not only will the airmen have to refuel our Spitfires, which swallow ninety gallons each, by hand from five-gallon drums, but also the transit aircraft that call in at Luqa during their nearly two thousand mile flight between Gibraltar and Egypt: these transit planes, consuming thousands of gallons between them, will have to be refueled by the airmen by hand in the darkness, with a continuous patrol of enemy aircraft dropping flares and high

explosives. Bomb splinters through a couple of Spitfires may sound simple enough to repair, but we have no spare parts . . . ., so Chiefy [the ground crew chief] has to search among other wrecked planes to find serviceable pieces.[11]

Malta fought back as best it could, but the enemy raiders were too many and too ravenous to be held in check or even slowed down. They simply overwhelmed the island's meager defenses. Lloyd's fighter force, down to three serviceable planes by the middle of the month, fought with great bravery and skill, but to little purpose against such long odds. As a French officer remarked in witnessing the famous Charge of the Light Brigade nearly a century before: "C'est magnifique, mais ce n'est pas la guerre." Only the guns could offer any real resistance. Zeroed in to throw up barrages over the few target areas likely to be attacked, they were able to create curtains of flak heavier than those over London during the Battle of Britain. In the first week of April the island's 124 heavy guns fired a daily average of sixty-nine rounds each, and the 160 Bofors, an average of fifty-nine. Over the course of the month a total of 160,000 shells were expended.[12] All this amounted to what one German pilot described as "a flying junkyard," but in the end it made little difference. Commenting on one of the heavier barrages, a British news correspondent on Malta at the time noted that although a few enemy planes were destroyed or damaged, most of them cut through it as though it simply weren't there:

There were occasions when the sky seemed to be filled with the puffs of exploding shells; I have heard the shrapnel raining down and I have marvelled that any plane could survive in a maelstrom of flak such as that which Malta's gunners have put into the air, but the Germans appeared to be quite unperturbed.[13]

Obviously, guns alone could not protect Malta. What was needed, if the island were to be saved, was an effective fighter force. But acquiring such a force would be no simple matter. It could not be done by dribbles. As Foreign Secretary Eden remarked somewhat contemptuously: "Nine Spitfires flicked off an old freighter is not good enough."* Something on a grander scale was called for—which is why Churchill asked President Roosevelt in early April for the loan of the U.S. supercarrier *Wasp:* "With her broad lifts and length capacity we estimate that *Wasp* could take in fifty or more Spitfires at a stroke . . . and give us a chance of inflicting a very severe and possibly decisive blow on the enemy."[14] Roosevelt replied at once: "*Wasp* is at

*The old freighter was the carrier *Argus,* which was actually a converted merchantman. Anthony Eden, *The Eden Memoirs: The Reckoning* (London, 1965), p. 325.

your disposal as you request." Thus, shortly after daybreak on the twentieth of the month, forty-seven Malta-bound Spitfires were flown off the USS *Wasp* standing 600 miles to the west. All but one reached the island safely.

The fate of these April Spitfires was every bit as tragic as that of the March convoy, and perhaps even more inexcusable. By late morning of the day the planes arrived, the enemy was over the aerodromes in force, bloodying the newcomers as they sat helplessly on the runways—but this was not until ninety minutes after the first Spit had landed and nearly half an hour after the appearance of the last straggler! Reports vary over how many of the planes were destroyed or damaged while still on the ground. Lloyd himself says seventeen. Others have put the total as high as thirty-five. Under the circumstances it seems surprising that there were any at all. It has been argued that, given the generous amount of time allowed them, every one of the Spitfires could have been airborne well before the enemy's arrival.

But, for reasons still not clear, they were not. Later Lloyd would maintain that the planes had not been properly checked out before leaving England and had reached him in poor condition for combat. Specifically, their guns were dirty and imperfectly synchronized, their radios unreliable, and their carburetors in need of cleaning. This could very well have been true, but was it cause enough for not having the planes aloft when the Germans appeared? One of the newly arrived pilots later commented upon the leisurely pace at which the aircraft were serviced and refueled. To him it bespoke a lack of urgency on the part of the Air Command. Apparently Air Marshal Lloyd had forgotten the ancient admonition of Euripides that "the god of war hates those who hesitate." As a result the Spitfires, flown in at such cost and hazard, never had a chance. By the end of the third day all but three were *spicca*—Maltese for "finished"—and the island was left with only six serviceable fighters. On April 27 Lloyd signaled Cairo and London that soon he would no longer be able to offer even token resistance to the enemy.[15]

Thus although at the end of April 1942 Malta continued to hold on, it was obvious that Field Marshal Kesselring had succeeded in carrying out Hitler's order to neutralize the island. With its surface and underwater navy driven from the scene, and its air force all but nonexistent, Malta no longer had any significance as a base for offensive operations. Axis supplies to North Africa could now pass in peace, save for occasional attacks by far-ranging raiders out of Alexandria. The decline in enemy shipping losses from 77 percent the previous November to less than 2 percent during the April blitz says a great deal about the strategic importance of Malta and Kesselring's success in countering it. In only one respect did Malta continue to play a positive role in the Mediterranean theater: Despite the incessant pounding of its runways and service facilities, Luqa somehow managed to continue its nighttime refueling of Wellingtons on their way to Egypt. With Kesselring's night-fighters hovering about, this was a dangerous operation, but, as will be seen later, it proved to be a highly successful one.*

Meanwhile, Malta's civilian population was suffering the torments of the damned. Periodically Governor Dobbie would reassure the people over rediffusion radio, which was piped into the larger shelters, that this was all part of God's inscrutable plan. And the Maltese didn't doubt for a moment that this was true. A judgment had been placed upon them by the Almighty for their sins, and only the intercession of the Blessed Virgin or the patron saint of their village could effect their deliverance. It was a terrible time to be alive. It would be hard to imagine how things could have been worse than they were in April 1942, when the island was running short of everything except death and desolation. Since mid-February the people had been on siege rations, which meant that they were slowly starving. At Marsa, where most of the island's flour was produced, workers considered themselves fortunate to be chosen to repair the bomb-damaged mills because they were allowed to keep the sweepings from the floor—a mixture of flour and dirt. In normal times a Maltese workingman might eat fifty ounces of bread a day. Now he was lucky to get a quarter of that, for although bread was not yet rationed, it was in short supply and usually contained additives.** Besides bread, an adult male could expect a biweekly ration of twelve ounces of canned meat, four ounces of canned fish, five ounces of rice, seven ounces of lard, and nine ounces of olive oil.[16] Ordinarily an enterprising housewife could supplement the above with a few nonrationed items, mainly fresh vegetables, but these were so scarce that they were obtainable only in small amounts, if at all. It was perhaps some consolation to the people to know that the governor himself ate no better. At the residency in San Anton, distinguished visitors on their way to and from Egypt lunched on dry bread and radish slices—and very little bread at that.

Along with hunger came the cold and often darkness. For years Malta had relied almost entirely upon kerosene for home fuel. Before the war a family

*See below, p. 202.

**Some additives, such as maize, were ordered by the government to stretch the bread supply. Others, of a nonnutritional nature including sawdust, were prohibited but were widely used nevertheless. By June 1942 there were more than a hundred inspectors checking on the weight and quality of bread produced by the commercial bakeries. See *Report on the Working of the Rationing Office, 1941–45,* p. 38, in Kissaun Collection, University of Malta.

ordinarily burned two to three gallons a week during the cold season, depending on the severity of the weather. By February 1942, however, the authorized allotment for an average-size family was down to two quarts a week. Thus, during one of the coldest and wettest winters in years, Maltese families received only a small fraction of what was needed to heat their homes, cook their food, and, for several days at a stretch when the electricity was out, burn their kerosene lamps. Given the options, all of them unpleasant, most of the islanders preferred to shiver through the winter, often in total darkness, in order to have enough fuel to prepare at least one hot meal a day. In one respect those families still living in the target areas were fortunate: After each raid the women would sift through the rubble of newly blitzed buildings in search of broken pieces of furniture to burn. From there it was only a short step to burning one's own possessions. Sometimes in desperation a father would smash his chicken coops or break up a good chair in order to warm his house for a sick child. Or even steal. Police records for the winter and early spring of that year show an epidemic of thefts involving clothing and blankets, often from military depots.[17] Even so, most people, including the governor and his family at the San Anton residency, were cold much of the time. "When the weather was at its worst," Sybil Dobbie would later recall, "we were able to heat one room for half a day."[18]

It was cold everywhere during that winter and much of April,* but nowhere more so than in the public shelters. As the intensity of the enemy raids increased during the winter months, the islanders spent more and more time in these cheerless underground vaults, and by April most people in and about the target areas were practically living in them. In some of the larger neighborhood shelters the government attached narrow benches to the walls to allow the old and the sick a place to sit, and in a few cases electric lights were installed. But these improvements were the exceptions. Generally the shelters remained as crude and unpleasant as before. In early January, after it had become clear that Kesselring meant to continue pounding the island, a Constitutionalist member of the Council of Government urged that immediate action be taken to upgrade conditions in the shelters. In particular, something needed to be done about sanitary facilities, lighting, physical hazards such as slippery steps, seepage and drainage, drafts, and lack of first-aid equipment. The council responded by setting up a committee to study the recommendations—which is another way of saying that the authorities continued to do very little to improve Malta's some 2000 shelters.[19] "We didn't

*Malta's average minimum temperature for the winter months is forty-eight degrees.

Kerosene ration.

want to make them too comfortable," one official is reported to have remarked:

We didn't want the people to develop a shelter mentality. We provided very few of the amenities. In fact, we *permitted* few as a matter of policy, for the good of the people themselves. Shelter living is unhealthful and psychologically damaging. We didn't want them to fall into that habit.[20]

The government did do one thing for the shelters, however, the effect of which was to make them even worse than before. In February it reversed its earlier position by permitting hammocks and deck chairs in the shelters, provided they came and went with their owners. This move was meant to enable the people to get some rest during the raids, but while benefiting a few, it only made life more miserable for the others. Soon the *Times* was receiving dozens of letters complaining that the presence of various kinds of chairs and cots in the shelters was causing intolerable congestion. It seemed that in every shelter there were always a few bullies who made it a practice to take over as much as six feet of floor space apiece so that they could stretch out in their deck chairs, or whatever, while women and children had to stand pressed together like sardines in a can. Finally in May, after the worst of the blitz was over, the authorities announced that they would take action against these offenders, but there is nothing to indicate that they ever did. On this as on other occasions the government seemed to be in agreement with the advice offered by the *Times of Malta* that "the best form of help which the people can give themselves and the officials concerned with shelter policy is to avoid unnecessary bickering, and to adapt themselves as well as they can to the conditions obtaining in their particular shelters."[21]

But conditions in the public shelters were hardly conducive to a spirit of good fellowship. "I dreaded going into those crowded, steaming, stinking, noisy dungeons," a stationer from Sliema would remark more than a generation later;

They were nothing but pest holes, with infants crying, and people moaning and praying and vomiting with fear, and others snoring away in their deck chairs with cotton stuffed in their ears. There were lice everywhere and fleas as big as your fist. About the only good thing was that there weren't any rats, at least not in our shelter. There wasn't room enough for them.[22]

Practically everyone agreed that the shelters were little better than torture chambers, but most people went there just the same, because what was outside was even worse. For more than four months running, a majority of the island's civilian population spent most of their time underground, while the Luftwaffe and their Italian friends engaged in their long orgy of destruction. It was a terrible, dehumanizing experience—and an exhausting one. A then middle-aged woman remembers going "in and out, up and down, morning, afternoon, and night, sometimes eight or nine times a day, month after month. We were all thoroughly worn out. I don't know how the old people could stand it. And of course we were all so terribly hungry."[23]

Worst of all, though, was the indescribable terror. With few exceptions the public shelters, while offering excellent blast protection, were not deep enough to be proof against a direct hit by the 500-kilogram bombs then being used by the Germans. And the people knew it. Herded together in their dark hole, which might prove to be their tomb, they wept and screamed with fright as they felt the bombs land about them. And they prayed as they had never prayed before: "Santa Marija, itfa'il bombi fil-bahar, jew fil hamija" (Holy Mary, let the bombs fall in the sea, or in the fields). A resident of Gudja, a village near the Luqa aerodrome, recalls a late afternoon raid during the height of the April blitz:

> With every explosion the ground shook so much that one would have thought that the shelter was made of cardboard. The women prayed desperately, but all seemed in vain. There was no indication that the air raid would ever stop. In fact, the terrifying noise got even worse. The ground trembled and you could see the expression of terror on everybody's face. We all huddled together, some clutching to each other. At one point the kappillan [priest], Dun Anton, who was in the shelter with us, told us to make an act of contrition and then gave us absolution. It was clear enough that the end was near. However, the end was not for us! After about two hours the noise died down, and we heard the sirens signaling that once more the raid was over. Once more our minds were at rest.[24]

On another part of the island a Maltese shopkeeper recalls a time when the enemy seemed to have zeroed in on his neighborhood shelter. With bombs raining down on all sides, he had no doubt that his time had come:

> You won't believe it if I told you that I was perfectly calm. But it's God's truth. I wasn't the least bit frightened. I remember saying to myself: "Well, if this is the end it's not so terrible after all." I tried to pray—but somehow I had forgotten the usual formula. Instead I mumbled something to God about being prepared to die, but if I was to live on, I begged him to spare me from mutilation. That was my predominant fear.[25]

Life, while far from pleasant, was decidedly more tolerable for the relatively small segment of the population with private shelters. This was especially true of those families, mainly in the vicinity of Grand Harbour, who had dug cubicles into the base of the ancient ramparts of the Knights and were protected overhead by fifty feet or more of solid rock. By the time of the April blitz there were several hundred of these cubicles in the fortifications guarding Valletta, Floriana, and the Three Cities area. Although originally intended as emergency shelters, most of them were now permanently occupied by families who had lost their homes or had tired of rushing for cover every time the siren sounded. Generally a cubicle consisted of one or two rooms, with an outside lean-to where the family did its cooking and laundry and spent the daylight hours between raids. Usually a canary cage could be seen hanging near the entrance. Sometimes a few hens and chickens were kept in little pens by the side of the lean-to. When the siren sounded and the red flag was raised over the palace in Valletta as a sign that planes were headed for the Grand Harbour area, everything outside, including the canary and poultry, was grabbed up and hustled into the cubicle. For identification the cubicles were numbered, and as a safety feature each was connected to one of its next-door neighbors by a small tunnel that served as an emergency exit. There was, of course, no running water, nor were there toilet facilities except for chamber pots, which the children emptied periodically into the harbor. While not the last word in gracious living, these cubicles offered probably the best combination of safety, privacy, and comfort anywhere on the island.

The shelters saved Malta. Without them the carnage would have been too much for any people to bear. Large areas of the island were leveled by enemy bombs. When Malta's chief medical officer visited the Three Cities soon after the April blitz, he could scarcely believe the extent of devastation. It seemed impossible to him that anyone could have survived. This was true to a lesser degree of Valletta, Floriana, Vittoriosa, Kalkara, Sliema, Gzira, and the villages near the aerodromes. The earlier evacuation of thousands of people from these areas had done much to keep the casualties down, but thousands of others had remained behind, and for them the shelters, with all their discomforts and indignities, meant nothing less than survival. With some exceptions:

In late March during a raid on Takali, a public shelter in neighboring Mosta sustained a direct hit that killed or mutilated more than half of the 122 people inside. In the village of Luqa, adjacent to the aerodrome, a shelter was flooded when the nearby reservoir was hit. Many of its occupants, unable to get out in time, were drowned. A government doctor who happened to be in Luqa at the time remembers standing by helplessly, listening to the sounds of the dying. As a medical man who served throughout the war, he would have many memories of human torment, but none would stir him more deeply or remain with him more vividly than the screams of those terrified people as they slowly drowned in their overcrowded bunker.[26] Two weeks earlier in the village of Kalkara, next to Vittoriosa, a bomb snapped a gas main and asphyxiated twenty-four people in a neighborhood shelter nearby. Rescue workers had to wear respirators to get out the dead. Their work was made more difficult by a ruptured water pipe that was slowly flooding the shelter. Afterwards there was some question as to which of the occupants had died of gas inhalation and which had fallen unconscious and drowned in the knee-deep water. On April 28 several people were buried alive by a direct hit on a shelter in Senglea. Their screams could be heard for hours as they slowly suffocated in the pitch-black darkness of their sealed tomb.[27]

Not even those private shelters dug into the base of the mighty fortifications of the Knights were entirely safe. Occasionally a bomb would land just outside the entrance to one of the cubicles, with results similar to those described in the following deposition by a seventeen-year-old Cospicua boy:

> During the 5–6 P.M. air raid on the 5th of April, 1942, I was in St. John's [public] shelter when I heard a bomb explode not far away. Karmanu Gafa and myself went out to investigate and saw smoke coming out of a private rock shelter in which Gafa's aunt, Mary Damato, lives with her husband and daughter. We approached and heard moans inside. Karmanu Gafa went inside with his cousin Salvo . . . and after some time they brought out Concetta Cutajar, Mary Damato's daughter, and her father, Joseph.
>
> Then Joseph Gafa and myself joined in and helped rescuing Mary Damato. I then went into the adjoining shelter where it was known there were five people still trapped. . . . Thick smoke was coming out of an inner chamber. I put on a respirator but could not see. We then obtained a candle and a lamp and made further attempts to enter the smouldering chamber after removing some of the broken material blocking the passage way. We soon discovered the body of Dennie Montague. I felt like fainting and went out.[28]

But such tragic incidents were mercifully rare. Throughout the almost incessant pounding of the April blitz only three hundred civilians were killed, an average of one person for every twenty-two tons of bombs dropped on the island, or eight for every enemy plane destroyed. There was, it is true, an element of luck involved—or, as many of the Maltese saw it, divine intervention—the most notable example being "the miracle of Mosta."

The Mosta church would be rather ordinary were it not for its magnificent dome, which is said to be the third largest in the world and is certainly one of the most beautiful. It is an object of great pride among the people of the village and the rest of the island as well. At about teatime on April 9 some three hundred parishioners were gathered inside the church awaiting the early evening services when the air raid siren sounded. This was nothing new. Living less than a mile from the Takali aerodrome, the villagers had spent much of their time in the shelters during the past few months. Mosta itself was not a target area, however, and for the most part had escaped serious damage—which perhaps explains why the people inside the church that afternoon chose to ignore the warning and remain where they were. As before, enemy action centered on the airstrips at Takali, but suddenly, about ten minutes into the raid, a 500-kilogram bomb came screaming down through the dome of the church, caromed off two of the interior walls, and amid a heavy cloud of limestone dust, skidded the entire length of the floor before coming to rest near the main entrance. Once the terrified congregation had filed past it and reached the outside, they discovered an identical bomb on the front steps. It too had failed to explode! Two heavy bombs had landed only a few yards apart—one in the crowded sanctuary—and yet not a person had suffered so much as a scratch, and aside from a neat hole in the dome, which was later repaired, and a few superficial gouges in the walls and floor, the building was undamaged. The Catholic church has never claimed that this was a miracle. But for the people of Mosta, especially those present that day, there could never be any doubt: "Oh, Mother Mary, you have spread your mantle so that the bombs could not hurt us."

But miracles notwithstanding, it was Malta's soft limestone, so readily available and so easily burrowed into, that enabled the island to withstand the enemy's ferocious onslaught—that and the remarkable ability of the Maltese people to bear up under such heavy and prolonged punishment. A few months later, when the worst had passed but the island's wounds remained largely unhealed, a priest in one of the Three Cities reflected upon the cruel hardships his parishioners had endured:

> If we look around us what do we see? Our habitations are destroyed; our streets are blocked; our families are scattered; our sanctuary, a precious gem so dear not only to our own people but to the Maltese in general—alas, our Basilica Church is a heap of ruins; our city is cut off from the rest of the Island through enemy action. Could we have suffered more? What else could we have suffered? We had to suffer all sorts of privations and fear. We had to part with dear friends and relatives. . . . Everything I

remember and I seem to live again for a moment those agonizing days and to feel once more the horror they inspired and the desolation then experienced.[29]

On an uncommonly quiet day in late April a Maltese admiralty worker stood atop one of the giant bastions of the Knights in Valletta and inspected the surrounding area. On all sides, land and water, there was ruin. In the harbors dozens of half-sunken ships, both merchantmen and naval craft, lay on their sides or with their bows pointing skyward as if in prayer. A thick film of oil covered the water. Nearby communities from Sliema to Cospicua were one continuous pile of rubble. "For as far as my eye could see, I could find nothing left to destroy."[30]

On April 15, at the height of the fury, King George VI awarded the George Cross to Malta "to honour her brave people . . . for a heroism and devotion that will long be famous." It was (and still is) the only time such an award has been conferred upon an entire people, and the news swept through the towns and villages of the island like a fresh breeze. There was much speechifying by officials, both British and Maltese; the *Times of Malta* gushed with pride and gratitude to His Most Gracious Majesty; and, from his new headquarters in Hamrun, Governor Dobbie thanked the king and promised that, with God's help, Malta "will not weaken but will endure until victory is won." The people themselves were genuinely pleased and more than a little flattered by the award. During the ensuing weeks thousands lined up to see the medal as it was moved from village to village for public viewing.

And yet, it would be untrue to state, as did a British writer, that "their main reaction was an upsurge of loyalty to the Crown and a determination to be worthy of the award."[31] To the extent that there *was* a main reaction, it seems to have been that, hmm, well yes, this George Cross business is a very nice gesture but it butters few parsnips. In fact, if the medal were intended to be a morale-booster, it not only failed in its purpose but actually produced a somewhat opposite effect: Here was the king himself seeming to say to the people of the island that this was all the empire had to offer them in their hour of greatest need. And it was simply not enough. Where was the mighty British navy? Where were the Hurricanes and Spitfires? Where were the convoys carrying the food and fuel Malta so badly needed? At night between raids silent figures scribbled "Hobz, mux George Cross" (Bread, not George Cross) on the walls of bombed-out buildings, while in the privacy of their homes neighbors asked one another if the award were not in fact meant to be an advanced obituary for the island.

Despite his fighting words, Governor Dobbie must have asked himself the same question. Later in the month he wrote to the Air Command requesting a bombing mission against Axis aerodromes in Sicily in order to relieve the pressure against Malta. "How would you do it?" Churchill asked his air chief:

> Could the Wellingtons fly from England to bomb Sicily, land on the possibly cratered fields of Malta, and return home the next night, dropping another load of bombs? If not Wellingtons, what aircraft would you use? It is quite understood that this would be very costly if it had to be done.[32]

"Out of the question," came the reply from the Air Ministry. And that was that. Meanwhile on April 18, three days after the island had been given its medal, the chiefs of staff in London informed the governor that they were abandoning earlier plans for sending a double convoy through to Malta from Gibraltar and Alexandria simultaneously. The approach from the west through the central Mediterranean narrows was judged to be too risky: "In the existing world-wide naval situation we cannot afford to have capital ships or aircraft carriers damaged; these ships must not therefore be exposed to attack from the powerful air force based in Sardinia and Sicily." Instead, a single convoy would be run from Alexandria. Five days later the chiefs notified Dobbie, with regret, that due to naval commitments elsewhere, the convoy from Alexandria would also have to be canceled.[33] The Admiralty now feared that there could be no reprovisioning of Malta before mid-June at the earliest. Until then the little island would simply have to survive on its own. How this was to be accomplished by a people already well on their way to starvation and virtually defenseless against the ravages of a bold and resourceful enemy was not made clear.

15 *Among Those Present*

The Friends of Howard Coffin

Many a soldier or sailor lies
Far from customary skies.
—YEATS

Takali is a pleasant place now. A few of the original quonset huts, where the airmen used to stay, still stand and are occupied by a variety of handcraft industries that sell Maltese weave and glassware to the thousands of tourists who pass through each year. Sections of the old runway have been hard-surfaced and are used from time to time for drag racing and driver training. The surrounding landscape remains much the same as it was then, with bright green onion fields scattered about the edges of the saucer-shaped hollow, and the nearby town of Mdina frowning down from its ancient bastions. The wind continues to swirl about the place as it did more than a generation ago when the Hurricanes, and later the Spitfires, came fluttering to earth like so many wounded sparrows. The story is told, and perhaps even believed by some of the older and more superstitious Maltese, that each spring the ghosts of the young men who were killed there come back to visit, and to drink again as they did then:

A toast to His Majesty's airforce,
and a toast to the next man to die.

Of the hundred or so Hurricane pilots stationed on Malta when Kesselring began his assault in December 1941, Howard Coffin was among the oldest. He was also an American, one of four who had flown in with a large British contingent that past August and the only one who would still be alive the following spring—although how he managed to survive is a mystery. On March 9, 1942, he noted laconically in his diary: "Shot down today for the third time. Rear gunner of a Ju 88 put a slug through my engine."[1]

He had been born and brought up in Los Angeles in a proper middle-class home. For two years during the early 1930s he had attended UCLA, but the depression put an end to that, and he became a drifter, working up and down the West Coast at a number of odd jobs and saving what money he could to take flying lessons. In September of 1939, soon after the war broke out in Europe, he tried to join the American Army Air Corps but was turned down because he was too old (twenty-seven) and hadn't had enough college. In January 1941 he was accepted into the RAF and midway through the following summer was sent to Malta as a Hurricane pilot. On his first day there he was shot down by an Italian Macchi and had to be fished out of the sea. By and large, however, life was neither perilous nor even unpleasant for Coffin during his first few months on the island. The Italian raids were something of a nuisance, but once one got used to them, they were little more than that.

During his off-duty hours, of which there were many that summer and autumn, he would often idle about the Terra Kumbo with his fellow pilots, talking shop and playing cards, or sometimes simply taking in the beauty of the place. The Terra Kumbo was an old palace outside of Rabat, a short bus ride from Takali. Once a private residence owned by a Maltese nobleman, it had been taken over by the British early in the war and turned into a billet for air officers and their batmen. Surrounded by gardens of flowers and lemon trees and perched high enough on a hill to offer a clear view of much of the island, it was one of Howard Coffin's favorite spots, until suddenly one day it took on the smell of death.

For most of the "Hurry-boys," as the fighter pilots were commonly called, the fleshpots of Valletta were Malta's main attraction. A night on the town usually began with a proper ablution at the Union Club, which claimed to have five of the forty hot bathtubs on the island. There, for the sum of nine pence, a chap could rid himself of the dust and sweat of Takali before heading for Maxime's Bar and Grill, which catered to "gentlefolks" (meaning officers only), or Captain Caruana's on Kingsway. Although little more than a hole in the wall, and a rather dingy one at that, Captain's was the most popular of all pilot hangouts, mainly because it was the only place on the island where decent liquor could still be had at reasonable prices. ("I saw the war coming on and put a few bottles aside.") Around the corner in back of the opera house was another well-frequented spot, Monico's restaurant-bar. There, as late as the summer of 1941, it was still possible to buy a frozen steak dinner for half a pound sterling (about two dollars), which was one-thirtieth of Howard Coffin's monthly pay as a pilot officer. Later in the evening, accommodations could be had at the Mayfair Hotel, where half a quid would cover the cost of a room for the night and two eggs for breakfast. For a negotiable surcharge a girl would be provided by a solemn-faced Maltese procurer known only as "Tony." Again, officers only.

Aside from the movies and a weekend dance or cultural presentation at the British Institute, there was little planned entertainment available for the pilots in Valletta or anywhere else on the island. However, they were usually able to make their own fun. It was a treat just to saunter down the streets of any town or village and bask in the adulation of the crowds. By all accounts the people of Malta opened their hearts and homes to the British troops in general—so much so that many chose to remain on the island after the war. But the fighter pilots were by far the sentimental favorites, mainly because they were recognized heroes, whose skills and bravery had been demonstrated so often in the skies over the island, as thousands looked on from below. They were, in the words of Air Marshal Lloyd, "immensely popular." Wherever they went, they were mobbed and cheered like movie stars, and sometimes, especially after a good day's result against the enemy, they were picked up and carried on the shoulders of the crowd. Men would tip their hats; women would curtsy; and children would flock after them, imitating their swagger and chanting "Hurry-boys! Hurry-boys!" It was all rather embarrassing. But quite nice.

With the coming of Kesselring that winter, life took on a more serious tone for Howard Coffin and his friends. "Ten warnings today," Coffin noted in his diary in early February 1942:

> Fifty-plus came over in the afternoon. Lost four more chaps. Cavan was jumped by a couple of 109Fs at 20,000 feet; he went straight down; saw his plane when it hit. Morrel crashed into a Focke-Wulf; nothing but splinters of fire. Parker was killed on the way down. Sorenson was wounded but picked up by an Air-Sea Rescue Boat; a Ju 88 blew it to bits.[2]

Four pilots killed within the space of a few hours, and on the following day perhaps as many more! "The British fighters deserve recognition for their bravery and maneuvering skill," Kesselring later wrote.[3] What he failed to mention was that, bravery and skill notwithstanding, against the Germans they were so overmatched that they seldom had a chance. Not only were they faced with numerical odds that ran as high as fifty to one against them, but they were also up against a better plane. The Hurricane, for all its power and sturdiness, was simply no match for the German Me 109, one of the finest fighters of the war. It could outdistance, outfire, and outmaneuver the Hurricane. Indeed, it could literally fly circles around it. "Intercepted three 109s," Coffin wrote in his diary on February 27. "Had a three-second burst at one of them. Damage claimed. . . . The 109s aren't so hot, when you can see them."[4] But with their great speed and maneuverability, seeing them was not always easy, and of course the real trick was to see them soon enough. Nobody said as much at the time, but to send a man aloft repeatedly in the face of such conditions was little short of premeditated murder. "Well, we all knew the odds," Coffin later remarked. "Every fighter pilot at Malta had to figure himself like a dead man on vacation. Some of us knew we were going to draw pretty short vacations, but after we got used to the idea it wasn't so bad. Every extra day was like a bonus."[5]

And yet it was a job that had to be done, although sometimes it was hard to understand why. Seldom did much good seem to come of it. On those rare occasions when a Hurricane managed to break through the protective shield of 109s and get a clear shot at the enemy bombers, its puny .303 caliber ammunition more often than not bounced off the stoutly armored Ju 88s like peas from a peashooter. This helps explain why during the entire month of January 1942, when there were 263 raids, British fighters shot down only six Axis bombers. Malta's fighter force obviously needed a more modern type plane that could fly faster and smarter, and shoot with more telling effect. In May such a plane would finally reach the island in sufficient numbers to make its presence felt. But by then it would be too late for most of Howard Coffin's friends at the Terra Kumbo and Captain Caruana's bar.

Some died harder than others. One day during a raid in late March a Hurricane landed at Luqa with its cockpit on fire and its pilot fried fast to the seat. His screams were so loud that they could be heard above the roar of the battle, until, after a few minutes, a fellow pilot walked onto the landing strip and shot him through the head.[6]

Others died stupidly. An off-duty pilot stood on a hillside not far from Saint Paul's Bay, watching a dogfight between a Hurricane and four 109s:

The enemy seems to slacken for a moment, their sharp-winged Messerschmitts drawing out to sea a little. The Hurricane, seizing the opportunity, dives into the cover of the hills. As it disappears from sight below the hill crests, there's a sharp burst of gunfire from the ground. From the Ground! The Ground! It was our own guns firing! Our own guns! With terrible anxiety I watch the Hurricane reappear. Its huge shape lifts over the skyline with part of its left wing breaking away. Uncontrollable, it plunges into the rocks; an exploding crimson flame scars the hill, while a smaller black shape, trailing blue smoke, bounces down, down, down towards the water; there at the water a second fire bursts out.

"A Hurricane or a Messerschmitt?" calls a Squadron Leader running toward us.

"A Hurricane," I reply.

"That's what I thought," he mutters.[7]

And then there were those who might better have died, but didn't. Periodically at night a bus would pull up outside Imtarfa military hospital near Rabat and pick up a load of the more seriously wounded, mostly pilots, whose bodies or minds had been ravaged by the butchery of battle. Some had lost limbs, others their sight, or sanity. Many were disfigured by burns or wounds that had torn away parts of their faces and left them looking like grotesque caricatures of humanity. At Luqa they were loaded onto an A29 Hudson and flown by way of Gibraltar to the United Kingdom, where today some may still be found in military hospitals—yesterday's heroes, alone and all but forgotten.

The first of the four Americans, Pilot Officer Peter Steele, was killed in early February when his plane was shot to pieces and crashed into the sea. Soon after, Pilot Officer Paul Tedford came down in flames. "Words cannot express how I feel at this moment," Coffin wrote in his diary. "I've lost a buddy, and our force has lost a wizard pilot."[8] Of the Americans, that left only Coffin and his young friend Junior Streets. Eddie Streets was a cocky kid from the Eastern Shore of Maryland. At the age of fourteen he had dropped out of school to wash dishes in a restaurant, where he saved enough money to learn how to fly. In the winter of 1940–41 he joined the RAF, was later commissioned as a pilot officer, and arrived at Malta with the others in August 1941. He was eighteen at the time, and at only five feet, two inches tall, had to sit on a cushion to see over the instrument panel of his plane. Because of his youth and size he was known as Junior, and soon became something of a squadron pet. He was especially close to Howard Coffin, who, being nearly a dozen years older, had an almost fatherly affection for the youngster.

As social secretary for the British Institute, the Marchesa Cissy Zimmerman saw a lot of Coffin and Streets over the course of several months:

They would attend our weekend dances more or less regularly, and at other times they would pop in to say hello and chat for awhile. Howard was very handsome and a nice man, and Junior, of course, was an absolute dear.

After the Germans returned that winter, they didn't come around so often, and when they did, it was sad to see how they had changed. In a matter of months they had aged years, and the old gaiety was gone. I remember quite clearly the last time I saw Junior. It must have been in early May. He seemed all adrift. He told me that his nerves were badly frayed, that he couldn't eat or sleep. He said he needed a leave badly but didn't think that he should ask for one since everyone else was in the same boat. He was very upset.

Not long after that I took a day off and caught a ride in an army lorry to my summer place at Saint Paul's Bay. On my way back the following afternoon I heard that there had been a direct hit on one of the officers' quarters in Rabat and that Junior and several other pilots had been killed.[9]

Coffin, who had been on duty during the attack, returned later in the day to sift through the ruins. The entire front of the Terra Kumbo had been blown off. All that was found of Junior was his hat and a Boy Scout knife he had been awarded years before for saving a young child's life. At the time of his death Pilot Officer Eddie Streets was nineteen years old.

Coffin remained on the island throughout that spring and summer, but he was a changed man. It was as if Junior's death had shattered his spirit. In early autumn when his tour was finally up, he dropped by the Institute to say good-bye to the Marchesa. America was in the war by then, and he had decided to go back and fight for his own country. Just before leaving Malta, he visited the quartermaster warehouse in Marsa where hundreds of duffel bags containing the personal effects of the dead were stored, awaiting shipment home. A few weeks earlier an enemy bomb had hit one end of the warehouse and blasted many of the bags to bits, so that the entire building was littered with fragments of pocket watches, love letters, snapshots, and other treasured possessions. Those bags belonging to his American friends had been spared, however, and one night in October they were loaded aboard a Gibraltar-bound Hudson, as Howard Coffin headed for home with all that remained of his three countrymen.

As for the rest of the Hurricane pilots who flew onto the island with him in the summer of 1941, well over a hundred in all, only six were still alive two years later. Most of the others had fallen over Malta during that sacrificial winter and spring of 1942, when the squadron commander kept shouting, "Dig him in," and, like Thomas Hardy's Drummer Hodge, they dug them in, "uncoffined—just as found."

The Dghajsaman

To the outsider the Maltese language is a baffling one. It seems to have more letters than it can find use for. As a result, it is not uncommon to come across a word like *dghajsa,* which is pronounced simply "dy-sa" and means "taxi-boat." The dghajsa has been a prominent feature of Maltese life since it was introduced to the island in the early sixteenth century, probably by Venetian traders. Although similar in purpose to the gondola, it differs considerably in size and configuration and is operated by an oarsman (called a *barklor*) standing in the bow. The dghajsa was, and still is, a common sight on the larger harbors of the island, where it is used mainly to ferry passengers from one side to the other. Given a calm sea, it is a pleasant and graceful way to travel.

Unlike the gondola, which is rather somber in appearance, the dghajsa has a happy look, bedecked as it is with brilliant colors inside and out. To its Maltese owner, for whom it provides a meager living at best, it is less a boat than a cherished member of the family, the object of much care and affection. In time, through special touches here and there, it comes to take on something of the personality of its owner and to share in his happiness and sorrow—which is why, on the occasion of a death in the family, the two large eyes on the point of its bow are painted shut in mourning.

Joseph Borg was nearly seventy when the war began. He had been a dghajsaman for almost as long as he could remember. He had begun as a cleaning boy at the age of nine and had eventually saved enough money to purchase his own boat, which he liked to think of as the handsomest on all of Grand Harbour. For over half a century he had supported himself and his family by carrying passengers and light freight between the Three Cities and Valletta. During that period he had painted the eyes of his dghajsa shut three times, twice when his only children died in infancy and again, just recently, when it had pleased the Almighty to take away his beloved wife.

The war had dealt a serious blow to Joey Borg's business. As the enemy continued to blast the harbor area, more and more people fled inland. Furthermore, most of those who remained were afraid to venture out into the harbor lest they get caught there during a raid. Worst of all, though, was the loss of Joey's best customer, the Royal Navy, which had largely avoided the island since the beginning of the war. During peacetime, when British warships were a common sight in Grand Harbour, he had done well by ferrying sailors from ship to shore for a penny a head. Sometimes, when a vessel was to be in port for a long time, he would rent out his services to it for two pounds a month. Like every other dghajsaman, Joey had his favorite ship. It was the destroyer *Zulu,* which by arrangement with its crew was his to take care of whenever it visited the island.

Early in the war Joey had become homeless when his house in Senglea was leveled by enemy bombs. After that he lived in one or another of the town's deep-rock shelters, or, when the weather was warm and enemy air activity light, in his boat, where he kept his few possessions. By the time the Germans returned in late 1941, his business had dropped to practically nothing, but he kept his dghajsa well scrubbed and continued to roam the harbor in search of customers. There was little else he could do, since he could neither read nor write and knew no other trade.

Then one day in January 1942, during an attack on the shipyards, his dghajsa was destroyed at dockside. It was one of the lesser casualties of the war, but for Joey Borg it was a shattering blow that deprived him not only of his livelihood but his purpose as well. For some weeks thereafter he lived off the bounty of friends. For the first time in his seventy-odd years he was a beggar. Dejected and humiliated, he prayed to the Blessed Virgin Mother for deliverance, and eventually his prayers were answered.

Although HMS *Zulu* had last visited the island several months before and had since been sent to distant waters, somehow word of the old man's misfortunes reached it. A sum of five pounds was raised among the crew and sent to him. To many people five pounds might not have seemed like much, but to Joey Borg it was more money than he had ever had before in his entire life, more than he could normally expect to earn in two months, even in peacetime. It was not enough to buy another dghajsa with, but it enabled him to rent one from a neighbor and get started again in business. For this he was immensely grateful to the Virgin and his friends on the *Zulu,* who, he vowed, would forever after ride free with Joey Borg. Of course, it wasn't the same as having his own boat, but he could scarcely complain about that. After all, at his age one couldn't expect to have everything, especially with a war on.[10]

"The Very Model of a Modern Major General"

"The Terrible Beak," as he was commonly known, was a bumptious, blustering man, entirely deserving of his reputation as a small-minded, stiff-necked martinet. He arrived on Malta to take over as general-officer-commanding in the winter of 1942, when an invasion of the island seemed imminent. His coming was something of a slap at Dobbie, for although the governor was to remain in nominal charge of the island's garrison, henceforth most major decisions affecting the army would be made by Beak, who would be answerable not to the governor, but to Cairo. In London the chiefs of staff officially explained the move as one designed to establish a closer working relationship between Malta and General Auchinleck's desert command, but it was no secret in military circles that Beak was being sent in for a sterner purpose: There had been reports that morale among the troops on Malta was sagging. After so many months of being pounded without any opportunity to pound back, they were said to have become listless, even slovenly. Apparently they had lost pride in themselves as soldiers. Well, Maj. Gen. D. M. W. Beak, V.C., would soon put a stop to that by administering a proper dose of old-fashioned military discipline—the sort for which he was so well remembered in Palestine and everywhere else he had trod.

"He was what the Americans would call 'a hot cookie,' " one of his subordinate officers would later recall, "but the British troops used another phrase for him." Soon after his arrival he made an unannounced inspection of the island's defense positions and was shocked by what he found: officers and men lying in bed during the middle of the day! (He immediately rousted them and sent them to their battle stations, although, as an aide explained, most of them had been kept up all night by enemy air attacks.) And the uniforms were a disgrace: missing buttons, torn pants, shoes run down at the heels. Small wonder morale was low. Sloth was rampant.

Shortly thereafter he held a meeting of all army officers at the Manoel Theatre in Valletta, where one well-placed bomb would have blown the lot of them to bits. "You're a bunch of lazy loafers," he shouted at them as he paraded back and forth on the stage, slapping his swagger stick against the palm of his hand as if to punctuate his remarks. "You're a disgrace to the uniform. [Slap, slap.] Well, all that's going to change, beginning now. [Slap, slap.] I want you all to get off your fat bottoms and get to your positions where you belong. From now on the officers and men of this garrison are going to look and act like soldiers, starting with all of *you,*" and he pointed at them menacingly with his swagger stick. Later, outside the theater he stopped a shabbily dressed captain and scolded him publicly for his appearance. When the officer explained that his barracks had been hit by a bomb the night before, leaving him with nothing but the clothes on his back, the Terrible Beak was unmoved. "Well," he replied, "that's no reason for not having a proper press in your trousers."

Within a week after his arrival on the island the general moved into his residency and as an act of defiance proceeded to run up the Union Jack. The Germans responded immediately by dropping a 500-kilogram bomb (which failed to explode) into his bathtub. Later, in quick succession, his aide was killed by shrapnel while leaving the Lascaris command post, the general himself barely missed being cut to shreds by a low-flying Me 109, and one morning while he was shaving, an enemy bomb blew away half his house and left him standing with razor in hand and no mirror (or wall) to gaze at. All this should have told him something, but it obviously didn't. Throughout what the troops on Malta would long remember as "Beak's reign of terror," he insisted upon acting as if the embattled island were just another peacetime garrison in need of a good shakedown. He delighted in holding dress parades and frequent inspections of uniforms and quarters. Even worse, he introduced a physical fitness program intended to promote "hardiness and agility." Among other things, the program included before-breakfast calisthenics and running in place with full battle kit, followed later in the day by a rapid hike (called a "mobility march") to some distant part of the island. By itself the program might not have been an entirely bad idea, but coming on top of regular duties and extra assignments, such as repairing the aerodrome runways, it soon reduced the troops (already weakened by short rations) to such a state of exhaustion that, had an invasion of the island occurred, they could scarcely have raised their rifles to contest it. As a captain of the Hampshires commented rather charitably: "The general appeared not to have a very keen understanding of the situation."

General Beak remained on the island until August, and the longer he stayed, the worse he got. By early summer the garrison, like the civilian population, was living on the raw edge of its nerves, and not much else. With so little to eat, the officers and men were losing weight at an alarming rate as they continued to carry on their duties amid persistent harassment from enemy aircraft. If ever there were a time for them to husband their energy, this was it, but the Terrible Beak kept pushing them to the outer limits of their endurance. "We must see to it that the men are kept busy," he announced to his staff. To give him his due, it must be said that he showed no favorites. Age and rank meant nothing to him, nor did he make any distinction between the Maltese and the British. All were abused equally, and all were deeply resentful. It simply wasn't fair. To be bombed, strafed, and half-starved by the enemy was bad enough, but to be "Beaked" by one's own command seemed an excessive cruelty. If troop morale had been sagging at the time of the general's arrival, it had bottomed out by the time he left.

Many years later a retired British officer who had served on the island during Beak's regime still found it hard to understand why the army had sent such a man there in the first place, or why he had been allowed to stay as long as he did—more than seven months during the most critical part of the siege. "Specimens like Beak should be kept at home on the parade ground," he muttered as he sat sipping his late-night brandy in the bar of a Sliema hotel. "But they never are, are they," he added ruefully. "Not in this man's army they aren't."

And then, staring solemnly into his glass as if fixed upon some faraway time and place: "We needed a soldier and they sent us a drillmaster. How bloody typical!"[11]

The Man Who Walked with the King

When most of the residents of Senglea, including his own wife and children, fled the village after the attack on the *Illustrious,* Dr. C. Jaccorini stayed behind to care for the few hundred of his neighbors who refused to leave—although it all seemed so senseless. Repeatedly he urged them to move. "You are living in a very dangerous place," he told them. "Why don't you go to the interior, like the others? Think of your children, if not of yourselves." But he might as well have saved his breath. They were determined to stay on, and, that being so, he felt that he must also.

For more than two years Dr. Jaccorini, a wiry little man in his late thirties, served as the only doctor in Senglea, doing what he could to care for the sick and wounded and bring new life into the world. During that time he had no home, save for the shelters where he caught what little sleep he could. Day and night he went wherever he was needed, whenever he was called for. Often for weeks at a time he had neither medicine nor bandages for his patients. Even aspirin tablets were all but impossible to obtain during the worst of the siege.

Conditions in Senglea were grotesque. The town lay in ruins, and each day brought added death and destruction. Life was primitive and ugly, and fear became the dominant passion. At times the doctor felt as though he had died and gone to hell—such as on the night he led a woman in labor out of a shelter and had to kick aside the rats in order to get through the rubble. How he managed to go on, day after day, month after month, was as much a mystery to him as to those about him:

> After a while everything seemed to converge on me. The suffering and squalor were terribly depressing, and the task of trying to care for so many patients, with no help and so little to work with, was exhausting. Physically and emotionally I simply wore myself out. My nerves became so frayed that it's surprising I could keep control of them. Every day I was sure would be my last. I was quite convinced that I was

dying. In my own mind I knew that nothing could save me, short of running away, and I couldn't bring myself to do that. I prayed that God would give me enough strength to carry on for just a little longer. And all the while I was so awfully afraid. Really, I was terror-stricken by the bombs. I have never been a brave man, you see.

Meanwhile the story of the Senglea doctor spread to other parts of the island, and, without his knowing it, he became something of a folk hero. When George VI came to Malta later in the war, he heard about the little doctor's remarkable dedication and was so moved that he did an unusual but altogether fitting thing: By special invitation the doctor of Senglea was invited to join the royal party on its inspection tour of that devastated town.

Which is how it happened that on June 20, 1943, Dr. Jaccorini laid aside his medical kit for an afternoon, put on his good suit, and went walking with the king.[12]

The Indomitable De Wolff

After the war broke out in the autumn of 1939 and her husband, a senior army officer, had been posted to France, she was urged by her friends and the colonial authorities to leave the island and return to the supposed safety of England. In those days British dependents were departing Malta in droves as fast as shipping became available. With the Italians likely to enter the war at any time, it would have been foolish not to—or so people said. But Marjorie De Wolff would have none of it. She had first arrived on the island in 1933 and had immediately fallen in love with it. Since then she had come to consider it her home, and, war or no war, she was determined to remain.

She was a feisty little woman in her early forties, with a reputation for getting things done. Perhaps because nature had denied her any children, she was almost obsessively fond of animals, and as head of the Royal Malta Society for the Prevention of Cruelty to Animals she worked tirelessly to protect them from neglect and abuse. In peacetime her job had been difficult enough (the Maltese have been known to mistreat their animals, especially their household pets), but with the entry of Italy into the war it became next to impossible. The bombs terrified the animals. Many became permanently deranged. Some ran into the sea and drowned. Others attacked humans or anything else that moved. In the Three Cities after the early raids the dogs looked like porcupines, their hair standing on end all over their bodies. Many pets were buried alive under the debris and cried pitifully until they died or were rescued. Several mutilated animals could be seen crouched in the corners of bombed-out buildings, whining with pain, while others dragged their damaged bodies pathetically to some out-of-the-way place to die. Their misery was compounded by the fact that when the people fled the target areas for the interior, they often left their pets behind, many of them locked indoors without access to food or water—but not for long, once Marjorie De Wolff got word of it.

As a close friend of Lady Dobbie, also an active member of the Royal Malta SPCA, Mrs. De Wolff was not without influence with the governor and was not at all hesitant to use it in behalf of the island's animals. Upon learning of the cruel conditions in the Three Cities, she persuaded him to order the local authorities to break down the doors of abandoned houses suspected of having animals inside. She was also given permission to round up all stray dogs and cats and, after a decent interval, dispose of them painlessly at the Society's shelter in Floriana. Before long, however, she was approached by the chief medical officer and asked to spare the cats in order to keep down the rats, who, as the bombings continued, were beginning to leave the sewers and become more aggressive.

So the cats were allowed to live, and in order that they not starve, Mrs. De Wolff arranged for donated food to be deposited daily by the Boy Scouts at certain abandoned spots in the Three Cities and, later, Valletta. "For a time we wondered whether the cats or rats got the food," she would later recall:

> The rats were rather fierce, you see, and some of them bigger than the cats and quite capable of killing them. But we were soon satisfied that the cats were in control, because after the first few days whenever a scout showed up at a distribution area, hundreds of them would be there to greet him.

As the bombings persisted and the number of homeless animals increased, it became apparent that the Malta SPCA would need outside help to continue its feeding program. An appeal was sent to the London chapter of the Society, which responded by sending several tons of pet food, some of it in the form of tiny biscuits individually stamped with a "V" for "Victory." However, by the time the cargo had made its long passage around Africa and completed its journey to Malta, conditions on the island had worsened considerably. The food shortage had begun to be felt, especially among the poorer residents of the island who were unable to keep up with rising prices. "So I'm afraid the biscuits never did reach the animals," Mrs. De Wolff explained. "The people got to them first, you see."

But worse things lay ahead for the animals. As the blockade of the island tightened and the food situation became more desperate, an increasing number ended up as stew meat, particularly the cats, who, when skinned, dressed, and sectioned, could be passed off as rabbits to the unwary. Diced dogmeat also found its way to the stewpot on occasion. Because of the many useful chores the island's horses performed, especially after motor vehicles had all but disappeared, they were considered too valuable to be slaughtered for food, but as the war continued, the cumulative effect of too much work and too little fodder did many of them in. Some horses actually died in their traces and were stripped of their flesh where they lay. "It was pathetic to see how the animals suffered," Mrs. De Wolff later commented. "They were all so wretchedly thin. During the worst of it even the rats were starving. But the dogs and cats were the worst. They were just skeletons—not an ounce of flesh on their bones. Still," she added sadly, "they flavored a stew."

Throughout the siege Marjorie De Wolff continued to watch out for the animals' interests as best she could, but with too many bombs and too little food, there was only so much she could do to ease their suffering. Besides, she had herself and the survival of the island to worry about—which taken together accounted for much of her time and energy. As she later remembered those days:

> Living in an interior village [Balzan], I commenced to take in refugees soon after the war began, and from that point on I was almost never without several in my home. There were dozens of them in all, although not at the same time of course. Most of them would come and stay for only a bit, but a few remained for over a year. At one time I had ten people living with me. Can you imagine such a thing? Eleven of us in all in my tiny house. But we had to take them in. I mean, it had to be done. They had no place else to go.
>
> Finally a time came when everyone had left and I was alone again. But that didn't last long. A few days later one of the authorities came to see me and told me to prepare to take in some more refugees, unless I preferred to have stores. I asked him what kind of stores, and he said tinned beef, several tons of it. I told him I thought I'd try the beef for a change. It would be easier on the nerves. But the next day my house was bombed, and that was that. Now *I* was a refugee.

During the early months of the war when only the Italians came over, Mrs. De Wolff had been contemptuous of the raids, like most other people on the island. But when the Germans arrived and dropped a giant bomb only half a block from her house, she changed her mind and contracted with Maltese masons to dig a private shelter in her garden. It was a hole some thirty feet deep, with a small square chamber at the bottom, which she outfitted with a cot, a folding chair, and a few candles.

Although Balzan was a considerable distance from any military target (the nearest being Takali two miles away), errant bombs sometimes fell on the little village. Thus, for weeks on end as the raids grew ever more frequent and ferocious, Mrs. De Wolff spent most of her nights, as well as many daylight hours, in her deep rock shelter, often in total darkness in order to save on candles—which, along with practically everything else on the island, had become hard to find. And then one day, while she waited in her underground vault only a few yards away, a German medium bomb tore into her house and gutted it:

Well, you can imagine what the place looked like. I didn't know really what to do, but I thought: "Pull yourself together, Marjorie De Wolff." A kind friend took me in, just up the street, and I stayed with her for a fortnight, during which I went back to my house and picked the silver out of the ruins—huge stones, great blocks of them, and dust. We tried to pick out whatever was left, but—well, I can't tell you what it was like. In any case, so it went.

Throughout the remainder of the war Marjorie De Wolff lived here and there as a visitor in other people's homes. ("They were so good. They did everything they could for me. They were so very sweet.") But it wasn't the same as having a house of her own. Often she would return to her place in Balzan, where, wandering among the ruins, she would recall the happy times spent there with her husband and friends and dream of the day when the war would be over and she could put things back together the way they had been before:

Oh, those were trying times. But they brought out the best in most of us, as well as the worst in a few. We were all together then, and we helped each other because we cared what happened to one another, you see. We worked side by side with a common purpose during those years. And on the whole I'd say that we did very well, wouldn't you? Yes, we did very well. Very well indeed.[13]

Warriors All

THE SWEEPER

Luciano Callus from the village of Siggiewi on the south side of the island joined the Royal Navy not long after the war began, and for the first two years served on a minesweeper in Grand Harbour. During the early months it was an easy job with little to do except keep up the ship and go on practice runs. But soon after the coming of the Germans in January 1941, all that changed. Fliegerkorps X, having had plenty of experience in the fjords of Norway, proved expert at laying down mines, so much so that within a few weeks after its arrival the major harbors of Malta and the coastal waters beyond were infested with them.

The mines were mainly of three types: those that floated freely, those that were tethered a few feet beneath the surface, and magnetic mines that rested on the bottom. The free-floaters were easily disposed of, simply by towing them out to sea and exploding them with rifle or machine-gun fire. Disposing of the other two types presented a good deal more difficulty and danger, however. The tethered mines, which were anchored to the bottom by heavy cords, were generally cleared by a minesweeper and an outrigger (called a paravane), separated from one another by as much as two hundred yards. Suspended between them at a depth of four to five fathoms they dragged a sharp serrated cable that severed the anchor cords and permitted the mines to bob to the surface. Like the free-floaters they were then towed outside the harbor and detonated by small-arms fire. This operation was not without its risks, for although the tethered mines were usually far enough beneath the surface to allow the shallow-draught sweepers to pass over them safely, such was not always the case:

April 8, 1978

To the Editor of the *Times of Malta*

Sir: Each year on April 8th my mind goes back to those days in the Second World War when I underwent a tragic experience on board HMV *Moor* [a boom-defense ship that doubled as a sweeper]. The rest of the ship's company consisting of my 29 comrades all lost their life when the ship hit an enemy mine and sank within a few minutes. I was the ship's diver and certainly had a very lucky escape as I was the sole survivor.

May God have mercy on my less fortunate comrades.

Yours truly,
Tony Mercieca, Marsa

The magnetic mines, commonly called "cucumbers," were the hardest of all to deal with. Among the more terrifying of the new weapons introduced by the Germans during the war, these mines were dropped from low-flying aircraft into the shallow parts of Malta's main harbors, where they waited on the bottom, ready to lunge up at passing ships. During the winter and spring of 1941, when they were sown almost nightly by the Luftwaffe, Luciano Callus spent much of his time aboard a converted wooden trawler trying to sweep Grand Harbour clear of them:

We used to crisscross the harbor towing a small wooden craft that looked something like a pontoon. There was a big four-inch electric coil on it that drew its current from our sweeper and was supposed to create a force field that would make the cucumbers jump up and explode some distance away from the pontoon. But this didn't work very well. For some reasons the cucumbers didn't always come up, and, when they did, they sometimes blew up the pontoon.

So then we tried dragging large pieces of metal behind us, which wasn't very effective either. Depth charges did better, but even with them you couldn't be sure. You just never knew how the cucumbers would behave. I remember once when a picket boat was sunk by one. Only a few minutes before, a cruiser had passed over the same spot and nothing had happened, but when this little picket boat came along, a cucumber jumped up and blew it to pieces. They were very notional, you see.

Minesweeping in Malta was a demanding, nerveracking business, not meant for the faint of heart. At times it could also be deadly, as the *Moor* disaster demonstrated. But what was perhaps worst of all for the men engaged in it was its apparent futility. Night after night during the periods of heavy attack, German bombers seeded the harbors with mines, and day after day the sweepers, continually harassed by enemy aircraft, fell further behind in their efforts to clear them. A flotilla of modern sweepers might have been able to keep pace, but Malta was forced to make do with considerably less. At the beginning of the war the island had a dozen regulation minesweepers. During the first year all but three were knocked out of action. To take up the slack, a motley collection of civilian boats, most of them fishing trawlers and tugs, were converted and pressed into service. Slow, cumbersome, and coal-burning (at a time when the island's coal reserves were already low and unlikely to be replenished), these makeshift craft were not the ideal answer to the problem of keeping the harbors clear of mines. But they did generally manage to maintain at least one open channel to the outside world. And that, after all, was what mattered most, for without it the little island would have been entirely cut off.*

On a day in early May 1941, as Luciano Callus looked on from his sweeper not more than a hundred yards away, the destroyer *Jersey* ran afoul of a magnetic mine while entering Grand Harbour:

The explosion broke the ship's back, right in the midsection. In no time at all the bow and stern pointed upward and both parts started to sink. I could see the matelots [sailors] trying to squeeze out through the portholes, but the holes were too small for them. They were screaming as the ship went under. Nearly all of them drowned, and I don't think they had even been hurt. But some got clear of the ship and started swimming around in the debris. "Save me! Save me!" they shouted when they saw us coming toward them. And we did, what few were left. We thought we had them all and were about to head in when we heard someone scream, "No, don't leave me! Please!" It was just a boy. He couldn't swim and was holding onto an icebox. We had to pry him loose, he was so frightened.

*As an added precaution, however, most of the convoys were preceded into Grand Harbour by their own sweepers.

A month or so later when the decomposed bodies began to surface through the portholes, it fell to the sweepers to scoop them up in nets and dispose of them at sea. One day about six weeks after the sinking, Luciano Callus and his mates sighted what appeared to be a large wad of cotton or wool bobbing up and down near the breakwater. As they gathered it into their net, they recognized the remains of what had once been a man. Embedded in the soft, fibrous mass were three small pieces of metal: a belt buckle, a religious medal, and a steel tag identifying this shapeless blob as having formerly belonged to the *Jersey*.

That night ashore Luciano Callus did an uncustomary thing: He took some of the money he had been saving to send to his father in Siggiewi, and, together with friends from the sweeper, visited a Cospicua pub and drank himself senseless.[14]

THE DECOY

In December 1940, not long after turning eighteen, Joseph Bartolo Parnis enlisted in the King's Own Malta Regiment. Despite his youth he soon proved himself to be a first-rate soldier and had risen to the rank of sergeant by the time his platoon was sent to Qrendi a few months later.

In those days, with so much force arrayed against them and so few means with which to combat it, the island's defenders used whatever weapons they could, and not the least of these was deception. It was common, for instance, to burn barrels of used oil in order to send up great clouds of smoke in hopes of convincing enemy planes that a certain area had recently been bombed and set ablaze. By so doing, a valuable supply depot or military installation might be spared from attack for days or even weeks. In the same spirit of delusion, perfectly good buildings were destroyed, or, more correctly, given the appearance of having been destroyed.

During the early summer of 1942, when most of the generating plants lay in ruins and barely enough electricity was being produced to provide for the needs of the hospitals and other vital services, the Germans made a sustained effort to knock out the island's last major plant, near Crucifix Hill in the Grand Harbour area. "You are hereby appointed . . . to do something to mislead them," the lieutenant governor notified Philip Pullicino, chief of civilian camouflage. That same day Pullicino rounded up nearly two hundred laborers and, soon after nightfall, put them to work with picks and sledgehammers knocking down the walls of the building, while taking care not to damage any of the machinery. The ruse proved a complete success. On the following morning, when the usual German reconnaissance plane flew over to take pictures of the previous day's damage, the power plant appeared to be in ruins. Thus, the enemy sought out other targets, and the slender stream of electricity, upon which so much depended, continued to flow.

The job assigned to Sgt. Bartolo Parnis and his platoon in Qrendi was also intended to deceive, again with the purpose of steering enemy aircraft away from a critical installation. It was a simple but highly imaginative charade, best described by the sergeant (later major) himself:

We constructed a fake airstrip running parallel and nearby to the one at Luqa. Actually, there was no construction to do. By day it was just an open field, but as soon as it got dark, we hurried and put out rows of lights on both sides of a long strip so that from above it appeared to be a landing field. Then we hauled out a few burnt-out planes and scattered them in different places along the strip in order to fool the flares. The enemy figured that this was Luqa and that the lights were on because we had planes coming in. Night after night they would pound us with bombs, and then, just before daylight, we would take up the lights and wheel the wrecked planes back under their camouflage nets, and the place would become an empty field again. In the meantime, after the enemy had finished with us and returned home, the lights of the real airstrip at Luqa would be turned on, and bombers on their way to Egypt could come in and land.

How well did this ruse work? Throughout the entire siege, day and night, the runway at Luqa remained open to incoming traffic. During the worst of the raids, from November 1941 to the following May, 529 replacement aircraft landed at Luqa on their way to Egypt—nearly half the total number of planes to reach the Middle East during that period. From February 25 to May 1, when the island was virtually at the mercy of the enemy, 339 made it through, most of them at night. And it is perhaps reasonable to suppose that, by drawing enemy fire down upon himself and his men, Sgt. Bartolo Parnis helped to make all this possible. At least there were those in high position who must have thought so. Why else would they have awarded the British Empire Medal to a mere decoy?[15]

THE GUNNER

September 21, 1977

Sir:

I came to Malta in the year 1938, one year before the war, my regiment in Malta was the 36th AA Regt. Royal Artillery at that time stationed at Tigne Barracks [near Sliema].

My first idea of war was when one of the Batteries went to Marsa Racecourse and made a gun position there, we used to be a happy crowd, especially in the Canteen . . ., in my time the Gun position was attacked many times, also I lost one of my friends on the gun when in action the Breach blew out and the Round exploded before firing of the gun, also we had a lot of Casualties from Rounds exploding outside the Barrel, it was not always the Bombs which caused the Casualties but sometimes accidents by being quick to fire or the noise of the shouting and the crack of the guns going every second, so you will understand what it was like to be a Anti Aircraft Gunner.

After a year I was moved with our Battery to Manoel Island, it was a nice place, but what a death trap it was in war time, one night a Complete Command Post was killed when they was off duty and went below in a shelter to sleep, because two Bombs dropped 500 lbs each one went clean through the roof, killing all the Command Post, the other Bomb got lodged in the roof of the shelter and never exploded, in that raid I lost some of my best friends of 20 to 25 years of age. One young soldier of the same Regiment was on the Predictor in the Command Post when a air raid was in progress, and one of the men looked round and he saw my friend still standing up, but he was dead with the Shrapnel going right through the tin helmet, making a big hole about 2 inches long.

When we had a break we used to go to the talkies at the old submarine depot and run back on the alarm signal, but I enjoyed those days, even if you was in danger of losing your life any minute.

The Batteries used to move to different places during the stay in Malta, I was in the Battery one day when the Officer said "Do you want to go to the talkies in Valletta. I have only a few spare Tickets." I am glad I never went because it was Bombed and about 200 people lost their lives, mostly Service Personal, but war is a terrible thing, you never say "I will be alive tomorrow or not" and the suffering left behind for the families, which are in England, away from Malta.

But the life of the Soldiers was not all air raids and alerts all the time, he used to get drunk and fight not only in the Bars but with his own friends that was there.

I used to get fed up sometimes because the siege was making me into a Corn Beef but we had to get used to it because there was nothing else to eat. . . . One day I remember I was near Qormi when the Air Raid was on, I did not go to the Shelter but stopped in the road, I will never forget the sight of the Guns flashing from different parts of the island, also the stick of Bombs starting from Corradino right across the fields, a stick of Bombs but how marvellous they were in a Straight Line as if you marked them out. so I say the Bombing pilots was very good at their job, and I do not blame the Germans because they have to bomb targets like the British Pilots, and some of the Pilots I saw (German) was very young, and you used to have pity because they are human Beings the same the world over, but the greatest part have to suffer for the higher up people in time of war.

But in war you must fight back because it is your life or the one you are fighting, and you must fight for the right things in life, Justice, Freedom, happiness, and to live a decent life for yourself and family.

Hope you enjoy this, it is the best I can do I am no educationist, Just a plain English ex-service man which remains forgotten now the was is over, and everyone has forgotten the times that meant a Slave or a person which is free to go where he likes and have a say in running the country he is in.

I remain
Your Obedient Servant
J[ohn] O[liver][16]

16 A Break in the Clouds

On a morning in late April 1942 a young British fighter-pilot joined his comrades at the officers' mess for breakfast. The meal, if it could be called that, was no more disgusting than the others he had eaten since coming to the island two weeks before.

> A sooted length of pale bacon flopped lifelessly over a partially fried piece of bread, both coldly congealed to the plate, and a mug of tea. Knowing that we are on a semi-starvation diet because of the siege, and knowing that oil from crashed aircraft, which we have to use for cooking, was responsible for the beastly taste of the bread and bacon, I had to accept it, but to my mind there was no excuse for the tea.[1]

Actually, though, there was. Water was in short supply because of the destruction of several mains and a lack of electricity with which to work the island's deep wells. Thus, the tea that morning had been made with the same water the beets had been boiled in the afternoon before. Earlier that day, at first light, the young pilot had stood on the balcony of his billet in the inland town of Naxxar, not far from Takali, looking out onto the parish church across the square.

> The cross leaned toward me and looked down upon me: a silent morning blessing accompanied by the bark of Bofors guns and the whine of engines. I felt terribly sad. I felt cut off from its blessing.[2]

But then suddenly, after more than five weeks of almost incessant bombing, the raids fell off dramatically. According to RAF figures, the number of Axis aircraft over Malta decreased from 220 on April 29 to 68 on the following day. And this was just the beginning: During the entire month of May enemy planes would drop less than 700 tons of bombs on the island, contrasted to ten times that amount during the April blitz. Perhaps equally significant, in early May for the first time since the beginning of Kesselring's air offensive some five months before, Italian bombers were back in force over the island, flying in their neat, textbook formations at 12,000 feet. "It was a comforting sight to look up and see the black crows, as we called them," a Maltese civilian later recalled. "It was like being visited by old friends. We felt that our prayers had been answered. God had sent back the Italians."[3]

Yes, but not quite like before. The reappearance of the Italians did not mean, as it had the previous spring, that the Luftwaffe had entirely abandoned the island. This time several squadrons of German bombers and Me 109 fighters would stay behind to help out their Italian friends. Still, by far the greater part of German air strength was moved elsewhere—mainly to the Russian front and to North Africa in support of Rommel. According to Field Marshal Kesselring, who would remain in Sicily, the Germans could no longer justify tying up so many of their planes in attacks against Malta. The island had been neutralized.[4] The job was now to keep it that way. Thus, enemy planes would continue to be a frequent, if no longer paralyzing, presence over Malta, strafing its harbor installations and aerodromes and depositing an average of 45,000 pounds of high explosives every twenty-four hours during the month of May. This was an almost negligible amount when contrasted to the pounding of the previous four months, but it was enough to worsen the ruin and add to the general suffering, especially in and about the main target areas, where the people continued to spend much of their time in the shelters. "Life is certainly tough here," a British fighter-pilot noted upon arriving on the island in early May. "The bombing is pretty well continuous all day. One lives only to destroy the Hun and hold him at bay; everything else—living conditions, sleep, food, and all the ordinary standards of life—have gone by the board."[5]

So, the enemy kept coming on, and, despite his diminished numbers, there was little Malta's garrison could do to oppose him—at least for the time being. "What we need," Air Marshal Lloyd wrote to London, "is Spitfires, Spitfires, and more Spitfires. And they must come in bulk, and not in dribs and drabs."[6] But, as always, there was the question of how to get them to the island. With all but one of Great Britain's carriers on assignment elsewhere, and that one (the *Eagle*) too small to do the job by itself, Churchill again called upon President Roosevelt for use of the *Wasp,* and again Roosevelt obliged.

Soon after daybreak on Saturday, May 9, the giant American carrier and HMS *Eagle,* standing together in a tranquil sea some 650 miles to the west of Malta, flew off sixty-four Spitfires, each fitted with an auxiliary fuel tank that was later jettisoned at sea. Within four hours all but three had reached the island safely, prompting a delighted Churchill to exclaim: "Who said a Wasp couldn't sting twice!" And this time there would be no repeat of the disaster of a few weeks before, when the enemy slaughtered the new arrivals on the ground. In accordance with a carefully arranged plan, the incoming Spitfires were met about an hour from the island by a Glenn Martin reconnaissance plane and ushered to their destination. Once over the aerodromes, all three of which would share in receiving the aircraft, the pilots circled at a low altitude well within the range of the Bofors and awaited their turn to put down. For landing purposes each plane had been assigned a number and upon touchdown was met by a rider on motorcycle who guided it to a nearby dispersal pen with a matching number. There, while a fresh Malta-based pilot squeezed into the cockpit, an RAF ground crew, aided by army personnel, refueled the craft by hand from five-gallon cans, readied its guns and radio, and otherwise prepared it for action. It was expected that the entire operation would take a quarter of an hour. As it turned out, however, most of the planes were back in the air within seven minutes, and some in less than five—in plenty of time to meet the enemy raiders head on as they flew in for the expected kill. Giving credit where credit was due, a British writer noted that, on this day of remarkable achievement by so many individuals and groups on both ends of "Operation Bowary" (as the fly-in was code-named), the principal heroes were the Malta ground crews. Had they worked less rapidly or well, the newly arrived Spitfires, like their ill-fated predecessors of the month before, would almost surely have never left the runway.[7]

The Axis got a surprise in the skies over Malta that day. For the first time during the war the island's defenders were able to send up a respectable number of first-rate fighters to challenge enemy raiders and, in the process, destroyed perhaps as many as a dozen of them. The May 9 Spitfires did not guarantee Malta local air superiority, as some British sources have claimed, nor would the arrival of seventeen more, flown in from the *Eagle* ten days later. The enemy would continue to hold a decided numerical edge in fighters, as well as in all other types of aircraft. However, the odds had been narrowed significantly, to the point where Malta no longer presented an easy target. From now on enemy raiders would have to pay a price for their attacks, and knowing this, they would tend to proceed with greater restraint. Thus, whereas during the first eight days of May, before the coming of the Spitfires, Axis planes dumped 550 tons of bombs on the island, for the remaining three weeks of the month, they dropped scarcely a quarter of that amount and in doing so lost a record forty aircraft.

The safe arrival of the Spitfires, then, was an event of tremendous importance for Malta. Without them the island could scarcely have held out during the late spring and summer of 1942, when conditions were so desperate that survival itself hung in the balance. At last the island's defenders had, in goodly number, a fighter that could measure up to anything the enemy could send against it. Although weighing about the same as the Hurricane, the Spitfire carried much heavier armament, which included, in addition to its four .303 machine guns, two 20-millimeter cannons capable of firing nearly 250 rounds of armor-piercing ammunition. Equally important were the plane's rapid rate of climb and slick maneuverability. Pilots marveled at its precision balance. "You could stick your arm out of the cockpit and the bloody kite would dip," one of them later remarked. "The enemy took on a new respect for us once the Spits arrived."[8]

But not even the best of planes can function for long without spare parts, especially in combat. And parts were extremely hard to come by, for unlike the planes themselves, spares had to be transported to the island as cargo, usually by ship because of their bulk or weight. With the enemy still in control of the sea approaches to Malta for a distance of several hundred miles, such an undertaking was hazardous, to say the least. It *could* succeed, however, as HMS *Welshman* demonstrated so often during the siege, but never more dramatically than on the day following the arrival of the May Spitfires, when the immediate availability of spares for the new planes was a matter of the highest urgency.

The *Welshman* was a great favorite among the islanders, for like its sister ship the *Breconshire,* which had been sunk at Marsaxlokk during the destruction of the March convoy, the *Welshman* repeatedly came to Malta's aid in time of dire need. Several times it ran the blockade, crammed to the gunwales with everything from dry milk and medicine to aircraft engines and Bofors shells. "We didn't like those trips," its first officer later commented. "We knew that sooner or later the Germans would get us."[9] And they did, but not until after the *Welshman* had given Malta the thin margin of supplies that would enable the island to survive.

Originally constructed as a minelayer, the *Welshman* had been converted into an armed blockade-runner early in the war, with the Malta run specifically in mind. Having a cargo capacity of under 400 tons, or barely twice that of a freighter submarine, it could scarcely hope to make a dent in the island's overall supply needs, no matter how many times it ran the blockade. Only merchantmen could do that. The *Welshman* could and did, however, provide at least a trickle of those items that were absolutely essential if the island were to hold out yet a bit longer. Realizing its value to Malta, the Germans and Italians did their best to destroy it. In fact, as far as they were concerned, it was one of the most sought-after British ships in the Mediterranean and certainly the most irritating. Repeated attempts were made to intercept it, sometimes by submarines lying in wait in the Sicilican narrows. Wild chases occurred; attacks against it were common; but for several months the little vessel managed to escape without serious damage. Many of the Maltese believed it to be under the protection of the Blessed Virgin. Perhaps so, but the *Welshman* was also one of the fastest ships afloat. With a top speed of forty knots, the land equivalent of forty-six miles per hour, it could, quite simply, outrun any vessel in sight, while presenting a highly elusive target for enemy aircraft. Churchill, who took a special liking to it and asked to be kept informed of its doings, called the ship his "greyhound of the sea."

But even with its great speed, which enabled it to make the 1000-mile run from Gibraltar to Malta in less than thirty-six hours, the *Welshman* would probably not have lasted long in such perilous waters had it not been for the uncommon gifts of its skipper, Capt. W. H. D. Friedberger. Besides being an artful seaman (and as bold as a bandit), Friedberger was a master of deception. In the early morning hours of May 8 the little vessel departed Gibraltar disguised as a French destroyer. With the Tricolor flying brazenly from its masthead, it proceeded nonchalantly eastward during the rest of that day and most of the next, hovering so close to the coast of North Africa that at times it entered well within French territorial waters. Twice German planes circled it and then dropped down to mast level for a closer look. On another occasion a French shore station called upon it to show its signal letters, but, having none, the ship simply sailed on, pretending not to have noticed. And then at dusk on the second day, as it stood a few miles off Cape Bon, Tunisia, the *Welshman* broke out the white ensign and made a run for it. Before dawn of the following day, Sunday, May 10, the little vessel cleared the breakwater of Grand Harbour and tied up at number 5 dock, alongside Senglea in French Creek.

Unloading began almost immediately and proceeded like clockwork. With troops from the Royal Artillery and the RAF working alongside Maltese stevedores, little time was lost in emptying the *Welshman*'s 340 tons of cargo (mostly Spitfire spares, antiaircraft shells, and aviation fuel) and transporting it to supply depots inland.[10] As expected, enemy aircraft did their best to sink the ship before it could be unloaded. Beginning soon after 8:00 A.M. several waves of German and Italian planes, totaling upwards of two hundred, attacked it continually for more than two hours. But this time, the enemy raiders were overmatched. Unlike before, smoke was put up over Grand Harbour, blanketing the *Welshman* with a grayish-green miasma that made the vessel virtually impossible to spot from above. But the enemy knew it was there and sent their Stukas down to destroy it, with a fury reminiscent of the attack on the *Illustrious* more than a year before. The response from the ground was awesome. With practically all of Malta's antiaircraft batteries zeroed in on a small segment of the sky directly over the ship, the *Welshman* barrage was the heaviest in history. For much of the morning, until the raids ended, the island's guns threw up what one artillery officer present during the attack described as "a fiery cone of steel."[11] Still, the Stukas came on, their pilots straining for a glimpse of the target through the smoke and then plunging boldly downward into the murderous field of flak. Forty, fifty of them in succession, with little or no regard for their own safety. "What an aerial monument of courage this scene is!" exclaimed a British observer as he watched a Stuka calmly position itself for its dive:

> In a strange way, although we were anxious for the safety of our precious ship, all our hearts are with the enemy plane: we are witnessing an act of superb courage. He's starting to dive. He's plummeting vertically downwards, down, down, down, down. He's hit! The whole tail has come off—the mass of the machine veers for one drunken moment sideways and upwards—the right wing snaps in two places—the fragments drop untidily behind the hill.[12]

Meanwhile, above the flak, Malta's newly arrived Spitfires were giving a good account of themselves. Coming from out of the sun, they brushed aside enemy fighters and homed in on the Ju 88s and high-flying Italian Cants 1007s with deadly effect. Most of the Spitfires' attention, however, was given to the Stukas, not only because they posed the greatest threat but also because, weighed down with heavy bombs, they presented excellent targets as they maneuvered for position before going into their dive. The toll of Axis aircraft was heavy, perhaps as many as twenty destroyed by the island's fighters and guns, as against a loss of only three Spitfires. Add to that the enemy raiders shot down the day before during their attempt to wipe out the incoming Spitfires, and the total exceeds thirty—or nearly as many as had been lost during the entire five weeks of the April blitz, with its some 11,500 sorties![13] Soon after the distressing news reached him, Count Ciano

Smoke for the Welshman.

noted in his diary: "In the last few days we and the Germans have lost many feathers over Malta."[14]

And to what end? Aside from inflicting further damage on the already prostrate Three Cities, the enemy's costly efforts gained them nothing. The Spitfires had succeeded in establishing themselves on the island, and the cargo brought in by the *Welshman* had been unloaded in a little more than five hours, virtually intact. As for the ship itself, shortly before noon after the major raids had ended, a visitor came aboard and was surprised to find so little damage, although the decks were littered with more than fifty tons of limestone rubble from nearby Senglea and Corradino Heights. Early that afternoon the *Welshman* crossed over to Marsa to take on diesel from the island's dangerously diminished fuel reserves. And then at eight o'clock that evening, as the skies were darkening over Grand Harbour, the little vessel was led out through the breakwater by the harbor's last surviving minesweeper to begin its uneventful dash back to Gibraltar:

> Our departure was most affecting [the ship's captain wrote]. The quiet of a shattered dockyard frontage . . . a circle of five burnt-out or sunken merchant vessels . . . then a ring of cheers which seemed to come from the bastions of Valletta and Senglea, and the singing of "Roll Out the Barrel," a tune which is vieux jeu, but nevertheless expresses the spirit of Malta.[15]

It had been a great weekend for Malta. No one could doubt that a glorious victory had been won. Throughout the island there was much rejoicing and public prayer. And yet . . . On the following afternoon an off-duty Spitfire pilot hitched a lorry ride to the town of Birkirkara, where, after rummaging through the barren shops in search of lace for his wife, he entered a local pub and bought a glass of warm goat's milk flavored with almonds. It was not the sort of drink he would have preferred, but it was all that was available—a sobering reminder that the events of recent days, however gratifying, had done little to alter the overall situation facing Malta. With the enemy still in firm control of all sea approaches, it was only a matter of time before the islanders, already badly undernourished, would be starved into submission, unless, as seemed unlikely, some way could be found of breaking through the blockade. And it would have to be done soon, because for Malta the hour was already late. Just the week before, the unthinkable had finally happened when bread, the chief staple of the Maltese diet, was added to the island's ration list.

Still, the victory in the skies over Malta that weekend was, as the poet Browning would have put it, "cause enough for calling forth that spot of joy." A shame that governor Dobbie, who had waited and prayed so long for such a triumph, was not on hand to witness it, although there are those who say that if he *had* been on hand, there would have been no such triumph. Late in the evening of May 7 the governor, along with his wife and daughter, left Malta forever. An hour or so earlier a Sunderland flying boat had arrived at Marsaxlokk Bay from Gibraltar with his successor aboard, and the two men had conferred briefly in a partially demolished shed overlooking the harbor. Then, with Dobbie and a small assemblage of military and civilian dignitaries looking on, the new governor was sworn in by the island's chief justice. That done, Dobbie joined his family on the Sunderland. But according to a British official on hand to see him leave, just before takeoff he stepped out onto the wing of the plane and stood there for a moment or two looking back at the island as if bidding it a final farewell. Silhouetted faintly against the horizon in his lieutenant general's uniform, which now hung loosely on his once robust frame, he appeared a gaunt and lonely figure.

For reasons of security the departure of the Dobbies was kept secret from all but their household staff and a few of the island's top officials. Even close personal friends were taken by surprise. The governor had hoped to broadcast a fitting good-bye to the islanders, with whom he had suffered so much over the past two years, but was dissuaded from doing so lest the enemy be alerted and lie in wait for him. Instead his farewell message appeared two days later in the island's newspapers. No explanation was given for his leaving, but the people generally assumed that it was for reasons of health. Sometime later Viscount Alanbrooke, who as chief of the Imperial General Staff (CIGS) had been the one to recommend that Dobbie be replaced, seemed to confirm this view when, without bothering to elaborate, he wrote of Dobbie that "the stress was beginning to tell on him."[16]

Actually, however, although the governor's health had obviously suffered during his long ordeal on Malta, it seems unlikely that this was the real cause of his removal. Many other reasons have been put forward (but never in print) by persons then in positions of authority:

He was not assertive enough. He lacked vigor. He seemed to feel that the war would be won by praying. Every time there was a raid he was on his knees.

He failed to see that the fate of Malta would be decided in the air. He was too much old army. He didn't trust aeroplanes or believe in them. To him the answer to everything was guns, guns, and more guns.

It was Dobbie's fault that the March convoy was lost. The people in London understood this, and as soon as they could, they replaced him. Notice that they were careful to have a new man in charge for the arrival of the *Welshman*. They wanted to make sure its cargo didn't end up at the bottom of the harbor.

Governor Dobbie was too easy on the civilians. Of course, with civilian morale such an important factor, perhaps this was the best thing. Still, time and again he neglected military necessity in order to spare the civilians as much as he could. For instance, he should have started rationing long before he did, and the same with labor conscription, which he never really did do effectively. It was almost as if he were afraid to put the people to the test.

There was a terrible feud between Dobbie and the COG [Gen. Beak]. It began with Dobbie's objecting to having the troops work or train on Sunday. But Beak went ahead anyway. Dobbie was furious. The feud became public knowledge and had an adverse effect on troop morale. Finally, it reached a point where either Dobbie or Beak had to go, and Alanbrooke chose Dobbie.[17]

To a greater or lesser degree Governor Dobbie was certainly guilty on each of the above accounts, but again it is unlikely that any of them, or all of them together, caused his removal. There was something else—something more compelling, and urgent. Years later in his history of World War II, Churchill wrote of the incident: "Disturbing news in April arrived about General Dobbie. Up to this moment he had been magnificent, and from all parts of the Empire eyes were turned on him." The key words are "up to this moment." Obviously something happened in April to shake Churchill's faith in the governor, and, according to the date of Alanbrooke's recommendation to replace him, it must have occurred soon after the middle of the month. The prime minister made no mention of what it was, but it was clearly no minor matter. He concluded his remarks on the subject by writing: "I received this news with very deep regret, and I did not at first accept what I was told. However, a successor had to be chosen."[18] All of this lends credibility to the following account by Melita Strickland, whose husband, Roger, it may be remembered, was head of the elected majority in the Council of Government:

I can tell you for certain that it was Roger who was responsible for Dobbie's being replaced. He was convinced that Dobbie was about to run up the white flag. One day—it was toward the middle of April after several weeks of almost constant bombing, and we wondered if there would ever be an end to it—one day he approached Roger and told him of his concern for the people. Despite his stiffness Dobbie was a very compassionate man, you see. "Strickland, I cannot ask them to suffer any more than they have," he said. Well, it was so clear to Roger that Dobbie was on the verge of surrender that he went to the lieutenant governor and [his deputy] Andrew Cohen and persuaded them to join him in forwarding this information to the Home Government and asking for Dobbie's removal. This was the "disturbing news" from Malta that Churchill referred to. It was all done very secretly. I doubt that Dobbie himself ever knew the real story behind his being relieved.[19]

So Malta lost its father figure—by all accounts a good man and by some a great one. There are those who say that the island could never have held on without him, that through the example of his unflagging belief in the ultimate goodness of God's plan, he gave its people the will and courage to stand fast during those first two years of the war, when Malta lay alone and vulnerable in a hostile sea. On the other hand, as a military commander he had his shortcomings. By and large the civilians were sorry to see him go. "He was a truly inspirational man," said one. "He brought out the best in all of us." The island's military leaders, although not saying so openly, were less chagrined. While recognizing Dobbie's many fine qualities (Lloyd called him "kind, hospitable, and very brave"), they were hardly satisfied with his showing as commandant of the island. What was needed, they agreed, was a man of greater vigor and enterprise. Dobbie's successor was said to have an abundance of both. His name was Gort, and he could scarcely have come at a more critical time.

In appearance he was a far cry from the monumental Dobbie. Neither especially tall nor especially short, he was somewhat inclined to stubbiness and given to a slight stoop. His face was pliant, almost cherubic, and his sad eyes seemed always on the verge of tears. If met in mufti in the street, he could easily have been mistaken for a college don with something ethereal on his mind. But his looks belied the man, for Gen. John Standish Surtees Prendergast Verecker, Viscount Gort, V.C., G.C.B., D.S.O., M.V.O., M.C., A.D.C., was every inch a soldier. Descended from a long line of military men, he had served in the army for nearly forty years and had learned his trade well. By the time World War II broke out, he was considered one of Britain's top three or four general officers and was placed in command of the British Expeditionary Force in France. The rout that followed was none of his doing. In fact, it was he who prevented it from becoming a complete disaster by extricating his army virtually intact from the beaches of Dunkirk in the spring of 1940. But glorious as it was, the evacuation of Dunkirk with its almost total loss of supplies and equipment, was a colossal defeat for the British, and since Gort had been the one to preside over it, not surprisingly he became something of a scapegoat. His next command, several rungs down the ladder, was as military governor of Gibraltar, where, if Franco's Spain had decided to enter the war, he no doubt would have been called upon to engineer another evacuation. When he arrived on Malta in early May 1942, he was fifty-six and hard as nails. He was also more than a little suspect, especially to the civilians. "We were undecided as to what to think," said one. "Obviously he was a great general. On the other hand we couldn't forget that he was the one who brought off Dunkirk, and we wondered if he might not have been sent to Malta for the same purpose."[20]

The situation confronting Malta at that time surely warranted such a suspicion. Not only were supplies of all kinds becoming critically low, but, of more immediate concern, it now appeared certain that the enemy would mount an invasion of the island some time in the near future. Malta had suffered invasion jitters before, most notably after the fall of Crete a year earlier, but this time the signs were unmistakable. In late April RAF reconnaissance flights from Malta began to spot additional landing strips being constructed not far from the regular runways at Gerbini, Sicily, one of the enemy's main air bases. At first it was thought they were intended for conventional aircraft, but a careful study of the pictures left little doubt that they were glider strips. By early June the strips appeared to have been completed, and as far as Malta knew, crated gliders could be hidden in the adjacent sheds, waiting to be assembled during the night for takeoff at early dawn.

The enemy's preparation had not progressed that far, but otherwise the British had read the situation correctly. Finally, after nearly two years, the Axis had concluded that Malta must be seized. This decision was due largely to the persistent urging of Field Marshal Kesselring, who in early April had managed to persuade Hitler that, with a major offensive about to be launched against the British in North Africa, it didn't make sense to allow an enemy base, no matter how prostrate, to remain standing astride Rommel's main supply lines. The invasion of Malta, set for the early morning hours of July 10, was to be a joint operation involving an airdrop of one German and one Italian division, followed by a seaborne landing in the vicinity of Marsaxlokk. Diversionary landings were to be made on Gozo just before dawn, while hundreds of dummy parachutists were to be dropped over the northern end of the main island. The entire operation, involving nearly 100,000 men, two dozen tanks, and a regiment of field guns, would be supported by combat and transport units of the Italian navy.

During May and much of June, while equipment and supplies were being assembled at half a dozen embarkation points in Sicily and southern Italy, the personnel assigned to take part in the invasion (code-named Herkules by the Germans and Operazione C-3 by the Italians) rehearsed their roles time and time again, down to the fussiest detail. Areas similar in terrain to Malta were chosen, and combat conditions akin to those anticipated in the actual invasion were simulated. Japanese military advisers were brought in to lend their expertise on amphibious procedures, while German and Italian staff officers kept a close watch on every phase and feature of the preparations. Meanwhile, with Teutonic thoroughness, Field Marshal Kesselring checked and rechecked the plans and pronounced them sound. "It can be done," he said.[21]

And most likely he was right. Against such a force the island's garrison of 30,000 to 35,000 British and Maltese troops probably wouldn't have stood much of a chance, even if they had been in top condition—and they were far from that. Having lived for several months on siege rations, they lacked energy and stamina and, in general, had lost something of their fighting edge. Furthermore, despite the small quantities brought in by the *Welshman* in early May, the garrison had grown dangerously short of aviation fuel and antiaircraft ammunition, both of which would be needed in goodly amounts against an airborne attack. By early June the shortage of antiaircraft shells had grown so acute that gun crews were forbidden to fire more than ten rounds a day each without special permission from headquarters. "The island would have fallen," a Maltese infantry officer declared years afterward. "The enemy would have paid a heavy price, but we simply didn't have the men or matériel to stand up against a major assault."[22] Kesselring agreed. "It would have been easy," he later wrote:

> We knew much about the enemy's disposition. Excellent aerial photographs had revealed every detail of his fortifications, coastal and flak guns, and field positions. We even knew the calibre of the coastal guns, and how many degrees they could be turned inland.[23]

The Führer wasn't so sure, however. From the first he had held serious reservations about Herkules. In fact, he almost immediately regretted having approved it. The awful cost of the Crete invasion and the narrow margin by which it had eluded disaster continued to haunt him. Besides, the manpower and equipment required for Herkules could be put to better use on the Russian front, where, Hitler was convinced, the war would eventually be won or lost. But it was the joint nature of the operation that worried him most. Frankly, he didn't trust the Italians. "Experience has shown," he confided to his advisers, "that they do not possess the necessary fighting spirit." He particularly distrusted the Italian navy and feared that at the first sign of danger it would bolt for home and leave the invasion force stranded on the island. "And then what?" he asked Gen. Kurt Student, the hero of Crete, who was also to head the Malta airdrop. "You'll be left there alone, sitting on your parachutes."[24]

By late May the Führer had decided to abandon Herkules as too risky, and he so informed the German High Command. The main problem now was how to back out of the operation without offending Mussolini, who had come to have high expectations for it. In a stall for time Hitler ordered the OKW to "proceed with the preparations for Herkules, but only theoretically."[25] In other words a charade while he sought to let his partner down easily. Given the Duce's sensitivity to slight, this might have been difficult had not the gods of war suddenly beamed upon the Axis. On June 21, after having resumed his desert offensive three weeks earlier, Rommel surprised everyone, including himself, by capturing the strongly fortified harbor of Tobruk, which had hitherto held out doggedly during the ebb and flow of military fortunes in North Africa. The fall of Tobruk was a disastrous defeat for the British. "A bitter moment," exclaimed Churchill. For the Axis, on the other hand, it was a tremendous victory that provided Rommel with excellent port facilities less than a hundred miles from the Egyptian border and, of more immediate importance, a mountain of supplies and equipment that Tobruk's 25,000 defenders had neglected to destroy in their haste to surrender. "The booty was gigantic," Rommel's chief of staff later wrote. "It consisted of supplies for 30,000 men for three months and more than 10,000 cubic meters of petrol."[26] Rommel was ecstatic. Filled with the euphoria of victory, he radioed Berlin that the invasion of Malta had become irrelevant. Hitler, grateful for any excuse (and particularly such a convincing one), was quick to agree and, under the circumstances, had little trouble winning over the Duce.

Thus, unbeknownst to the Maltese, who would continue to live in its shadow for months to come, Operation Herkules was officially aborted. Kesselring was appalled. To him Malta remained the key to victory or defeat in Africa. Upon learning that the invasion had been called off, he pleaded with the Führer to change his mind, "but a wireless message from Hitler told me that this was no further business of mine." Thus rebuffed, the field marshal decided after much soul-searching to let the matter drop. "For such a judgment," he later wrote, "I feel myself responsible before history."[27]

17 *Lean Times*

Within two weeks after the fall of Tobruk, Rommel had chased the Eighth Army 300 miles eastward, all the way to El Alamein. There, running into stiffening British resistance, he paused to regroup, barely seventy-five miles from Alexandria. None of this was the best of news for Malta. "Well, we were really quite shocked," Melita Strickland would later recall:

> With the nearest friendly face almost a thousand miles away, we felt terribly isolated and alone. And we were certain now that the invasion would come at any moment. I remember Roger telling me at this time that, in case he was unable to do it for me, I must be prepared to kill myself rather than be taken alive by the Germans.[1]

Aside from further dampening their spirits, however, Rommel's advance into Egypt would do little to worsen the condition or prospects of the islanders. Even before the enemy's most recent thrust eastward, surface shipping from Alexandria to Malta had been rendered all but impossible by the Luftwaffe's tight control over the narrow sea passage between Crete and the hump of Cyrenaica. This much had been sadly borne out by the fate of Operation Vigorous just before the fall of Tobruk.

Vigorous was the larger of two convoys that set out simultaneously for Malta from different ends of the Mediterranean on June 12. Composed of eleven merchantmen carrying upwards of 60,000 tons of precious cargo, it departed Alexandria in the company of forty-six naval vessels—an altogether imposing armada. However, upon approaching the narrows between Crete and Cyrenaica ("bomb alley"), the ships came under repeated attack from enemy aircraft and sustained heavy damage. This, coupled with a report that the Italian fleet was rapidly closing from a distance of less than 150 miles, caused the convoy to turn about and head back to home port.

Meanwhile, Operation Harpoon from Gibraltar had also run into trouble. Consisting of six merchantmen, with an escort of twenty-nine warships, the convoy was badly bloodied while passing through the Sicilian straits. It continued on to its destination, however, where Malta's new governor, Lord Gort, had made certain that the island was properly prepared to receive it. More than 2500 troops and civilians, including inmates from the boys' reform school, had been alerted to report at an hour's notice to unload the ships. Some 500 trucks were standing by in the harbor area, ready to hustle the cargo to inland storage depots along well laid-out routes marked by colored arrows and overseen by teams of special constables. The island's guns were zeroed in over Grand Harbour in anticipation of a barrage, smoke pots were in place, and on the runways of all three aerodromes Malta's now battle-hardened Spitfires waited in readiness.

Finally, late in the afternoon of June 15, the battered remnants of Operation Harpoon cleared the breakwater. Only two of its cargo ships had made it through the blockade—at a cost of eleven merchant and naval vessels destroyed and an equal number damaged. From atop the bastions on both sides of the harbor, thousands of islanders who had come to cheer the convoy in, watched in grim silence. There was, as Air Marshal Lloyd noted, little cause for rejoicing. Two supply ships out of a total of seventeen from both convoys was a sorry score indeed. "We received about 15,000 tons from the two ships that arrived," the lieutenant governor announced a few days later after the vessels had been safely unloaded. "That is something and certainly a help, but it is a very small part of what we hoped for."[2] What made the situation even worse, although the people were not informed of this, was the fact that close to two months would be needed to ready another convoy, and it was certainly no secret that without additional supplies Malta would be hard put to hold out that long. As a young Spitfire pilot noted in his diary at this time: "We have very little petrol, very little food, no reliefs, and practically no ammunition."[3]

The failure of the June convoys came as a shock to the islanders. For several months they had been living on what amounted to a slow-starvation diet of 1200 to 1500 calories a day, and now it appeared that they would have to get by on even less. On June 20, five days after the arrival of the two ships, Lt. Gov. Edward Jackson went on rediffusion radio and informed the people of what to expect: "I have come here this evening to tell you plainly what our arrangements are, and I shall tell you the worst." With no outside help in sight, Malta would have to survive for an indefinite period on what remained of its reserve stores, plus what little produce could be grown locally. The key to the entire situation was the island's bread supply: "We know that our present [bread] ration cannot be reduced and it will not be reduced." Practically everything else would, however:

> In examining our position we first calculated the time for which our bread would last. The calculation gave us a certain date which I shall call our "Target Date," the date to aim at. Our new task was to see how we could make other vital necessities last to the Target Date.

In other words, Jackson explained, all of the island's provisions, including military stores, would be measured against the bread, so that everything would run out at the same time. After all, it would make little sense to have gasoline or cigarettes left over if there were no bread to eat; nor, conversely, would it make sense to have any bread remaining if the island lacked the other essentials, such as fuel for cooking and running the generators. Although not explicitly stated, the authorities clearly meant to see to it that if Malta were squeezed into submission, it would have precious little left to turn over to the enemy. Not that such an event were likely to occur:

> I cannot tell you when the Target Date is but it is far enough off to give ample opportunity for fresh supplies to reach us before our present stocks run out. England will not forget us and her Navy and Air Force will see us through.[4]

According to a British journalist on the island at the time, the Maltese people "accepted the situation, generally, with the utmost tolerance . . . and they remained at heart willing to endure all things in the effort to maintain the resistance of their island."[5] Well, not exactly. Having already gone hungry for so long, having sold their watches and wedding rings in order to buy a few dozen eggs and potatoes on the black market to keep their ribs from caving in, having seen their infants and old people waste away from lack of proper nutrition, they were hardly inclined to receive such news with "the utmost tolerance." However, there wasn't much else they could do about it, except grumble. And this only within modest limits, for too much grumbling could be construed as defeatism, and, as the government repeatedly warned the islanders, defeatism would simply not be tolerated. "People are writing to me and saying that we cannot now be supplied," the head of the

Information Office commented at this time. "Now, people who speak and write like that are QUISLINGS! Every effort will be made to replenish our stocks. . . . Woe to those who in any way seek to imperil our determination."[6]

As expected, the authorities didn"t wait long to introduce a further reduction in rations. As of July 1, each adult male was to receive the following allotments twice a month until further notice:

Rice	2 oz.
Preserved meat	12 oz.
Preserved fish	11 oz.
Cheese	1¾ oz.
Fats	5¼ oz.
Edible oil	8½ oz.
Sugar	11 oz.
Soap	7 oz.
Matches	2 boxes (small)
Kerosene	⅜ gal.
Tea	1 oz.
Coffee	2½ oz.

For edible items these rations came to a total of fifty-six ounces (down six from the month before)—or less than four ounces a day. However, the overall allotments were considerably skimpier than even these figures would indicate, for women and children received less than men, on the grounds that men were bigger and had to work harder. Furthermore, the larger the family size, the smaller the average per capita amount of each item allowed. Thus, a household composed of a husband, wife, and three children received not ten ounces of rice but only seven and not sixty ounces of preserved meat but only twenty-four. Larger families received proportionately even less.[7]

Besides these semimonthly rations every person on the island was to receive thirteen ounces of bread each day, an increase of two and a half ounces over the per diem allowance of the two previous months. Since bread was the main staple of the Maltese diet, this increase came as a welcome surprise, even though thirteen ounces was still well below half the normal daily per capita consumption. At the same time, however, the government announced its intention to introduce "further variation in the composition of bread to meet the supply situation while preserving the full nutritional value of the staple food."[8] In other words, more adulteration—which would certainly not be well received by the Maltese people, who thought very highly of their bread and resented having it "faked up."

Aside from the meager allotments listed above, the islanders had to rely upon homegrown products, which, as mentioned earlier, were not rationed because of their scarcity. They *were* price-controlled, however, although with many items the prices were well beyond the reach of most islanders. For instance, in June the official cost of a dozen eggs was four shillings and six pence (about ninety-two cents), nearly a day's pay for the average government worker.[9] But no need to worry about official prices, because little attention was paid to them anyway. In fact, most local food items that were not immediately snapped up by the government for consignment to the military or the new communal kitchens* soon disappeared into the black market. Thus, although the shelves of the island's grocers were more often than not bare of produce, a few carrots or cauliflowers could usually be found under the counter for those customers willing to pay the price. And the price was often several times that fixed by law. Consider, for example, the following comparative figures for local food products in the summer of 1942.[10]

	Government-controlled Prices	*Black Market Prices*
1 doz. eggs	4s. 6d.	30s.
1 chicken	8s.	25s.
1 orange	4d.	2s. 6d.
1 lettuce	1½d.	5d.
1 tomato	4d.	6d.
1 rotolo (28 oz.) onions	6d.	2s.
1 rotolo peaches	2s.	16s.
1 rotolo French beans	11d.	4s.

(One shilling is approximately twenty cents; one pence is approximately two cents.)

Rationed goods, many of them stolen from bakeries and government warehouses, also appeared on the black market, but in such small quantities that they were a negligible factor in the overall pattern of food distribution among the islanders. In fact, prices for these goods were usually prohibitively high for all but the rich. In July 1942, for instance, the cost of a halfpenny loaf of bread or a fourpenny rotolo of sugar ran as high as ten shillings.[11]

The black market not only operated openly, it flourished. "We all knew it was wrong," a resident of Pieta later explained, "but we went along with it anyway because we were so wretchedly hungry."[12] Those who had anything to spend squandered it willingly for "a little something extra," like a winza

*See below, p. 227. *et seq.*

of supposedly nonexistent potatoes or a rotolo of green beans hidden beneath the cloth skirt of a vendor's cart. "There was no meat," a Sliema resident would recall, "but if you had a friend who knew one of those sly butchers, he would take you there, and you could get a bone with a little skin wrapped around it, for which you would pay through the nose."[13] Sixpence for a cauliflower, twenty pounds for a sack of flour—what difference did it make? The important thing was to survive. First went the wages, then the family savings, followed by jewelry, household effects, furniture, and anything else of value, including religious treasures.

For those persons too poor, too proud, or (in a few cases) too prominent to buy on the black market, life could be very hard indeed. "Well, I nearly starved," Melita Strickland would recall a generation later:

> Roger divided his time between the Council of Government and his regiment and was seldom at home, so I had to get along on my own. Fortunately, I had a goat and a very small vegetable patch, but even so I don't see how I managed to stay alive. Roger had absolutely forbidden me to buy anything on the black market. He said that we should set an example for others. Naturally, I didn't pay any attention to him, and as soon as he was out of sight, I would be running frantically all over town trying to buy whatever I could.
>
> But nobody would sell me anything. Since I was the wife of the government's majority leader, the shopkeepers were afraid to take a chance with me. I suppose they thought I would turn them in or something like that. When it came to dealing with *me,* none of them had ever heard of such a thing as a black market. So, my friends were buying all sorts of lovely things like chocolate bars, and I couldn't even find an egg.
>
> I became terribly weak. Everything was such an effort. Finally, toward the end of the siege, I would spend three or four days a week in bed so as to conserve my strength. Otherwise, I doubt that I could have lasted from one ration period to the next. Looking back on it, I really wonder how I kept going.[14]

Generally it was the poor who suffered the most, however. With their large families and disproportionately smaller rations, they now led a day-to-day, hand-to-mouth existence, hovering on the very verge of starvation. For them, having nothing of value to exchange, the bounties of the black market were hopelessly out of reach, unless of course they chose to steal. And, as the food situation grew more desperate, an increasing number of them did. By the summer of 1942 thousands of normally honest islanders had turned to theft as, literally, a way of life. The bolder among them robbed government supply dumps and warehouses, usually making away with small quantities of anything from bully beef to binoculars, some of which would be kept for family use and the rest bartered for food or fuel on the black market. Others broke into bakeries in search of flour and bread or, more frequently, into shops and private homes with the hope of finding food or items that might be exchanged for food with a black marketeer. The police records for this period are filled with reports of robberies, most of them involving trivial amounts but, in the aggregate, accounting for several thousand pounds' worth of stolen property:

> June 21, 1942: Somebody or *bodies* broke into a military mess hall near Zabbar and stole 2 tins of corned beef, 10 tins of fish, 2 tins of margarine, and 5 lbs. of powdered milk.
>
> Also Zabbar, somebody broke into a private residence and stole 1 small tin of margarine and 2 lbs of tea, and 2 gals. of kerosene.[15]

Petty theft of this sort carried a penalty of ten days for the first offense and anywhere from a month to two years for subsequent offenses. However, arrests were exceedingly rare, partly because the thieves had the good sense to do their stealing during air raids when most people were confined to the shelters and partly because the police and special constables were usually looking in the opposite direction. "I saw nothing," was their stock reply, and the higher authorities were inclined to let it go at that.

Officially, of course, the government frowned upon the black market and the cruel inequities it caused. "We must be altogether in the task that is before us," Lieutenant Governor Jackson reminded the people. "*It must be the same for everyone.* We must be able to feel as we see each other passing by on the street, that we are really all together in this task, enduring whatever has to be endured."[16] But it *wasn't* the same for everyone, and by all accounts, official measures to make it that way fell far short of the mark—so much so that many of the islanders wondered if the authorities were really interested in doing away with the black market or even slowing it down. True, there was much huffing and puffing by the government, resulting in a profusion of regulations ostensibly meant to resolve the problem. For example, as time passed, penalties were made more severe, so that by July petty black-marketeering (amounts under five pounds) was punishable by fines ranging from ten to fifty pounds, while offenses on a grander scale carried sentences of up to five years imprisonment.[17]

The fact is, however, that few people were ever arrested and even fewer convicted. In all fairness it should be noted that the islanders were generally reluctant to report black-market activity, often because they themselves were caught up in it (either as buyers or sellers), and even more reluctant to testify against it in court. Still, in view of the scope of the operation and the number of people involved, the government's meager record of conviction is hard to understand. Years later Dr. Jaccorini offered the opinion that the black market was "unofficially condoned by the government. It seemed to serve a useful purpose."[18] A British officer who remained stationed on the island throughout the siege was more explicit:

> The black market was a necessity. The quantities that were sold on it wouldn't have amounted to anything if they had been divided evenly among the entire population. So why not let at least some of the people get enough to make a difference? But what people? The answer to that was plain old-fashioned capitalism. Those who had the money to pay were able to buy; the others weren't. It was as simple as that. It may not have been very nice, but under the circumstances there was no better way.[19]

Not everyone would agree. "My blood still boils when I think of it," a Sliema man exclaimed many years after the war:

> Thousands of little children went without milk, but the big shots always managed to have Rikotta [cheese] at their fancy parties. Don't talk to me about "share and share alike." Money talked. If you had it, you could buy anything. If you didn't, you damn-near starved. . . . The black market was despicable.[20]

As if the island's food situation weren't already bad enough, Malta's early harvest that year was far below normal. The causes of this short-fall included the now almost total lack of commercial fertilizer, the damage done standing crops by the enemy's intensive bombing that spring, and the ever-growing amount of farmland taken over by Air Marshal Lloyd for his runway extensions and dispersal strips. However, the bitterest blow of all, the partial failure of the spring potato crop, has a story all its own.

As mentioned earlier, potatoes were Malta's most bountiful crop. Originally the island had produced mainly "White Elephants," a Mediterranean variety well suited to Malta's climate and soil. Because of its bland taste, however, it was not highly valued as an export item and was eventually abandoned by the Maltese in favor of the Irish potato. Besides finding a ready acceptance in the commodity markets of Amsterdam and London, the Irish potato proved more prolific than the White Elephant and at least its equal in all other respects save one: Unlike its predecessor, the Irish potato could not reseed itself in Malta's warm climate. Thus, for each planting, seed potatoes had to be brought in from outside, usually Scotland or Northern Ireland. Whereas in peacetime this presented no great difficulty, once the island fell under siege, shipments of seed potatoes, like everything else, had a hard time against the blockade. Thus in late 1941 the island's authorities, forced to come up with another source of supply, switched to a variety of potato then being grown on Cyprus and proceeded to import some 2000 tons by submarine and small surface vessel for Malta's 1942 spring planting. But the Cyprus potato failed to respond well to its new surroundings—which helps explain why, at the worst possible time, Malta's spring potato harvest dropped to little more than 8000 tons, less than half the average prewar yield.[21] By early July potatoes had virtually disappeared from the island, except for a few winzas on the black market, where they sold for exorbitant prices.

All things considered, then, it is not surprising that the islanders failed to set a very ample table during the summer of 1942. On a July evening just before a new issue of rations was due, the Marchesa Cissy Zimmerman sat down to a dinner of one sardine and ten peas, and felt fortunate to have that much. Returning home from work on a horse-bus one afternoon, a passenger turned to the stranger beside him and unburdened himself of a story that might have been told with minor variations by thousands of islanders that summer:

> I have five children. The youngest is nine. It breaks my heart to hear them squabbling over bread. They steal one another's and lock themselves in the closet and eat it. My wife is always crying over this misfortune which has overtaken us. She and I give up half our ration to the children. We have one slice each for supper. I press her to take a second, the last in the dish, but she refuses. She says she's not hungry. In my turn I refuse it too, but soon after our hands shoot out simultaneously for it. This makes us red in the face. We laugh in embarrassment. Then I say, well if that's the case we'll share it. After that we pick off the crumbs one by one.[22]

But the shortage of food, bad as it was, was only one of many scarcities facing the islanders. Indeed, it often seemed that everything was in short supply, except lines to wait in. Cigarettes, for example, were so scarce that men stood in queues for hours to purchase a single pack of Flags or Woodbines, expected to last an entire week. Confirmed smokers turned in desperation to dried fig leaves. Lemon and strawberry leaves were also popular—but hardly a substitute for the real thing:

> How often on one of those visits to the cinema could one watch those pictures depicting celluloid people nonchalantly lighting a cigarette, only to grind it out immediately into so many shreds of tobacco. And the groans from many throats as they thought of their own meagre allotment and the rubbish they had smoked by necessity, if only to soothe their tired nerves.[23]

Soap, toothpaste, razor blades, shaving cream, nursing nipples, fountain pens, writing paper, and a thousand other items ordinarily taken for granted had long since disappeared from the shops. Articles of clothing were now irreplaceable, and there was nothing to mend them with, unless a person were prepared to spend a pound (four dollars!) for a penny spool of thread.

Aside from food, however, it was the acute shortage of fuel that was most sorely felt. Coal, which the British should certainly have stockpiled in greater quantities, was nearly extinct. Black oil, intended mainly as ships' fuel but now being used to power the island's emergency generators and other essential machinery, was down so low that the authorities doubted it would last as long as the bread. The strictest economies were practiced. Electricity for civilian use was cut off throughout the island, save for the hospitals and the movie theaters. The latter were allowed to remain open to boost morale—but without aisle lights or overhead fans, just the projectors. The only other exception was a few hours of rediffusion radio, again to help keep the people's spirits up. Military personnel and furloughed dockyard workers were assigned by the government to scavenge through ruined buildings for splintered wood to fuel the island's flour mills and bakeries. For a time the authorities even considered commandeering all wooden products, including furniture and window frames, but eventually dismissed the idea as too extreme. In July a government bounty was introduced for the collection of dried thistles.[24] Meanwhile, gasoline had become so scarce that Lord Gort had taken to riding a bicycle even on his official rounds, and all but a few of the island's regular buses had been retired in favor of horse-drawn wagons.

But it was the shortage of kerosene that had the most serious effect upon the day-to-day life of the average person, for kerosene was the all-purpose fuel in most homes, and the lack of it led to considerable inconvenience and hardship. Fortunately, with the coming of warm weather, heating was no longer necessary. Cooking still had to be done, however, as well as innumerable other household chores, such as dishwashing and laundry, that ordinarily required hot water. Furthermore, once the electricity had been cut off, kerosene became the principal, and virtually only, source of illumination. For all this the semimonthly ration of one and a half quarts per person was puny indeed, and when this amount was reduced by half in early July, the situation became impossible. The military were no better off. "A crashed aeroplane was a windfall in those days," Air Marshal Lloyd later wrote. "The oil would provide an extra hot drink for a day or so."[25]

To ease the hardship caused by the growing shortage of food and kerosene, and to economize on the consumption of both, the government had

Maltese soldiers foraging for wood.

begun setting up communal feeding centers back in March of 1942. By July there were nearly one hundred of these centers, or "Victory Kitchens" as they were commonly called, serving more than 30,000 hot meals each day. Eventually, as centers came to be located in all parts of the island, they would provide daily feeding for 200,000 people, or about three-quarters of the total population. Usually situated in an abandoned shop with a large V painted on the front, each Victory Kitchen served a noon and evening meal, either one of which (but not both) any civilian could obtain by paying the sum of sixpence and surrendering half his ration slips for that day.

It is hard to imagine how the island's poor could have survived without the Victory Kitchens. Among other things, they served as distribution centers through which scarce nonrationed foods became available to everyone in more or less equal amounts, rather than ending up in the stomachs of the highest bidders. And yet, from the first they were the subject of bitter criticism. By all accounts the food was terrible. The main dish was a watery soup containing a few chunks of sausage or goat, a tiny sampling of local produce that the government managed to requisition before it disappeared into the black market, and bits and pieces of whatever else came to hand, including (some claimed) dog, cat, and even donkey. As a change from the soup, the kitchens occasionally offered a thin slice of what was officially called "veal loaf" but was actually a combination of goat and horse—strong enough to bring tears to the eyes of anyone able to eat it. "The food was absolutely disgusting," Melita Strickland later said of the Victory Kitchens. "The smell alone was enough to spoil a person's appetite. I would have starved before eating that slop. And I nearly did."[26] Cissy Zimmerman agreed: "The meals really were dreadful. Not only was the food itself pretty awful, but it was poorly prepared. The vegetables were usually only half-cooked and were often dirty, and I recall finding long goat hairs in my soup."[27] Fortunately, the servings were so skimpy that they probably didn't do anyone much harm. An English housewife would long remember her family's first communal meal. For herself and two children she received four tiny pieces of sausage and fifteen peas floating about in three pints of tasteless tomato broth.

Besides criticism of the food itself, there was a rising chorus of complaints about the way the communal feeding program was operated. The queues were said to be too long; meals were often served as much as an hour late; persons near the end of the line usually ended up with cold food; some people received larger portions than others, and so on. But the commonest complaint was that the Maltese personnel serving the food (most of them, it was claimed, the relatives of bureaucrats) were ill tempered and rude. "They seemed to resent our presence. They made us feel like beggars, even though we were paying for the meals and giving up our ration slips."[28] It was also noticed and widely commented upon that these same employees, and their families as well (!), appeared remarkably well fed. No need to wonder why: They were obviously pilfering food intended for the stewpot. Riots broke out, one of them serious enough to end in a protest march to the governor's residency at San Anton. Finally, in early August, the authorities felt it necessary to set up a committee to investigate and report on the communal feeding program. The committee's findings: The Victory Kitchens were a good idea; but they were poorly run, partly because their management board included a lawyer, an engineer, a retired soldier, and a politician—but not a single member with even the remotest experience in food-handling. In essence the committee agreed with the prevailing view that the kitchens were guilty of bad food, bad preparation, and bad manners, and that there was indeed considerable pilferage among the employees. Worse yet, instead of effecting a savings in Malta's rapidly dwindling kerosene supply, the Victory Kitchens were actually hastening its depletion. On October 7 the committee recommended that the kitchens be closed, but by the time the government got around to acting on the recommendation, the arrival of relief food supplies had made the entire matter largely irrelevant.[29]

For those who frequented the Victory Kitchens, and ultimately most people did, goat meat became a fast friend—or, better to say, acquaintance. It was one of the main staples of the stewpot and a major source of what little protein the islanders received. The slaughter of Malta's 35,000 goats had been going on for several months as the island's shepherds, faced with a growing shortage of fodder for their animals (and food for themselves), repeatedly thinned their herds. Not until late June, however, after nearly 70 percent of the goats had already been killed, did the authorities belatedly step in and requisition those that remained for the communal feeding program. It was the government's last card in the desperate game of survival, and the time had come to play it. By mid-July the Victory Kitchens were receiving more than 1000 goats each week.

The slaughter of the goats meant the virtual end of Malta's fresh milk supply. A few hundred of the choicest animals were spared to supplement the island's rapidly diminishing reserves of canned milk and the small shipments of dry milk brought in from time to time by submarine from Alexandria. But the sum total of milk available fell far short of providing adequately even for those who absolutely had to have it. As of early July only nonnursing children under ten years of age and expectant mothers were permitted allotments—and even they in meager amounts; The father of a nine-month-old infant whose mother was no longer able to nurse it, was much relieved when he was granted a doctor's permit to purchase six cans of milk. "But imagine my surprise," he wrote to the *Times,* "when I was informed that the issue had to last a month! On normal feeding a child nine months old consumes one tin of milk in just under a day and a half. How am I to feed my child for the rest of the month?"[30]

So it went. As July wore on, the islanders found little to cheer about. Hungry, ragged, and bone-tired, they lived from one day to the next, harassed around the clock by enemy aircraft and plagued by fears that the invasion of the island, still thought to be imminent, might snuff out their lives at any hour. And all the while they could only guess which meal would be their last, for the government, in its wisdom, had seen fit not to tell them when the target date would be. Beset by more miseries than they had ever before imagined, the people of Malta had good reason to ask themselves, and one another, if things could possibly get worse.

18 Life among the Ruins

Somehow during that harried summer of 1942 life went on. A district medical officer, who moved freely among the people and saw them at their best and their worst, marveled at their ability to persevere in the face of so much adversity and so little hope:

> Even though deprived of virtually all the things that one has a right to expect from life, they continued to go about their business and, by and large, retained their good humor and good sense and gentleness. In the morning after a night of enemy air attacks, the wife would boil a little tea, and that plus a bite of bread would be all for breakfast. Her husband would go off hungry to the dockyard and work in danger all day long, while the wife did the washing and hung it out to dry amid the ruins. Throughout the day she would stand in queues for bread or kerosene or something else, perhaps cigarettes for her husband, and often come back without anything. All around was death and misery, but these people chatted and gossiped and laughed, and at night when the husband came home, he was cheerful and always asked first: "How are you and the children? Are you all right? How did you spend the day?"[1]

And yet, the cruel attrition of the past several months had exacted a heavy toll. When Field Marshal Alanbrooke visited the island in midsummer to confer with Gort, he found conditions "distinctly depressing, to put it mildly." The people were terribly emaciated, some little more than walking skeletons. The target date, estimated at somewhere around September 1, was still a month away, but Gort warned Alanbrooke that if a convoy didn't arrive well before then, the islanders would be too weak to unload it. At about this time two transport planes left by night for Cairo, carrying a few dozen of the island's worst afflicted mothers and children. When they disembarked at their destination, grown men wept at the sight of them.

Clearly Malta was dying by degrees, and the end appeared not far away. Their bodies wasted by months of hunger, the people became progressively more lethargic and disoriented as the island drew ever closer to starvation. Life in all quarters, civilian and military alike, seemed to have slipped into a lower gear. Everything had become harder and slower. The most trivial task was now a major undertaking, and the simplest decision a matter of immense complexity. "What I remember most clearly about those days is not the hunger," a Maltese officer would later state, "but the awful, awful fatigue. We were absolutely fagged. The point was reached at which I just couldn't keep my eyes open. If I didn't keep moving, I was apt to go to sleep standing up and fall over."[2]

Under the circumstances it is not surprising that the islanders came down with a variety of diseases and other ailments, among them such potential killers as tuberculosis, pneumonia, and pellagra, all of which would reach disturbing proportions. Dysentery and other acute intestinal disorders were also common, along with a multitude of lesser afflictions, including the infamous "Malta Dog," a particularly virulent stomach flu that seemed to single out newly arrived pilots as its special victims. "From time to time a great hand within my stomach seems to grip, squeeze and crush all my inner parts," one of them wrote in describing "the dog," which occasionally kept as many as half the island's fighter personnel grounded.[3]

Malnutrition, with its erosive effect upon the body's natural resistance, was undoubtedly the major underlying cause of the people's worsening health. The high incidence of stomach ulcers suggests, however, that stress was also a factor. So were the island's appalling sanitary conditions, especially in the main target areas, where most water and sewer systems had long ago stopped functioning and the residents often emptied their "excreta buckets" into the gutters. The brief but widespread visitation of typhoid in the summer of 1942 appears to have been caused by the infiltration of sewage into the island's drinking water, or possibly by the increasingly common use of human excrement as a substitute for commercial fertilizer, now no longer obtainable. Whatever the reasons for Malta's mounting health problems, in 1942 its death rate, which before the war had hovered around twenty per thousand, jumped to thirty-two—an astonishing eight points above that of the year before and by far the highest ever recorded on the island.[4] As usual it was the helpless who fared worst: The mortality rate among mental patients rose from a prewar 5 percent to 26 percent, while among infants in their first year of life, death claimed fully a third.[5]

By far the most prevalent disease at this time, and the only one to reach truly epidemic proportions, was the mange, or, as it was more commonly called, scabies. Caused by a tiny, ticklike parasite and transmitted by physical contact, the disease first appeared on the island in late 1940 and spread like wildfire. By autumn 1941 it had become a scourge, and by the following spring was completely out of control. Although not fatal or in most cases even disabling, it was an exceedingly unpleasant affliction. Similar in some ways to poison ivy, it caused its victims to break out in skin blisters and lesions that itched furiously and were quickly spread by scratching to all other parts of the body.

At one time or another a majority of the islanders came down with scabies, many of them repeatedly during the two-year period when the disease was rampant. Indeed, it often seemed in those days as though scratching had become Malta's favorite pastime. It was quite common to see a person rubbing his back on a lamppost or the corner of a building like a bear against a tree. In some cases the itching was so severe that it simply could not be denied, even if it meant gouging oneself into a mass of bloody sores. The government recommended bathing the infected areas with warm soapy water, which was probably sound medical advice but not very practical for people who had neither the soap to wash with nor kerosene to heat the water. Eventually some of those most seriously affected would be admitted to the hospital. There they would be sponged and, if the timing were right, daubed with sulfa ointment brought in periodically by submarine. Generally after four or five days they would be pronounced cured and sent home, where, chances were strong, they would soon become reinfected by rubbing up against their neighbors in an overcrowded shelter or cigarette queue. Not until late 1943, after the war had passed the island by and living conditions had become less congested, was scabies finally brought under control. Until then it would continue to figure as just another barb, albeit a very irritating one, in Malta's crown of thorns.

The medical authorities did their best to cope with the island's worsening health crisis, and in a few cases, such as the 1942 typhoid inoculation program, they succeeded admirably. By and large, however, there was little they could do. Several thousand people still inhabited the filth-ridden rubble of the principal target areas; 85,000 more lived as refugees in the grossly overcrowded inland villages; and the entire population suffered from months of hunger, fatigue, and the anxieties of war. Against such odds as these the island's health officials could hardly have been expected to have much of an effect. Furthermore, as time went on they had progressively less to work with. By the summer of 1942 all of Malta's hospitals had been damaged by enemy air attacks, some so extensively that patients had to be moved into schools and convents and even special underground shelters. Enemy action also destroyed a considerable amount of irreplaceable medical equipment, although far more of it simply wore out from overuse or lack of replacement parts. At one point in the spring of 1942 there was only one X-ray machine on the entire island available full-time for civilian use.[6]

It was the shortage of medication that was the most keenly felt, however. With uncustomary initiative the British had stockpiled the island with large quantities of medical supplies during the Abyssinian crisis. But that was in 1935. During the years since then most of the medicines had lost their potency, and when the need arose for them early in the war, they were found to be useless. Why more was not subsequently done to replace them during those months when shipping was moving virtually unmolested into Malta is not clear. At any rate, by early 1942 the general public found it all but impossible to obtain even the commonest sort of pill, such as aspirin. At the very time that the government was warning the people against the dangers of coughing or sneezing in the shelters, there wasn't a single bottle of cough medicine, or a lozenge, or an inhaler to be had on the entire island. The same could be said for bandages, ointments, antiseptics, and even eyeglasses. What few medical items there were, brought in from time to time by submarines, were found almost exclusively in the hospitals, but even there supplies were so limited in amount and kind that doctors had difficulty medicating their patients properly. These shortages, together with the physical deterioration of the buildings themselves and their equipment, helps explain why of the some 4000 persons admitted with infectious diseases to Malta's hospitals in 1942 one out of every six died, and of admissions for all causes, no matter how trivial, one out of eight.[7] In May the island's health officials, appalled at the rising death rate, especially among the children, persuaded London to put aside its pride and ask Mussolini for a simple humanitarian gesture. The following entry from Count Ciano's diary gives some indication of the sort of enemy Malta was up against:

> The English would like to send some hospital ships to Malta. Our Navy agrees in principle, but the Germans are against it. The Duce decides against it, especially because his experience has taught him "the many things it is possible to hide in hospital ships when the blockade would otherwise prevent their passage. Last winter we were able to deliver some truly timely supplies of petrol to Benghasi by making use of white ships"—ships of the Italian Red Cross.[8]

A curious feature of the health situation in Malta during the siege was the steady drop in mental ailments. At the outset of the war medical officials had expanded the asylum at Attard in expectation of a substantial increase in mental cases, but quite the opposite occurred, as shown by the following record of mental patients listed on hospital registers (Gozo not included):[9]

June 30, 1940	915
September 30, 1940	823
December 31, 1940	785
March 31, 1941	756
June 30, 1941	713
September 30, 1941	720
December 31, 1941	705
March 31, 1942	698
June 30, 1942	682

It has been theorized that the intense physical and emotional pressures caused by the siege produced a sort of psychological imperative that enabled people to go beyond their normal breaking point. Simply stated, the islanders were too preoccupied with survival to give in to mental stress. This would perhaps account for the fact that in neighboring Gozo, which was practically untouched by enemy attacks, the number of newly registrered mental patients during the war was nearly five times as high proportionately as on the main island. This theory might also explain why, once the siege had been lifted, Malta's incidence of mental disorders stopped its more than two-year decline, and, as if by way of compensation, began to rise dramatically. By the war's end it had reached its highest level in nearly a century.[10]

For most of the islanders, normally a gregarious people, social life all but ground to a halt during that unhappy summer of 1942. Hungry, tired, and overmatched by the wickedly hot weather, they preferred to spend their off-hours at home, moving about as little as possible. Besides, there wasn't much else a person could do. Private gatherings as well as public functions had practically ceased to be. All restaurants and coffee shops were closed for lack of anything to serve, as were all but a few of the island's bars, including most of the neighborhood pubs. Even the band clubs, so central to the social life of the villages, had been shut down. Indeed, hardly a place was left open anywhere on the island where friends could sit and chat over a cigarette and a glass of beer. Not that this really mattered much because cigarettes had virtually disappeared, and at ten shillings a bottle (twenty times its prewar price), beer was way beyond the reach of the average worker.[11] For a special afternoon or evening out, there was the British Institute in Valletta, which, despite its multiple wounds, remained open during most of the siege. But the Institute drew mainly from the island's upper-class element. With its penchant for poetry readings and chamber music, it was too high-toned for the population at large.

If a person were desperate enough for entertainment or merely a change of surroundings, he could always go to the movies. However, with the overhead fans shut down, the theaters were apt to be insufferably hot and smelly. Besides, most of the films were "oldies" that had been making the rounds of the various villages for months and had been seen at least once by practically everybody. In fact, it was not uncommon for a person to attend the same movie half a dozen times. A young British soldier is said to have seen Ralph Richardson in *Four Feathers* twenty-six times—a record of sorts. Not surprisingly, as the siege wore on, more and more civilians preferred to stay home and listen to "The Bones of The Dinosaur" on their rediffusion radio.

Perhaps the hardest blow of all to the island's social life was the suspension of many of its religious celebrations, with their crowd-pleasing color and excitement and overall holiday atmosphere. All *festas* were canceled, as were most other public processions and ceremonies. Time-honored religious customs dating back as far as the Middle Ages were temporarily done away with, including the deeply moving Candelmas ceremony in which each year priests from all the villages on the island come to Valletta to present the traditional long candles to the head man. Fearful that these ceremonies, which invariably drew large crowds, would attract enemy raiders, the palace persuaded the church to dispense with them until a more suitable time. When the Government went a step further, however, and suggested that for the sake of manpower needs *all* religious holidays be suspended, the church bridled, and Governor Dobbie had the good sense not to push the matter.[12]

As a rule the church cooperated fully with the civilian and military authorities during the war. This came as something of a surprise, since many of the higher clergy, having been educated and groomed in Rome, were known to have a strong Italian bias. However, the head of the Maltese church, Bishop Dom Maurus Caruana, was a staunch anglophile who succeeded in keeping his hierarchy at least outwardly loyal and guiding the church in a salutary direction. A close friend of Governor Dobbie, whom he greatly admired for his piety, the bishop was more than generous in his support of the war effort: Monasteries and friaries were placed at the disposal of the government for use as refugee centers and hospitals; dietary and other dispensations were granted as concessions to the wartime conditions on the island; and, as mentioned above, many of the traditional religious ceremonies were suspended, including (in deference to the curfew) Christmas midnight mass. One sacrifice that proved particularly hard to accept, for clergy and people alike, was the silencing of the church bells, which were to be rung only as a signal of invasion. For as long as the islanders could remember, the bells of their village church had sounded several times a day, not only to toll the hour but, more important, to remind the people of the presence of the Almighty in their midst. When the bells no longer rang, the villages seemed strangely diminished, as if cut off from the voice of God.

As the summer ground on and the quality of life on Malta continued to worsen, civilian morale became a matter of paramount concern to the authorities. How much longer would the people hold fast in their will to resist? Could they reasonably be expected to remain loyal (or at least docile) as they watched their children waste away to skin and bones, or would they rise up in desperation and plunder what little remained of the island's reserved food supplies—or even attempt to turn Malta over to the enemy? Sometime earlier the lieutenant governor had ordered all protection officers to submit monthly morale reports for their districts, with any questionable or suspicious behavior described in detail. These reports have since disappeared, but there is no reason to believe that they were at any time negative. In fact, all indications are that throughout the siege the islanders remained, if not thoroughly committed, then at least resigned to doing what the authorities asked of them.

Some of those persons in the best position to know have claimed that this was due to the deep affection the Maltese had for the British. "There was a very warm feeling toward them, a marvelous feeling," the Marchesa Zimmerman remarked some years later:

> There was nothing, *nothing,* we wouldn't have done for them. When everything was so short and we were so hungry, we said to one another: "This is what God sent us. Let us pray." It never even occurred to us to blame the British, and under no circumstances would we have abandoned them.[13]

Others have disagreed, however, some rather strongly. "Of course we were true-blue. We had no choice in the matter," a Maltese teacher declared long afterward:

> We were thoroughly cowed. We didn't even dare complain, at least not openly. You see, there was a concerted campaign against grumbling, which the British linked to defeatism and even fifth-columnism. Posters and slogans were everywhere, warning against "pro-Italian elements" who might try to undermine the people's morale and help the enemy by spreading discontent. The people were afraid that if they com-

plained about conditions they would be torn away from their families and sent to a detention camp, or even deported like the others. So we did what we were told and pretended not to mind.[14]

It was considered risky even to comment unfavorably upon the vagaries of the war, especially as they pertained to Malta itself. Shortly after an enemy raid on the Luqa aerodrome in mid-July 1942, Frank De Domenico stood with a friend atop one of the walls of Fort St. Angelo in Vittoriosa and watched as huge clouds of black smoke rose up from the target area:

"Ara, Joey, il-bombi laqtu mahzen tal-petrol!"
(Look, Joe, the bombs have hit a fuel dump!)

"Le. Dak m'hux tlief taxix."
(No. It's only grass.)

"Imma, mela dah m'hux taxix. Ara d-duttan, tiela', kemm hu iswed."
(But of course it's not grass. See how black and high the smoke rises.)

"Frank, dak taxix, u jekk taf x'inhu tajjeb ghalik, tghid li hu taxix."
(Frank, it's grass, and if you know what's good for you, you'll say it's grass.)[15]

But whether they acted as they did out of friendship or fear, there can be no denying that the Maltese stood faithfully by the British throughout the entire siege, fulfilling their assigned roles with rare courage and dedication. Despite all dangers, difficulties of transportation, concern for the safety of their families, and the ravages of hunger and fatigue, they continued to show up for work each day as if nothing were amiss. Even during the worst of the blitz, in April 1942, absenteeism and tardiness were negligible. And yet, it appears that the government never really trusted them, at least not enough to take them into its confidence. During the course of the conflict the authorities repeatedly fed the people false information or no information at all, in order to keep unpleasant news from reaching them.

The principal instrument of deception was the Office of Information, headed by Maj. Francis Gerard, a tireless dissembler whose main job was to prevent the people from finding out just how bad things really were. Toward this end his office released a brief situation report each afternoon at five o'clock, which was published the following morning in the *Times of Malta* and the Maltese language paper, *Il Berqa*. Supposedly a factual summary of the day's military action affecting the island, the situation report was not above twisting the news, or even repressing it, when Major Gerard felt that the war effort would be better served thereby. Sometimes this practice was carried to senseless extremes, as when the ferocious attack on the *Illustrious*, certainly no secret on the island, was not even mentioned until ten days after it had occurred. Even then, in describing it the report conceded only that "some slight damage was done to civilian property in Senglea," which everyone knew was a lie. "Well, not a lie exactly," Gerard's Maltese assistant, George Zarb, would later argue:

> We were simply withholding part of the truth. We often did that as a matter of policy, so as not to shock the people, you understand. If the news were bad, we tried to release it in trickles. Major Gerard used to say: "If the news is good, make it better. If its bad, don't hit them with it all at once."[16]

Since most of the news those days *was* bad, the situation reports were usually couched in such vague language that, while appearing to provide information, they actually said very little: "Enemy action over the southern part of the island today resulted in some slight damage to civilian property," ran a typical report. "Enemy raiders were engaged by our antiaircraft and planes from our fighter command. A number of raiders were destroyed or damaged." But the reports seldom specified *where* on the southern part of the island, *how much* property damage, or *how many* raiders destroyed. It was all very irritating to the islanders, most of whom had a pretty good notion of what was going on but would have appreciated more detailed and accurate information. The phrase "some slight damage to civilian property" (a great favorite of the Information Office) was particularly galling. When applied inappropriately, as was often the case, it sounded insensitive—even callous. In a letter to the editor of the *Times* one reader protested:

> It is quite a puzzle to find out [from the situation report] the number of casualties suffered by enemy planes. . . .
>
> Another thing which is unsatisfactory is the cool, indifferent manner in which damage is mentioned. The other day, when enemy bombs destroyed a dozen houses in Sliema, the situation report said that there was "some slight damage to civilian property."[17]

In response to such grumbling the Information Office maintained that it was necessary to conceal certain matters of military importance from the enemy. While this was undoubtedly true, was it possible that the enemy didn't know how many of its own planes had been lost, or, with such excellent aerial reconnaissance, was unaware of the general extent of damage its bombs had caused, and where? "It was hard to escape the feeling that the authorities were more concerned with keeping us in the dark than the enemy," Frank De Domenico commented years afterward.[18]

At the same time, the Information Office shielded the islanders from the more dreary aspects of the situation abroad, such as the continuing German penetration into Russia, by sifting and often doctoring incoming news. In its daily official newspaper, the *Bulletin,* and its more ambitious *Weekly Bulletin,* the Information Office provided the people with all they were supposed to know about the progress of the war. And to make sure they were told nothing more or different, it maintained strict censorship over the island's press and rediffusion radio. "After the electricity went out in early 1942 and we were no longer able to pick up foreign broadcasts, we had only a vague notion of what was really going on in the outside world," De Domenico explained:

> By then we were getting practically no mail, because of the blockade. When we did get some, it was by submarine or sometimes bombers on their way to Alex. But that meant less space for powdered milk and medicine and chocolate bars, etc. So there wasn't very much mail those days and, what little there was, was heavily censored. We really had to depend for our news upon what the Information Office told us through the press and over the rediffusion radio. Of course we knew that the British weren't always telling us the truth, and it hurt us not to be taken into their confidence. After all, we were like brothers to them, like links in the same chain. Or so we thought.[19]

In some ways this was the hardest burden of all—not knowing about the true progress of the war. During that brutal summer of 1942, when so few avenues of truth were open to them, the people of the island fell prey to all sorts of rumors and false reports, many profoundly disturbing: A friend in a neighboring village knew a man whose nephew worked on the runway at Luqa and had overheard a British pilot say that a giant convoy from Gibraltar had been driven back with great loss, and it was doubtful another would be attempted. A servant at Admiralty House told a cousin of the widow who lived beside the church that the British fleet had been ordered to abandon Alexandria. Prime Minister Churchill had been killed by a bomb; the *kappillan* (priest) himself had said so, and he had got the news directly from the bishop.

Some of the more unpleasant rumors came by way of propaganda broadcasts beamed at Malta from Italy. Although from the beginning of the war, listening to Italian radio, including the opera, was illegal, many people did so anyway, using makeshift antennas that could be quickly dismantled if the need arose. Even after the electricity was shut off, a few sets were kept operating by the use of hand generators. Items of interest that were picked up soon became common knowledge among the islanders, including the mixed offerings of Rome's version of Tokyo Rose, a supposedly Maltese woman who showered her listeners nightly with Axis propaganda, some of it none too cordial:

Greetings to my friends in Malta. How do you like taking it? There will be more for you tonight. Tonight will be a very good night, because the moon is out. Tonight you are not going to sleep. Tonight you are going to take it!

At times, however, she could be very nice, as when she played opera and sympathized with them for all their suffering and sorrow, even calling some of the islanders by name! She found it hard to understand why her Maltese friends continued to sacrifice themselves and their country to the selfish interests of their British masters, especially when it was well known that the British had all but lost the war. Hitler had taken Moscow; Rommel was on the move again; and, the most glorious news of all, a huge naval battle in the eastern Mediterranean had destroyed the British fleet. Of course, everyone understood that she was lying. If the truth were known, she probably wasn't even Maltese. A real Maltese woman would hardly have been brazen enough to speak out on such matters—certainly not over the radio. Still, she seemed to know a great deal about what was going on. Could it be that some of the things she said were true? If so, which ones? It was enough to set a person wondering, in spite of himself.[20]

And all the while the air attacks continued, although the enemy planes no longer came over in massive numbers as they had earlier. The raids were now mainly small-scale, hit-and-run forays, carried out by German fighters during the day and small numbers of Italian high-level bombers at night, with some support from Ju 88s and Dorniers. The fighters were especially unnerving. Armed with light bombs, as well as cannons and machine guns, they would approach Malta at only a few feet above the surface of the sea and attempt to sneak in beneath the radar and listening devices. Once over the island they would blaze away at it from altitudes of usually no more than a couple of hundred feet, until, having exhausted their ammunition, they would veer out to sea and head back to Sicily. All within a matter of a few minutes.

They seldom came in groups of more than ten, but they came often and hit hard. When spotted in time they were highly vulnerable to the island's gunners and Spitfires, and their losses ran high, sometimes as many as a dozen planes a day. During the first two weeks of July, a period of especially brisk activity, the marauders were reported to have lost 102 aircraft—an inflated figure, no doubt, but close enough to indicate that, with Malta's fighter force now up to nearly 150 planes, air attacks against the island had become a costly undertaking.[21] Still, Kesselring was obviously willing to pay the price. And able as well: In mid-July, Air Marshal Lloyd, in a farewell message to the islanders before giving way to his successor, Sir Keith Park, announced that despite the enemy's continuing losses the number of Axis aircraft on Sicily (about 450) had remained more or less the same since May, meaning that replacements were constantly being brought in. The point of the air marshal's remarks was that Malta could be proud of the fact that it was using up enemy air strength badly needed elsewhere, which was true enough, although many of the islanders probably didn't view the situation in exactly that light.[22]

The intruder raids, as they were called, rarely did much military damage, nor did the nightly bombing runs. But military damage was no longer the enemy's main concern. Although the raiders continued to pound the aerodromes and to a lesser extent the dockyards, their principal purpose now was to wear down what little resistance the islanders had left. Unlike before, the enemy attackers were deliberately targeting the civilian population. Terrorize them with rooftop raids. Ravage their villages with indiscriminate strafing and bombing. Keep the people running to and from the shelters, where at this time of year as Kipling said of a different time and place, "the 'eat would make your bloomin' eyebrows crawl," and the stench was beyond all belief. Force them to spend their nights in those squalid, steaming holes, gasping for air and squabbling with their neighbors for an extra inch of space. Torment them around the clock with anxiety and fear.

To help accomplish this, the raiders resorted to some ugly tactics, including the widespread use of antipersonnel devices, such as pocket-sized bombs disguised as thermos bottles, fountain pens, and jackknives—the sort of thing one's neighbor might drop on his way to work. Designed to explode when handled in a certain way, they would usually lie harmlessly in the streets and fields, waiting to be picked up and jostled by some unsuspecting boob (hence the expression "booby trap"). Of course, they were especially tempting to children, which is perhaps what the enemy intended. In the little inland town of Lija, not far from the governor's residency, a boy of fourteen proudly brought home what he supposed to be a thermos bottle and blew up himself and his entire family. The Maltese author Laurence Mizzi recalls a similar incident in his boyhood village of Gudja on the south side of the island:

> I can well remember the day my friend died. His mother was a widow. Being the youngest of the family and fatherless, my friend was always by his mother's side.

> She simply doted on him. Never did he do anything without her knowing. One day while they were working in the fields, the boy found a thermos flask and decided to take it home. On arrival he found that it was not an ordinary flask and being curious he decided to try and open it and find out what it contained. He got a hammer and started to hit it. . . . I don't think he managed to hit it more than once. What a cruel and senseless way to die![23]

In addition to the antipersonnel devices, the Axis made extensive use of delayed-action bombs as instruments of terror. It is impossible to say how many were dropped on Malta during the summer of that year, but they must have numbered in the hundreds. And they were nerve-racking, to say the least. Whereas a conventional bomb would explode on impact and be done with it, a DA would usually carom around a bit before coming to rest in the gutter or in someone's doorway, where it would tick away for perhaps several hours before going off. In the town of Mosta one landed a few feet from the only unblocked entrance to a public shelter, forcing its occupants to remain in their underground vault for nearly twelve hours until the bomb was defused by a special team of sappers. Many of the DAs were set to explode at mealtime while people were queued up at the Victory Kitchens; others were timed for the middle of the night, when human nature is most prone to panic.

And then there were the duds—conventional bombs that were meant to explode on impact but through some malfunction failed to do so. Often they would lie in the streets for days before overworked bomb-disposal units took them to nearby fields and detonated them with machine-gun fire. Sometimes the disposal units arrived too late, as on a day in late July, only hours after an eight-year-old boy in Cospicua discovered an unexploded bomb in a rubble pile near his home and began throwing rocks at it. There was never a trace of him found. At the *kappillan's* suggestion his parents buried his good suit of clothes and a favorite toy.

There seemed to be little the island's garrison could do to put a stop to this mayhem, or even slacken its pace. Enemy planes were shot down in impressive numbers, but others immediately took their place. Furthermore, as July drew to a close, it was becoming increasingly apparent that the defenders were losing some of their sting. Each day their effectiveness weakened, as they were able to bring less and less firepower to bear against the intruders. The main problem was an acute shortage of the necessary wherewithal to keep Malta's guns and fighters operational. By late July antiaircraft ammunition had reached such short supply that each gun on the island was allowed to fire no more than five shells a day, a severe restriction allround but especially so for the Bofors because of their rapid rate of fire. To exceed this allotment without written permission from above could mean a reprimand or even court-martial for the gunnery officer in charge.

Malta's aircraft were also badly hobbled by shortages, so much so that as the summer wore on they were forced to cut down more and more on their flight time. Replacement parts were practically exhausted. When the island's air equipment officer was ordered by the air-officer-commanding to prepare a list of what Malta's air force needed in the way of spares, he suggested that it would be easier and more sensible to prepare a list of what *wasn't* needed, since virtually everything was broken, worn out, or depleted. Furthermore, aviation gas was down to less than a ten-day supply, and reserves of engine coolant were almost completely gone. Occasionally cargo submarines would arrive from Alexandria carrying loads of gasoline and glycol coolant, while every so often antiaircraft ammunition and aircraft replacement parts were flown in at night by transport plane, also from Alexandria. But all this, although gratefully received, was but a trickle, the merest fraction of the garrison's needs. And the cost ran high: Submarines and bombers alike needed large amounts of precious fuel for their return to base. A transport plane, for instance, required more than 600 gallons of aviation gas for the trip back to Alexandria, a fair exchange for a planeload of badly needed parts and ammunition, but still, under the circumstances, a painful price to pay.

And to what end? By the beginning of August, Malta was rapidly running out of time. Its 300,000 civilian and military personnel were already well on their way to starvation, and the pitifully meager remains of the island's food supply couldn't be expected to last longer than a few more weeks at most. Children had already taken to stuffing their empty stomachs with carobs, which in ordinary times had been considered fit only for fodder. In their villages at night the people, hungry, desperately tired, and more than a little afraid, discussed among themselves their island's chances for survival and concluded that, short of surrender, they were none too good. If Malta were to be saved, more would be needed than a few cases of carburetors and coolant sneaked through the blockade in dribbles. Nothing less than the arrival of a major convoy could do the job. But, as everyone knew, this was not likely to happen. Indeed, with the approaches to the island still controlled by the Axis for hundreds of miles in all directions, such an event would require a miracle.

19 The Miracle of Santa Marija

Only three hundred yards from the barrack blocks at Takali stood the remains of an extraordinary building, a large, sprawling villa that had been constructed before the war by an elderly couple as a monument to their long and happy life together. Every room had been designed and furnished in a different style after a special country or region the two had visited. Because of its size and proximity to the aerodrome, the enemy must have thought the building important and from almost the beginning of the war had bombed it repeatedly, scoring direct hits on some of its wings and tearing off bits and pieces of the main structure. By the summer of 1942 only the outer shell of the villa remained standing. Remarkably durable and singularly out-of-place, it seemed the very model of elegance and composure amid the havoc of battle. British pilots called it "The Mad House," and several of them, like young Denis Barnham who had flow into Malta with his paintbox tucked between his legs, would sit for hours during the cool of early morning or evening, attempting to capture its changing moods on canvas.

Such bizarre scenes were not uncommon that summer as Malta lay dying. Throughout the island hungry, ragged people waited in line, sometimes during air raids, to purchase tickets for the next month's drawing of the government lottery, while knowing full well that for Malta it was doubtful there would be a next month. In the Great Fosse, not far from the joint command post in Lascaris tunnel, a piano appeared one day, no doubt salvaged by its owner from his bombed-out home nearby. At night scores of people gathered around to sing Maltese songs and such current British favorites as "White Cliffs of Dover" and "I'll Be Seeing You." Almost daily, dozens of sallow, hollow-cheeked children, beating on tin cans and tooting whistles, marched down Kingsway in Valletta in a macabre parade that might have been staged by the theater of the grotesque. Their energy quickly spent, they would rest from time to time amid the ruins until forced to move on by the rats. In the countryside, where enemy bombs had fallen on bone-dry fields or struck a dirt road, huge clouds of dust would billow up for hundreds of feet into the sky and, when the air was still, hover there for hours, all but blotting out the sun.

On August 2, as visiting Field Marshal Alanbrooke was about to leave the island following his brief meeting with Gort, he decided to let the governor in on a secret. Poor Gort had lost a great deal of weight and was obviously rather feeble. Nevertheless, he continued to do twice as much work as anyone else, while drawing the same rations. As mentioned before, he traveled everywhere by bicycle, despite the stifling midsummer heat, which even the native Maltese found overpowering. Frequently, he would have to carry his bicycle over piles of rubble, an exercise that would have tired a much younger man. Not surprisingly, his spirits had suffered along with his body, and, as Alanbrooke later explained, it was to "dispel his gloom" that he took the governor into his confidence: Big events were in the offing in North Africa. The British Eighth Army at El Alamein was building up a powerful force that would be unleashed against Rommel sometime in October. With any luck, it would send him scurrying all the way back to Tripoli, where he would run up against an American expeditionary force moving eastward from Algeria and Tunisia. If things went as planned, the enemy might be cleared from North Africa by as early as the end of the year.

Naturally, this announcement came as welcome news to Gort. A victory over Rommel would give a tremendous boost to Allied arms. Unfortunately, though, for Malta it would come too late. Barring the unexpected, the island would be in enemy hands long before then, and Gort, together with his 35,000-man garrison, would be languishing in a prisoner-of-war camp, except perhaps for a few Maltese troops who might manage to disappear back into the civilian population. In the barracks and gun pits the men now talked openly of being taken prisoner ("going in the bag")—not a pleasant prospect, to be sure. Some of them pondered the possibility of escaping to Tunisia and being interned by the French. Others, including Gort himself for a time, spoke of making their way to southern Italy and fighting in the hills as irregulars. But this was pure romancing. The men had no way of getting off the island, and even if they had, they were in no condition to survive for long behind enemy lines. Sadly wasted by the privations of the past several months, they were in even worse shape than the civilian population, for, while receiving essentially the same amount of nourishment, they had been called upon to perform more strenuous duties, including the job of keeping the runways repaired. "By midsummer our food situation had become very bad indeed," a British infantry officer recalled a generation later. "For a meal we might be given three spoonfuls of lentils, a bit of hardtack, and a single sardine. God knows this was not much, but it was all there was."[1]

In early August a new ration list was issued by the Office of Food Distribution. Each civilian was now to receive ten-and-one-half ounces of bread, down from a previous thirteen. In addition, a member of, say, a family of six was entitled to an average daily allotment of approximately one-quarter of an ounce of rice, three-fifths of an ounce of corned beef and an equal amount of canned fish, two-thirds of an ounce of fats (half butter and half lard or margarine), two-ninths of a pint of edible oil, one-and-one-half ounces of sugar, and one-eighth of an ounce of tea. Rather than try to get by on such meager fare, however, most of the islanders now chose to surrender some of their ration coupons for a daily meal at one of the Victory Kitchens, where the food, however foul, was more plentiful and had the added attraction of being served hot. By now food had become an obsession. It was difficult to think of anything else, especially for the children. A Maltese teacher in Valletta would later remember how her little brother used to sleep with his bowl beside him on his pillow in the family shelter. When he awoke in the morning his first words were invariably: "How long before we go to the Victory Kitchen?" Throughout the island thousands of starving children constantly nagged their parents for more food, and when it was denied them, they asked the unanswerable question: Why was it that, after they prayed so hard for their daily bread, it pleased God to send them down so little?[2]

On Malta few crops come into harvest during the hot summer months. Tomatoes are the main exception, and during the first two weeks of August that year the island's biggest tomato crop in a decade flooded the market. This was indeed a blessing from above, for which the islanders were duly grateful to the Virgin Mother—not that tomatoes offered much nourishment, but they at least gave some relief to a gnawing stomach and did much to take the stink of goat from the Victory Kitchen soup. What was really needed, however, was not tomatoes but protein. A cubic inch of corned beef or tunny, or an ounce of "veal loaf" from the Victory Kitchen, was not enough to sustain life for very long, and yet the prospects for increasing the protein amounts, or even continuing them much longer at the same level, were dim indeed. By now virtually all of the island's rabbits and poultry had been slaughtered, and its goat herd was down to 5000 head, or less than one for every fifty inhabitants. What remained of the island's fishing fleet (an estimated two-thirds of it had been destroyed) might have helped to provide protein, but defense regulations prevented the boats from going out at night because on radar they could be mistaken for landing craft. And in the daytime they were helpless against strafing by the enemy, who had no intention of permitting Malta to fatten up on fish. On August 11 the government authorized the director of agriculture to begin scheduling all remaining livestock for slaughter at the public abattoir.[3] Horses were not included. They would be needed to help close up shop.

Meanwhile in London, Malta had not been forgotten. Convinced that if the little island were reprovisioned it could again play a key role in the battle for North Africa, Prime Minister Churchill was determined to push through a relief convoy, regardless of cost. Food, of course, was Malta's most pressing need, but food alone would not be enough. Oil, for fueling the island's power plants, bakeries, and pumping stations, was also absolutely essential. "Without it," a British writer later explained, "the whole complex of community life on the island would have broken down."[4] Furthermore, if Malta were to reemerge as an effective base of operations against enemy shipping, oil would be needed to fuel the submarine and surface raiders of the Royal Navy. In late July the Tenth Submarine Flotilla had slipped quietly back into Marsamxett Harbour and had immediately begun to take a toll of Rommel's supply ships. But with the island's oil reserves down to under 4000 tons, these operations were necessarily limited in their range and frequency and, it appeared, would soon have to be abandoned altogether.

Given the enemy's hammerlock on Malta, getting supplies of any kind to the island would be extremely difficult, if not impossible. Getting oil there in the quantity needed would be especially perilous because it would require a large tanker, which, due to the nature of its cargo and its lack of speed, would be highly vulnerable to attack, particularly by submarine. Indeed, if a tanker were to stand even a ghost of a chance in the fierce encounter bound to result from any attempt to relieve Malta, it would have to be able to outrun enemy subs. This meant a speed of at least fourteen knots, and there was no tanker that fast flying the British flag. The Americans had one, however, and so again Churchill turned to President Roosevelt for help, and again Roosevelt was happy to oblige.

The *Ohio,* barely two years old when sequestered from the Texaco Oil Company in the summer of 1942, was a marvel for its time. Capable of speeds in excess of sixteen knots, it was the fastest tanker afloat and, with a capacity of 120,000 barrels of oil, the largest ever constructed. After being turned over to a British crew at the Clyde in Scotland, where it was outfitted with additional antiaircraft guns and loaded to the gunwales with diesel and kerosene, the *Ohio,* now flying the red duster of the British merchant marine, put out to sea shortly before dusk on August 2 as part of a convoy called Pedestal.

Eight days later, soon after dark on August 10, the convoy made its way through the Straits of Gibraltar to begin its desperate run to Malta. Although shrouded by a heavy fog, it did not pass unnoticed by Axis spies, who infested both sides of the Straits and immediately notified Berlin and Rome of their sightings. However, their reports were superfluous, for the Axis command had known about Pedestal for some time, which is not surprising, given the lack of security surrounding the convoy. From the first the British could hardly have been more open about the operation if they had advertised it in the newspapers. At English docks where the merchantmen took on their cargoes, shipping crates were plainly stamped "Malta," and at clubs in London and Gibraltar the convoy was a common topic of conversation. "I have often wondered how the enemy could have had this concentration of forces ready at the right moment," a British admiral later testified before the House of Lords when the matter was under investigation, "but in view of this extraordinary carelessness, one can be surprised at nothing."[5] The concentration of forces referred to by the admiral included every available enemy submarine and light surface raider in the central and western Mediterranean, together with an estimated 540 serviceable aircraft on Sardinia and Sicily—all lying in wait for the kill. "Tomorrow will be a hard-fought day," Count Ciano noted in his diary upon learning that the British ships had cleared Gibraltar.[6]

Operation Pedestal was by far the largest convoy ever to enter the Mediterranean. In addition to fourteen merchantmen it contained seventy naval craft, many of them on loan from escort duty in the North Atlantic and Arctic. Included in their number were two battleships, four carriers, seven cruisers, thirty-three destroyers, and two dozen submarines, minesweepers, and other lesser craft. Like the *Ohio,* the other merchant ships were the best available—sturdy, well-constructed vessels capable of fifteen knots or better. In the aggregate their cargoes totaled more than 110,000 tons of food, ammunition, tinned aviation gas, and hundreds of other badly needed items, all distributed evenly among the various ships so that each vessel carried a cross section of the convoy's overall cargo. In this way if a given ship were sunk, something of everything would be lost, rather than everything of something. The only exception to this arrangement was the *Ohio,* which carried all of the black oil. This meant that even if the rest of the convoy were to make it to Malta safely and the *Ohio* didn't, the entire effort would be for naught. In a very real sense the *Ohio* carried the fate of Malta in its holds. Without its precious fuel, no amount of food would make much difference. The members of the convoy understood this. So did the enemy.

Shortly after noon on the first day out of Gibraltar, the battle was joined when a German submarine put four torpedoes into the starboard side of the carrier *Eagle*. This intrepid ship, which had off-flown so many fighters to Malta during the past several months, sank in less than eight minutes, taking all but four of her planes to the bottom with her—a full quarter of the convoy's air cover. What followed was one of the bloodiest and most ferocious air-sea engagements of the entire war, waged over a distance of some 500 miles, as Operation Pedestal fought desperately to reach the safety of Grand Harbour. For more than two days, almost without let-up, enemy dive bombers and torpedo planes hurled themselves at the convoy, while attack submarines and E-boats stalked their prey with deadly effect amid some of the most treacherous mine fields in the world. Only the main Italian fleet, short of fuel (and, some said, courage), was missing from the action. Had it not been, the convoy would certainly have been obliterated. Even so, the losses were appalling.

On Malta the people waited, and prayed, and talked of little else. For a week rumors had been circulating that a giant relief expedition was on its way, and now, although there had been no official confirmation, who could doubt that these rumors were true. Every available lorry and ambulance stood in readiness along the quays in French and Dockyard creeks, waiting to hustle away the convoy's cargo and wounded. Bridges of lighters had been laid out to buoys in the harbor where some of the ships would be tying up. Stevedores had been put on instant notice, and dozens of additional Bofors guns had been brought into position around Grand Harbour to provide maximum antiaircraft protection for the convoy once it arrived. Meanwhile, as Malta-based reconnaissance pilots brought back reports of a great battle at sea not far to the west, hundreds of people rimmed the cliffs at Dingli on the south side of the island, from where eastbound traffic could first be spotted, and watched in anxious vigil for any sign of their salvation.

Finally, on the afternoon of August 13, a tiny speck appeared on the distant horizon, followed shortly by a second, and then a third. Within an hour the news had spread by word of mouth over much of the island, and crowds of thousands shouting "Wasal il-Konvoy!" (The convoy is coming!) converged on Grand Harbour, where they clambered to the tops of the ancient walls and bastions that lined the bay. At the tip of Valletta beside the cratered remains of Fort St. Elmo a band was playing martial music, while thirsty soldiers at a Bofors site nearby huddled in the shade of their gun and sucked on grapes as they waited in the withering heat. Near the Upper Barracca, not far from where Governor Gort and his staff were standing, a lone vendor moved among the people, peddling raw beans to anyone willing and able to pay the price—not a very tempting treat but about all there was left to sell on the island. Overhead the sky trembled with the roar of dozens of Spitfires patroling the harbor area against possible enemy intruders.

At 6:18 P.M., with its guns pointed upward and its gun crews stripped to the waist and stained with blood, the cargo carrier *Port Chalmers* cleared the breakwater and entered Grand Harbour, followed in quick order by the *Melbourne Star* and the *Rochester Castle*. A tremendous cheer went up from the crowd, as the little band at St. Elmo greeted the ships with the inevitable "Roll Out the Barrel." People shouted, waved their arms wildly, and danced little jigs of joy. Others broke down and cried uncontrollably. Several fell to their knees and gave thanks to the Almighty: "Imbierka is-sapienza t'Alla! Waslu!" (They have arrived! Blessed be God's wisdom!). For those who were there the experience was unforgettable. "There would never be another like it for any of us," one of them exclaimed nearly forty years later. "It was an unbelievably stirring moment. It still lives with me as if it happened only yesterday. I think of it often, and when I do, I am not ashamed to say, my throat begins to tighten, and I am overcome with emotion."[7]

But the elation of the crowd was short-lived. A reporter for the *Times of Malta* noted that as the three ships moved into position at the foot of the harbor and their ugly wounds became visible, the people grew strangely quiet. By now it was generally known that the convoy had contained more than a dozen merchantmen. But where were the others? None could be spotted on the horizon, although the sea was as smooth as glass. And the condition of those ships that had just arrived was hardly reassuring. All had sustained damage, and one of them, the *Rochester Castle,* had been so severely mangled that its gunwales were barely above water by the time it reached its mooring. On the following noon a fourth cargo ship, the *Brisbane Star,* its bow blown clear away and its holds badly flooded, limped into the harbor. It was the only arrival during a long and watchful day. By dusk, with the rest of the convoy well overdue and none of its ships in sight, the mood of the island had turned somber. It now seemed likely that all of the remaining merchantmen, with their thousands of tons of precious supplies, had either been destroyed or forced to turn back—which was, in fact, very close to what had actually happened. Nine of the ten had indeed been sunk. The other, the indispensable *Ohio,* entered Grand Harbour at eight o'clock the following morning, after what must be counted as one of the greatest maritime marvels of the war.

The giant tanker had been partially disabled in the early evening of August 12, 800 miles or so east of Gibraltar, when an enemy torpedo slammed into its bow, leaving a gash twenty-seven feet long and twenty-four feet high. At nine o'clock the next morning, soon after suffering further damage from a 500-pound bomb, the ship was severely jolted by a Ju 88 that crashed into the sea less than fifty feet away and ricocheted onto the *Ohio*'s foredeck, starting several fires that were soon brought under control. At ten o'clock two sticks of bombs straddled the tanker and lifted it clean out of the water. A few minutes later a Stuka dive bomber splashed down nearby and bounced onto the ship's poop deck with a shattering impact. By now the *Ohio* was on a five-degree list, had taken on 10,000 tons of water, and was settling at the rate of six inches an hour. Shortly before noon, while it was still some ninety miles from Grand Harbour, its engines finally gave out.

Attempts were made to take the tanker in tow, and by six o'clock that evening the *Ohio* was again heading toward Malta. But with only a single destroyer and a minesweeper to do the towing, its progress was painfully slow. By eight o'clock the following morning, August 14, it had covered only twenty miles, during which it had received a direct hit from a Stuka on its forward extremity. Shortly thereafter two other destroyers, a second minesweeper, and several motor launches arrived and joined the towing operation, just in time to see the tanker barely missed by a 1000-pound bomb that tore a gaping hole in its stern, through which seawater came pouring in. For the rest of that day the *Ohio* was pulled along at an average speed of better than two knots, as its pumps strained to stem the rising tide inside and dozens of Spitfires from Takali provided almost constant protection overhead. Shortly before sunset the Dingli Cliffs were sighted, but by this time it had become extremely doubtful that the tanker could be kept afloat long enough to reach the island. Indeed, it was now riding so low that its midsection showed barely two feet of freeboard. As if to demonstrate how far the ship had settled, one of its gunners leaned over the side and scooped up a bucket of seawater with which to cool his Bofors barrel. But the *Ohio* had not come all this way and withstood so much punishment only to founder within sight of its destination. That night an old paddle-wheel tug was sent

Children welcoming the Santa Marija convoy.

The Ohio *entering Grand Harbour.*

out from the island to help with the tow, and as a last desperate measure the commander of the rescue flotilla ordered his two sturdiest destroyers to come alongside the tanker and prop it up between them.

Which is how the *Ohio* entered Grand Harbour the following morning, Saturday, August 15, as the crowd looked on in wonder from the surrounding heights. With its hull held together in places by little more than its outer plating and its long center deck thoroughly awash, the giant tanker was eased past the breakwater by its two destroyer attendants, which kept the helpless vessel shouldered between them like some drunken friend. The people, their spirits again resurgent, did not doubt for a moment that they were witnessing a miracle, the miracle of Santa Marija, for was it not true that this floating ruin had run the enemy's gauntlet and reached the safety of the island in defiance of all reason? And surely it was no mere coincidence that this most singular event had occurred during the final hours of the Novena to our Lady, a nine-day period of intense prayer that ends with the Festa of the Assumption of the Virgin Mary, one of the holiest of all religious celebrations for the Maltese. Who could deny that the Blessed Mother in her infinite mercy had seen fit to spare this great ship, along with the rest, that the island might live on to glorify her name? Let others speak of Operation Pedestal. To the Maltese the great relief expedition of August 1942 would always be known as the Santa Marija Convoy.

By half past nine the *Ohio* had secured to its mooring near the base of the harbor, where almost immediately pumping crews boarded the ship and began unloading its priceless cargo. As it yielded up its last gallon of oil and seawater rushed in, the tanker groaned and sank slowly to the bottom. But not until after it had received a farewell wireless communication from the commanding officer of the convoy. It read: "To *Ohio* stop I'm proud to have met you message ends."

20 "With Wonder and with Gratitude"

Despite its awesome losses, Operation Pedestal saved Malta. More than that: With fuel now available the little island was able to resume its offensive strikes against Rommel's supply lines and thereby figure prominently in the enemy's final defeat in North Africa. This is not to say that Pedestal put an end to the people's privations. There would still be many lean days ahead during which the islanders would have to continue to skimp—with many items even more so than before. But those few battered ships that succeeded in running the enemy blockade carried with them enough essential provisions to enable Malta to hold out until late autumn. By then, after Rommel's defeat at El Alamein and the landing of American forces in Algeria, Axis power in North Africa would be so badly weakened that it would no longer be able to dominate the approaches to the island.

In late November a convoy of four merchantmen carrying 35,000 tons reached Grand Harbour from Alexandria with only minor damage, and during the next month two more convoys brought in a total of 175,000 tons without even being challenged. In the meantime, except for a brief blitz in mid-October just prior to Alamein, enemy air activity against Malta had all but ceased, mainly because of the transfer of badly needed Axis aircraft to other fronts. By the end of the year there could be little doubt that the battle for Malta had ended. And for those who bothered to weigh the matter, it was clear that the issue had really been decided during those blistering days of the preceding August when the battered remains of a desperate and altogether heroic relief expedition staggered into Grand Harbour to rescue the island from what seemed at the time certain and imminent surrender.

So the little island had hung on after all. But the price was monstrously high. Records show that 1486 civilians were killed, 1846 seriously injured, and 1932 slightly injured by the enemy's 1199 air raids. These are the official figures.[1] As for the *actual* count, who can say? It was common practice for a family to deliberately conceal the death of a member in order to keep drawing his rations. Also, a widespread fear of doctors and hospitals prevented many of the wounded from reporting their condition to the authorities. And what of the untold numbers of islanders who, though they escaped the war's shells, were nonetheless its victims: the elderly who perished from heart attacks brought on by fright or the exertion of rushing to the shelters; the infants who died of malnutrition; the people of all ages who succumbed to war-related diseases; plus, the legions of those who survived the siege, but only with their health seriously, and in some cases permanently, impaired? The real level of casualties can only be guessed at, and under the circumstances (including a lack of agreement as to what constitutes an actual casualty) one person's guess is perhaps as good as another's. But among those in the best position to judge there is general agreement that the overall count approached 15,000, or roughly 5 percent of the island's total population.

Property damage, most of it in the densely settled southeast quadrant of the island, was staggering. The Three Cities area was virtually flattened. The chart below, composed of official government figures, presents a grim picture. In addition, incalculable damage was done to the island's water and sewer systems, power lines, buses, monuments and statues, public and private wells, fields, fences, and livestock. Altogether an appalling amount of devastation, but not surprising in view of the fact that Malta had been hit with more than 15,000 tons of high explosives—a mere dusting by today's megaton standards, but at that time the heaviest and most prolonged bombing ever inflicted on so small an area.

The real story of human misery, however, can seldom be told by statistics. *People* suffer, not numbers. On a June day more than a generation later George Zarb, retired businessman, sat amidst the elegance of his private club in Valletta, sipping his afternoon sherry and reminiscing about the not-so-good old days.

Throughout the war Zarb had stayed on in Valletta. He would have preferred to move with his neighbors to the relative safety of the interior, but the long, irregular hours of his job at the Information Office made that im-

WAR DAMAGE TO MALTESE BUILDINGS

	A	B	C	D	Total
Private premises	5,524	5,077	4,848	14,225	29,674
Churches, convents, etc.	11	32	21	47	111
Institutes, hospitals, colleges, etc.	4	23	10	13	50
Theaters, clubs, hotels	10	11	8	7	36
Auberges, palaces, villas	4	10	9	23	46
Government offices, banks, garages, etc.	4	14	5	8	31
Factories, bakeries, flour mills	14	23	18	24	79

A = totally damaged; B = damaged, requiring demolition; C = damaged, but not requiring demolition; D = damaged slightly.

Source: Statistical Abstract of the Maltese Islands, 1946 (Valletta, Malta, 1947), p. 76.

possible. His wife, although terrified by the bombs, insisted on staying with him. On the morning of April 23, 1942, a day of almost constant air raids, a baby boy was born to the young couple at their home on South Street, which up to then had somehow escaped serious damage. Minutes later a delayed-action bomb exploded outside the door and rocked the house so violently that the mother and infant were torn from their bed and thrown fifteen feet against the far wall of the room. Although neither was badly hurt, the emotional trauma so affected the mother that she was thereafter unable to nurse the baby. Even in ordinary times this would have brought great sadness and shame to any Maltese woman, but in those days, when almost no milk was available, it could have meant something much worse: literally a matter of life or death.

For a week the infant lived off his prenatal fat, receiving no nourishment except an occasional drop of sugar water. Each day, as his parents looked on helplessly, he grew weaker. "We prayed, oh how we prayed, that God would spare our son. And finally our prayers were answered." On the eighth day an allotment of dry milk was obtained from a shipment brought in by submarine, barely in time to save the baby's life. But the doctor feared that the prolonged lack of nourishment had caused permanent brain damage and that the child would be mentally retarded. Thus, for the next several years the parents waited and watched and attempted to interpret the signs. "It was a terribly hard time for my wife and me," George Zarb recalled. "It really wasn't until the boy entered school and started bringing home high marks that we dared feel he was all right."

And, of course, for the Zarbs, like everyone else in wartime Malta, there were also the more ordinary hardships and tragedies to contend with: the loss of loved ones; the constant, nerve-racking fear and anxiety; the gnawing hunger; the fatigue and awful sense of isolation; the discomfort and indignities of the shelters; and the unavoidable, everlasting filth. But to George Zarb all else paled before the sheer horror of an early morning encounter shortly before the siege was lifted, when the island's fortunes and the people's spirits were at their lowest. He had just left the neighborhood shelter following a night of raids and was on his way home with his infant son cradled in his arms. Along the way it was necessary to pass between two narrowly separated piles of rubble, and in the first light of dawn he was able to make out the presence of half a dozen or more rats crouching motionless on the top of each—big, ugly, gray-black brutes who had developed a taste for human flesh from feeding on corpses, and now appeared to be lying in wait for him. As he entered the path between the two mounds, several of the rats lunged through the air and attached themselves to him and his child. "It was the most terrifying moment of my life," Zarb exclaimed:

> If I live to be a hundred, it will always be with me, like only yesterday,. I still shudder whenever I think of it, and often at night, now forty years later, I dream about those rats, and I wake up covered with sweat and ask myself: "How, dear God, did we ever survive those awful times?"[2]

But the point is that Malta *did* survive and, by doing so, played a highly important role in turning back the barbarians. Almost certainly the island was the determining factor in the contest for control of the Mediterranean and North Africa. As a necessary fuel stop for aircraft on their way to Egypt, it performed an invaluable service for the Army of the Nile and later the Eighth Army; and by occupying the attention, often for months at a time, of hundreds of enemy planes that might otherwise have been used to good advantage in the desert, it provided another important assist. But the island's greatest contribution to the ultimate Allied victory in the Mediterranean theater was the slaughter it inflicted on enemy shipping. According to Italian sources, from the day of Italy's entry into the war in June 1940 through November 1942, Malta-based surface vessels, submarines, and aircraft sank or damaged over half a million tons of cargo intended for Axis forces in North Africa. As Rommel himself ruefully remarked as he waited for supplies that never arrived: "Malta . . . has the lives of many thousands of German and Italian soldiers on its conscience."[3]

It could be argued, moreover, that the influence of Malta reached far beyond the Mediterranean theater to affect the overall course, and quite possibly even the outcome, of the war itself. If the little island had not stood in the way, might Hitler have perhaps been more amenable to a major strike through North Africa at Britain's Middle East oil fields, as urged upon him by Admiral Raeder? Or, if the Duce had captured Malta early in the war and thereby gained a trophy to display to his people, would he have still felt compelled to launch his foolish attack on Greece, which forced Hitler into an unwanted Balkan campaign and figured heavily in his postponement of the invasion of Russia by six critical weeks? In any event, Axis fortunes would surely have benefited, perhaps decisively, if the 1200 first-line combat planes (and their crews) that were shot down during the more-than-two-year attempt to neutralize Malta had been available for use elsewhere—say, at Stalingrad in the autumn 1942. None of this is meant to suggest that Malta won the war for the Allies. Still, as the *New York Times* later remarked: "If we want to find the spot where the tide began to turn, Malta is as good as any."[4]

Much has been made of the little island that wouldn't quit, and of its beleaguered people whose uncommon courage and endurance counted for so much during those early years of the war when, as Churchill put it, "hardship was our garment." But among the accolades no finer or more fitting can be found than the tribute paid the island fortress by President Roosevelt during his brief visit in December 1943. In a message to the Maltese people, now inscribed on a plaque outside the Parliament Building (formerly the palace) in Valletta, the president recalled those tormented times of the recent past when "under repeated fire from the skies, Malta stood alone . . . in the center of the sea, one tiny bright flame in the darkness—a beacon of hope for the clearer days that have come." Such valor would not soon be forgotten:

> Malta's bright story of human fortitude and courage will be read by posterity with wonder and with gratitude throughout all the ages. What was done on this island maintained the highest traditions of gallant men and women who from the beginning of time have lived and died to preserve civilization for all mankind.

Notes

CHAPTER 1

1. Brian Blouet, *A Short History of Malta* (New York, 1967), p. 41.
2. Andrew B. Cunningham, *A Sailor's Odyssey* (New York, 1951), p. 177.

CHAPTER 2

1. Albert Ganado, interview with author, Malta, March 6, 1978.
2. Pierre D'Amato, interview with author, Malta, November 26, 1977.
3. Cecilia Zimmerman, interview with author, Malta, June 12, 1978.

CHAPTER 3

1. B. A. Pond, interview with author, Malta, March 24, 1978.
2. Frank De Domenico, *An Island Beleaguered* (Valletta, Malta, 1946), pp. 5–7.
3. William Dobbie, *A Very Present Help* (London, 1945), p. 79.
4. Cunningham, pp. 241–57 passim.
5. Miscellaneous Papers, Michael Kissaun Collection, Melitensia Room, University of Malta.
6. *Statistical Abstract of the Maltese Islands, 1946* (Valletta, Malta, 1947), p. xxvii.
7. Joseph Bartolo Parnis, interview with author, Malta, May 30, 1978.
8. Pond interview. See also Hugh Lloyd, *Briefed to Attack* (London, 1949), p. 137. Lloyd makes an almost identical statement: "True, there was a token defense, but its intention was to prevent the Axis from rowing ashore."
9. Maltese shopkeeper, interview with author, April 14, 1978. Name withheld on request.
10. *Statistical Abstract, 1946,* p. xxvii. See also *Malta Government Gazette* (1939–40), p. 720.
11. *Gazette,* pp. 720–23.
12. "Instructions . . . on Air Attacks, 1935," Government pamphlet in Joseph Wettinger Papers, in possession of Godfrey Wettinger, Malta.

13. Elia Galea, interview with author, Malta, November 21, 1977.
14. "General Instructions to Special Constables, May 31, 1940," Government circular in Joseph Wettinger Papers.
15. J. Aquilina, interview with author, Malta, June 20, 1978.
16. Zimmerman interview.
17. "Instructions on Gas Attacks," Government pamphlet in Wettinger Papers.
18. Elia Galea interview.
19. C. Jaccorini, interview with author, Malta, December 13, 1977.
20. Frank De Domenico, interview with author, Malta, January 7, 1978.

CHAPTER 4

1. De Domenico, p. 9.
2. Malcolm Muggeridge, ed., *Ciano's Diary, 1939–43* (London, 1947), p. 249.
3. Stewart Perowne, *The Siege within the Walls* (London, 1970), p. 58.
4. Albert Kesselring, *Memoirs* (London, 1953), p. 123.
5. Raymond de Belot, *The Struggle for the Mediterranean, 1939–1945* (Princeton, N.J., 1951), p. 44.
6. *Ciano's Diary*, p. 279.
7. de Belot, p. 155.
8. Anthony Eden, *The Eden Memoirs: The Reckoning* (London, 1965), p. 140.
9. Giulio Douhet, *The Command of the Air* (New York, 1942. Translated from the Italian by Dino Ferrari, second edition, 1927).
10. For these and other comments by the Italian press, see *Time,* June 10, 1940.
11. "General Instructions to Special Constables," June 3, 1940.
12. Ganado interview.
13. See, for instance, "General Instructions to Special Constables," May 31, 1940.
14. D'Amato interview.
15. Marjorie De Wolff, interview with author, Malta, October 22, 1977.
16. J. Aquilina interview.
17. *Newsweek,* June 17, 1940, p. 16.

CHAPTER 5

1. Charles Boffa, *The Second Great Siege: Malta, 1940–42* (Hamrun, Malta, 1970), p. 18.
2. Cunningham, p. 231.
3. *Times of Malta,* June 13, 1940.
4. Special Constable Joseph Wettinger's Record Book, in Joseph Wettinger Papers.
5. C. Jaccorini interview.
6. Joseph Wettinger Papers.
7. Kenneth Poolman, *Faith, Hope, and Charity* (London, 1954), p. 62.
8. Mario Jaccorini, interview with author, Malta, November 23, 1977.
9. Zimmerman interview. See also Special Constable Leonardo Sacco's Record Book, in Sacco Collection, Melitensia Room, University of Malta.
10. Rita Grima, interview with author, Malta, November 15, 1977.
11. Boffa, p. 21.
12. "Archpriest de Brincat Address, October 18, 1942, on the Occasion of the Display of the George Cross to the People of Senglea," printed leaflet in Miscellaneous Papers, Kissaun Collection, University of Malta.
13. Boffa, p. 21.
14. Frank De Domenico interview.
15. Cunningham, p. 236.
16. George Zarb, interview with author, Malta, February 2, 1978.

CHAPTER 6

1. Winston Churchill, *Their Finest Hour* (Boston, 1949), pp. 440–44.
2. Royal Air Force, *The Air Battle of Malta: The Official Account of the R.A.F. in Malta, June 1940 to November 1942* (London, 1944), p. 8.
3. I. S. O. Playfair, *The Mediterranean and the Middle East* (London, 1954), III, 203n.
4. Churchill, *Finest Hour,* p. 500.
5. *Times of Malta,* October–November 1940.
6. Cunningham, pp. 258–59.
7. Luciano Callus, interview with author, Malta, February 21, 1978.
8. Bartolo Parnis interview; also, C. Jaccorini interview.
9. L. A. Borg, interview with author, Malta, October 31, 1977.
10. Vincent Tabone, interview with author, Malta, November 4, 1977.
11. *Times of Malta,* June 12, 1940.
12. T. Fsadni, *Id-Dumnikant Maltin fi zmien il-Gwerra, 1939–1945* (Valletta, Malta 1978).
13. Elia Galea interview.
14. Joseph Galea, interview with author, Malta, January 28, 1978.
15. J. Aquilina interview.

CHAPTER 7

1. Frank De Domenico interview.
2. Elia Galea interview.
3. Ibid.
4. Francis Gerard, *Malta Magnificent* (London, 1943), p. 67.
5. Rosa Judge, "I Remember . . .," *Sunday Times of Malta,* December 18, 1977.
6. *Times of Malta,* July 18–26, 1940.
7. Joseph Wettinger Papers. For vigilance against quislings, see especially Defense Order #323, June 27, 1940.
8. Joseph Wettinger Papers.
9. Roger Vella Bonavita, interview with author, Malta, October 20, 1977.
10. Playfair, I, 312.
11. The story of Operation White is told in detail in Ian Cameron, *Red Duster, White Ensign* (London, 1959), pp. 52–61. For a more authoritative account, see Playfair, I, 243–44.
12. Cunningham, p. 378.
13. Churchill, *Finest Hour,* p. 453.
14. William Dobbie, pp. 25–28.
15. Melita Strickland, interview with author, Malta, June 9, 1978.
16. De Wolff interview.
17. Strickland interview.
18. William Dobbie, pp. 11–12.
19. Strickland interview.
20. Zarb interview.

CHAPTER 8

1. *Gazette* (1940), pp. 956, 1069, 1143, 1242. See also *Debates of the Council of Government* (1940), II, 33; IV, 1394.
2. On gasoline restrictions, see *Gazette* (1940), pp. 688, 1010. See also *Times of Malta,* July 4, 1940.
3. De Domenico, p. 39.
4. Strickland interview.
5. Emanuel Aquilina, interview with author, Malta, May 24, 1978.

6. *Debates* (1940), IV, 1137.
7. De Domenico, p. 31.
8. Ibid.
9. *Ciano's Diary,* p. 297.
10. de Belot, p. 77.
11. *Ciano's Diary,* p. 309.
12. Ibid., pp. 307–15.
13. RAF, p. 17.
14. Churchill, *Finest Hour,* p. 504.
15. *Ciano's Diary,* p. 316.
16. Ibid., p. 321.

CHAPTER 9

1. Winston Churchill, *The Grand Alliance* (London, 1950), p. 13.
2. Sybil Dobbie, *Grace under Malta* (London, 1944), p. 77.
3. Cunningham, p. 303.
4. J. R. Thachrah, "The Strategic Element in British Policy in the Western Mediterranean, 1939–1942," (Typescript, dated 1975, Melitensia Room, University of Malta).
5. *Times of Malta,* January 15, 1941.
6. Godfrey Wettinger, interview with author, Malta, October 12, 1977.
7. Emanuel Tonna, *Floriana in Wartime* (Valletta, Malta, 1969), p. 36.
8. De Domenico, p. 52.
9. Borg interview.
10. Victor Jaccorini, interview with author, Malta, November 23, 1977.
11. Elia Galea interview.
12. *Times of Malta,* January 20–23, 1941.
13. Frank De Domenico interview.
14. *Times of Malta,* January 21, 1941.

CHAPTER 10

1. Christina Nolte, "German Mediterranean Strategy and Malta" (Thesis, 1977, University of Malta), pp. 22–32.
2. Frank De Domenico interview.
3. Cunningham, p. 319.
4. Ibid., p. 322.
5. Ibid., p. 364.
6. Alexander Stewart, interview with author, Malta, June 8, 1978.
7. Bartolo Parnis interview.
8. Cameron, pp. 92–93.
9. Diary of a British airman, in possession of Richard Mifsud, Malta. I am indebted to Mr. Mifsud for permission to use this material.
10. Tonna, *Floriana in Wartime,* p. 43.
11. Zimmerman interview.
12. Gerard, p. 105.
13. Paul Cassar, *Medical History of Malta* (London, 1964), p. 560.
14. Inspector, Special Constabulary, Record Book, March 8, May 24, 1941, in Joseph Wettinger Papers.
15. Boffa, p. 105.
16. Government Order #345, in *Gazette* (1940), p. 687.
17. Government Order #309, in *Gazette* (1941), p. 549.
18. Elia Galea interview.

19. *Times of Malta,* April 18, 1941.
20. Frank De Domenico interview.
21. *Times of Malta,* March 10, 1941.
22. See, especially, *Debates* (1941), V, 1684.
23. *Information Service Bulletin,* June 4, 1941.
24. Ibid., May 28, 1941. This figure was released by the government in answer to criticism of the shelter program by the Nationalist members of the Council of Government. The announcement was apparently meant to justify the lack of progress in shelter construction, but it raised more questions than it answered—such as *why* there were so few hammers available.
25. Frank De Domenico interview. His charge of stinginess is supported somewhat by the government's announcement in late April that the people were free to electrify the public shelters, provided they did so at their own expense. See *Times of Malta,* April 28, 1941.
26. Sybil Dobbie, p. 63.
27. *Debates* (1942), VII, 820.
28. Strickland interview.
29. D'Amato interview.
30. Pond interview.
31. Strickland interview. According to Strickland, her husband Roger, in his position as leader of the elected majority of the Council of Government, had come out months earlier in favor of conscription but had been dissuaded by the British authorities from pursuing the matter.
32. Frank De Domenico interview. Also Bartolo Parnis and Stewart interviews.
33. Nolte, p. 39.
34. Ibid., pp. 37–40.

CHAPTER 11

1. B. H. Liddell Hart, *History of the Second World War* (London, 1970), p. 137.
2. C. Bekker, *The Luftwaffe War Diaries* (London, 1967), p. 370.
3. Hart, p. 137.
4. Nolte, p. 55.
5. The unit was sent first to Greece and then to the eastern front.
6. William Dobbie, pp. 76–81.
7. Joseph Galea interview.
8. *Times of Malta,* July 22, 1941.
9. *Ciano's Diary,* pp. 354, 437.
10. Playfair, II, 269, 276.
11. This account of the Italian attack on Grand Harbour is based mainly on the following sources: Playfair, II, 270–72; RAF, pp. 35–38; Winston Ramsay, ed. *After the Battle: Malta during WW II* (London, 1975), pp. 33–37; George Hogan, *Malta: The Triumphant Years* (London, 1978), pp. 52–56; *Times of Malta,* July 27–28, 1941; Borg interview. Since no two of these sources agree on all particulars, I took the liberty of "blending" a bit for the sake of presenting what seems to me to be the most accurate reconstruction of the attack.
12. Strickland interview.
13. *Debates* (1941), V, 2165.
14. This figure does not include 9,300 acres of animal fodder (mostly "sullah," or red clover). Unless otherwise noted all information on agricultural production in this paragraph is based on figures taken from *Statistical Abstract, 1946,* p. 19.
15. Miscellaneous Papers, Kissaun Collection, University of Malta.
16. *Gazette* (1941), p. 587.

17. The entire rationing program was administered by a staff of 43 people at an annual cost of £4,490 (4.07 pence per person on the island). See "Report of the Working of the Ration Office, 1941–1945," in Miscellaneous Papers, Kissaun Collection, University of Malta.
18. *Gazette* (1941), pp. 207–8; also *Debates* (1941), V, 2080.
19. *Gazette* (1941), pp. 588, 753, 857, 1084.
20. *Times of Malta,* June 22, 1941.

CHAPTER 12

1. Lloyd, p. 32.
2. Ibid., p. 208.
3. Ibid., pp. 24–29.
4. Ibid., pp. 60–62. Estimates of enemy shipping destroyed during this period vary widely. Lloyd places the total of "destroyed and damaged" at close to half a million tons. The 150,000 figure for tonnage sunk is Churchill's. See his *The Grand Alliance,* pp. 432–33. See also Cunningham, p. 411, and RAF, p. 34.
5. Lloyd, pp. 60–62.
6. By the end of 1941 the number of Maltese civilians employed by the military had risen from 4,000 to 17,000. The number employed by the civilian government had grown from 2,600 to 8,200. *Debates* (1942), VI, 87.
7. Perowne, p. 91. See also Cajus Bekker, *Hitler's Naval War* (London, 1974), p. 242.
8. *Ciano's Diary,* p. 404.
9. Ibid., p. 413.
10. Bekker, *Naval War,* p. 242.
11. Ibid.
12. Directive #38, as cited in H. R. Trevor-Roper, ed., *Hitler's War Directives* (London, 1964), p. 105. See also Albert Kesselring, *Memoirs* (London, 1953), pp. 103–04.
13. *Ciano's Diary,* p. 395.
14. Frank De Domenico interview. Ultimately the British would pay the Maltese £3,000,000 in property compensation, which, according to many informed Maltese, covered less than half the cost.
15. *Times of Malta,* August 5, 1942.
16. J. Aquilina interview.
17. Carmel Chetcuti, interview with author, Malta, October 15, 1977. See also *Debates* (1941), VI, 139; *Gazette* (1941), pp. 61–86.
18. *Gazette* (1941), p. 1033.
19. Ibid., p. 611.
20. J. Aquilina interview.
21. Churchill, *Grand Alliance,* p. 540.

CHAPTER 13

1. Cunningham, p. 439.
2. *Times of Malta,* January 6, 1942.
3. Ibid., January 21, 1942.
4. Kesselring, p. 121.
5. Lloyd, pp. 94, 145.
6. Kesselring, p. 109. Official British figures agree: 18.8% for January and 12.8% for February. See Playfair, III, 161.
7. Churchill, *Alliance,* p. 177.
8. Kesselring, p. 109.
9. *Debates* (1942), VI, 231.

10. P. P. Ferriol, "When Sir Ugo Mifsud Died for Maltese Liberty," *The Maltese Review,* IX (January–March 1952), pp. 8–15.
11. *Debates* (1942), VI, 240.
12. Strickland interview.
13. Ganado interview.
14. Ferriol, p. 8.
15. Ganado interview.
16. John Oliver to the Rev. Joseph Micallef, September 24, 1977, in possession of the author, courtesy of Fr. Micallef. The official casualty count appears in *Information Service Bulletin,* February 17, 1942.
17. *Times of Malta,* January 17, 1942.
18. Tonna, *Wartime,* p. 47.
19. Playfair, III, 160–61.
20. Hogan, p. 103.
21. RAF, p. 52.
22. De Domenico, p. 126.
23. Pond interview.
24. RAF, p. 51.
25. Lloyd, p. 159.
26. Pond interview.
27. Peter Shankland and Anthony Hunter, *Malta Convoy* (London, 1963), p. 42.

CHAPTER 14

1. *Times of Malta,* June 2, 1942.
2. Special Constable Record Book, Michael Kissaun Collection, National Bibliotheca, Valletta.
3. RAF, p. 55.
4. Zimmerman interview.
5. Stewart interview.
6. Playfair, III, 179.
7. Bekker, *Luftwaffe,* p. 239.
8. Ibid.
9. Callus interview.
10. Lloyd, p. 176.
11. Denis Barnham, *One Man's Window* (London, 1956), p. 70.
12. Playfair, III, 179. See also H. E. C. Weldon, "The Artillery Defense of Malta," *Journal of Royal Artillery,* LXXIX, No. 1 (1952), 27.
13. R. Leslie Oliver, *Malta Besieged* (London, 1944), p. 26.
14. Winston Churchill, *The Hinge of Fate* (London, 1951), pp. 299–300.
15. RAF, p. 61.
16. *Report on Rationing,* Appendix A.
17. Kissaun Record Book, National Bibliotheca, Valletta.
18. Sybil Dobbie, p. 111.
19. *Debates* (1942), VI, 179–83.
20. Frank De Domenico interview.
21. *Times of Malta,* January 13, 1942.
22. Interview, April 14, 1978. Name withheld on request.
23. Mrs. Joseph Galea, interview with author, Malta, January 28, 1978.
24. Laurence Mizzi, *Dhanen Tal-Guerra* (Valletta, Malta, 1975), pp. 27–28.
25. De Domenico, p. 142.
26. Joseph Galea interview.
27. Miscellaneous Papers, Kissaun Collection, University of Malta.

28. Ibid.
29. "Archpriest de Brincat Address."
30. Frank De Domenico interview.
31. Ian Bisset, *The George Cross* (London, 1961), p. 133.
32. Churchill, *Hinge of Fate,* p. 765.
33. Playfair, III, 183.

CHAPTER 15

1. W. L. River, *Malta Story: Based on the Diary and Experiences of Flying Officer Howard M. Coffin, RAF* (New York, 1943), foreword (n.p.)
2. Ibid., p. 116.
3. Kesselring, p. 122.
4. River, foreword (n.p.)
5. Ibid., p. 21.
6. Pond interview.
7. Barnham, p. 97.
8. River, foreword (n.p.).
9. Zimmerman interview.
10. *Times of Malta,* March 1942. See also *Sunday Times of Malta,* March 15, 1942.
11. This sketch of General Beak is based on the aforementioned interviews with Pond, Strickland, Zimmerman, and Bartolo Parnis. See also Hogan, pp. 48–49.
12. C. Jaccorini interview.
13. De Wolff interview.
14. Callus interview.
15. Bartolo Parnis interview. See also Lloyd, p. 179.
16. John Oliver to Fr. Joseph Micallef, September 24, 1977, in possession of the author.

CHAPTER 16

1. Barnham, p. 91.
2. Ibid., p. 89.
3. Frank De Domenico interview.
4. Kesselring, p. 122.
5. RAF, p. 67.
6. Ibid., p. 174.
7. Cameron, p. 192.
8. Richard Beck, interview with author, Malta, October 27, 1977.
9. Judge, "I Remember," *Sunday Times of Malta.* The *Welshman* was finally sunk off Tobruk in February 1943. For more on the *Welshman,* see Cameron, pp. 195–202; A. Samut Tagliaferro, "The Malta Convoys of World War II," *Armed Forces of Malta Journal,* XXVII (April 1977).
10. In addition to the stores, the *Welshman* brought more than a hundred RAF technicians, mainly mechanics for the new Spitfires.
11. The story of the *Welshman* barrage is well told in Weldon, pp. 20–27.
12. Barnham, pp. 128–29.
13. RAF, p. 71; see also Bekker, *Luftwaffe Diaries,* p. 242.
14. *Ciano's Diary,* p. 469.
15. Cameron, p. 201.
16. Arthur Bryant, *The Turn of the Tide, 1939–1943: A Study Based on the Diaries and Autobiographical Notes of Field Marshal The VisCount Alanbrooke* (London, 1957), p. 306.

17. Excerpts from previously cited interviews with Bartolo Parnis, Ganado, Pond, Stewart, and Zarb, although not necessarily in the order given.
18. Churchill, *Hinge of Fate,* p. 305.
19. Strickland interview.
20. Zarb interview.
21. For the rise and fall of Operation Herkules, see the unpublished account by German Air General Paul Deichmann, "Luftlandeaktion Malta," Hoover Library Manuscript Collection, Stanford University. Written ten years after the event, the general's account contains several inaccuracies, especially dates, but is nevertheless highly informative.
22. Bartolo Parnis interview.
23. Bekker, *Luftwaffe,* p. 244.
24. Nolte, p. 101; also Bekker, *Naval War,* pp. 253–54.
25. Bekker, *Naval War,* p. 254.
26. Churchill, *Hinge of Fate,* p. 377.
27. Kesselring, p. 123.

CHAPTER 17

1. Strickland interview.
2. *Times of Malta,* June 21, 1942.
3. Barnham, p. 203.
4. *Times of Malta,* June 21, 1942.
5. Oliver, p. 82.
6. *Times of Malta,* July 2, 1942.
7. *Report on Rationing,* Appendix A.
8. *Debates* (1942), V, 2162.
9. *Times of Malta,* July 12, 1942.
10. Government prices are taken from *Gazette* (1942), p. 600. Black market prices come from De Domenico, p. 168, and aforementioned interviews with Strickland and Chetcuti. Also, Anthony Gauci, interview with author, Malta, September 22, 1977.
11. De Domenico, p. 168.
12. E. Aquilina interview.
13. Frank De Domenico interview.
14. Strickland interview.
15. Kissaun Collection, National Bibliotheca, Valletta.
16. De Domenico, p. 170.
17. *Gazette* (1942), pp. 512, 515.
18. C. Jaccorini interview.
19. Pond interview.
20. Frank De Domenico interview.
21. *Statistical Abstracts, 1946,* p. 19.
22. De Domenico, p. 160.
23. RAF, p. 91.
24. *Debates* (1942), VII, 1014.
25. Lloyd, p. 194.
26. Strickland interview.
27. Zimmerman interview.
28. Elia Galea interview.
29. Saviour Sciberras, "The Council of Government during World War II, 1940–43" (Thesis, 1972, University of Malta), p. 130.
30. *Times of Malta,* July 4, 1942. Limited allotments of milk, mainly canned, were also available to the island's hospitals. See *Debates* (1942), VII, 700.

CHAPTER 18

1. Joseph Galea interview.
2. Alfred Samut Tagliaferro, interview with author, Malta, November 18, 1977.
3. Barnham, p. 126. Not mentioned here among Malta's wartime diseases is polio, which struck the island severely, but not until November 1942, three months after the siege had been eased by the Santa Marija convoy. See chapter 19.
4. *Statistical Abstracts, 1946,* p. 9. Although included in the mortality figures, the number of civilians killed during 1942 as a direct result of enemy action represented only a small proportion of the total deaths and therefore did not have an appreciable effect upon the overall rate.
5. Cassar, *Medical History,* pp. 564, 567–68. Pellagra was responsible for more than half of all the deaths among mental patients.
6. Wettinger interview.
7. *Statistical Abstracts, 1946,* p. xv. See also Cassar, p. 561.
8. *Ciano's Diary,* p. 471.
9. *Gazette* (1940–1942).
10. Cassar, p. 560.
11. Since beer, wine, and other spirits were designated as luxury items, they were neither rationed nor price–controlled.
12. *Gazette* (1942), p. 224.
13. Zimmerman interview.
14. Wettinger interview.
15. Frank De Domenico interview.
16. Zarb interview.
17. *Times of Malta,* July 10, 1942.
18. Frank De Domenico interview.
19. Ibid.
20. Zimmerman interview.
21. Lloyd, p. 229.
22. *Times of Malta,* July 16, 1942.
23. Mizzi, pp. 28–29.

CHAPTER 19

1. Pond interview.
2. Marie Magro, interview with author, Malta, June 2, 1978.
3. *Gazette* (1942), p. 643.
4. Shankland and Hunter, p. 40.
5. Oliver, p. 87.
6. *Ciano's Diary,* p. 495.
7. Frank De Domenico interview.

CHAPTER 20

1. *Statistical Abstracts, 1946,* p. xii.
2. Zarb interview.
3. Shankland and Hunter, p. 20.
4. As quoted in Hogan, p. 163.

Bibliography

INTERVIEWS

Perhaps the most informative, and certainly the most interesting and original, material that went into this book came from interviews and informal conversations with a large number of people who were present on the island at the time of the siege and were either participants in or witnesses to the events and conditions described. Among those whose recollections proved especially valuable were the following:

Name	*Role during Siege*
Emanuel Aquilina	Military chauffeur for Air Marshal Lloyd
Prof. J. Aquilina	Lecturer, University of Malta
The Marchesa Cecilia Zimmerman, Barbaro of Saint George	Social secretary, British Institute
Maj. Joseph Bartolo Parnis	Sergeant (later lieutenant), KOMR
Prof. Richard Beck	Wellington pilot
Lt. Col. L. A. Borg	Antiaircraft officer, RMA
Luciano Callus	Crew member of minesweeper
Carmel Chetcuti	Schoolboy
Dr. Pierre D'Amato	Conscript, KOMR
Frank De Domenico	Cable operator
Mrs. Frank De Domenico	Housewife
Sr. M. Deguara	Schoolgirl
Marjorie De Wolff	Head, Royal Malta SPCA
Elia Galea	Schoolteacher

Name	*Role during Siege*
Mrs. Elia Galea	Schoolteacher
Dr. Joseph Galea	District medical officer
Mrs. Joseph Galea	Housewife
Dr. Albert Ganado	University student
Anthony Gauci	Enlistee, KOMR
Dr. C. Jaccorini	Physician
Fr. Mario Jaccorini	Schoolboy
Fr. Victor Jaccorini	Schoolboy
Marie Magro	Schoolgirl
Maj. B. A. Pond	Sergeant (later lieutenant), West Kent Regiment
Brig. Alfred Samut Tagliaferro	Officer, RMA
Col. Alexander Stewart	Officer, KOMR
Melita Strickland	Wife of the elected majority leader, Council of Government
Dr. Vincent Tabone	Physician
Fr. Andrew Vella	Seminarian
Roger Vella Bonavita	Schoolboy
Dr. Godfrey Wettinger	Schoolboy
George Zarb	Assistant to the director, Office of Information

UNPUBLISHED SOURCES

Air Raid Precaution Officers' Reports (miscellaneous), 1940–42. Palace Archives, Valletta.

Correspondence between the Government of Malta and the Colonial Office, 1940–42. Palace Archives, Valletta.

Deichmann, Paul Air General. "Luftlandeaktion Malta." Unpublished typescript, Hoover Library Manuscript Collection, Stanford University.

Kissaun, Michael. Inspector of Regular Police (Eastern Division). Record Books. National Bibliotheka, Valletta.

Michael Kissaun Miscellaneous Papers. Melitensia Room, University of Malta.

Nolte, Christina. "German Mediterranean Strategy and Malta." Thesis, 1977, Department of History, University of Malta.

Sacco, Leonard. Inspector, Special Constabulary. Miscellaneous Papers. Melitensia Room, University of Malta.

Sciberras, Saviour. "The Council of Government during World War II, 1940–43." Thesis, 1972, Department of History, University of Malta.

Thachrah, J. R. "The Strategic Element in British Policy in the Western Mediterranean, 1939–42." Typescript, 1975, University of Malta.

Wettinger, Joseph. Inspector, Special Constabulary, Record Books and Miscellaneous Papers. In possession of Dr. Godfrey Wettinger, Mellieha.

GOVERNMENT DOCUMENTS

Debates of the Council of Government, 1939–42.
Malta Blue Book, 1932.
Malta Government Gazette, 1940–42.
Report on the Working of the Rationing Office, 1941–45.
Statistical Abstract of the Maltese Islands, 1946.

NEWSPAPERS AND MAGAZINES

Information Service Daily Bulletin, 1940–42.
Information Service Weekly Bulletin, 1940–42.
Newsweek, 1940.
Sunday Times of Malta, 1940–42.
Time, June 1940.
Times of Malta, 1940–42.

BOOKS AND ARTICLES

Barnham, Denis. *One Man's Window*. London: Wm. Kimber, Ltd., 1956.
Bartimeus [pseud.] et al. *The Epic of Malta*. London: Odhams Press, 1943.
———. *Malta Invicta*. London: Chatto & Windus, 1942.
Bekker, Cajus. *Hitler's Naval War*. London: Macdonald, 1974.
———. *The Luftwaffe Diaries*. London: Macdonald, 1967.
Beurling, George. *Malta Spitfire*. New York: Farrar & Rinehart, 1943.
Bisset, Ian. *The George Cross*. London: McGibbon & Kee, 1961.
Blouet, Brian. *A Short History of Malta*. New York: Praeger, 1967.
Boffa, Charles. *The Second Great Siege: Malta, 1940–42*. Hamrun, Malta: Saint Joseph's Home, 1970.
Bryant, Arthur. *The Turn of the Tide, 1939–1943: A Study Based on the Diaries and Autobiographical Notes of Field Marshal The Viscount Alanbrooke*. London: Collins, 1957.
Cameron, Ian [pseud.]. *Red Duster, White Ensign*. London: Frederick Muller, 1959.
Cassar, George. "Gozo during World War II," *Malta Year Book, 1964,* Sliema, Malta: De La Salle Brothers Publication, 1965, 300–14.
Cassar, Paul. *A Medical History of Malta*. London: Wellcome Historical Medical Library, 1964.
Churchill, Winston. *The Grand Alliance*. London: Cassell & Co., 1950.
———. *The Hinge of Fate*. London: Cassell & Co., 1951.
———. *Their Finest Hour*. Boston: Houghton Mifflin, 1949.
Cunningham, Andrew B. *A Sailor's Odyssey*. New York: Dutton, 1951.
de Belot, Raymond. *The Struggle for the Mediterranean, 1939–45*. Princeton, N.J.: Princeton University Press, 1951.
De Domenico, Frank. *An Island Beleaguered*. Valletta, Malta: Giov. Muscat, 1946.
Dobbie, Sybil. *Grace Under Malta*. London: Lindsay Drummond, 1944.
Dobbie, William. *A Very Present Help*. London: Marshall, Morgan, & Scott, 1945.

Douhet, Giulio. *The Command of the Air.* New York: Coward-McCann, 1942 (translated from the Italian by Dino Ferrari, second edition, 1927).
Eade, Charles, ed. *The Unrelenting Struggle: War Speeches by . . . Winston Churchill.* London: Cassell & Co., 1942.
Eden, Anthony. *The Eden Memoirs: The Reckoning.* London: Cassell & Co., 1965.
Ferriol, P. P. "When Sir Ugo Mifsud Died for Maltese Liberty," *Maltese Review,* IX (January–March 1952), 5–15.
Fsadni, T. *Id-Dumnikant Maltin fi zmien il-Gwerra, 1939–45.* Valletta, Malta: Dominican Publications, 1978.
Galea, Michael. "Malta: Diary of a War, 1941–45," *Armed Forces of Malta Journal,* No. 28 (October 1977).
Gerard, Francis. *Malta Magnificent.* London: Cassell & Co., 1943.
Guedalla, P. *The Middle East, 1940–42.* London: Hodder & Stoughton, 1944.
Hanson, Baldwin. *The Crucial Years, 1939–41.* New York: Harper & Row, 1976.
Hart, B. H. Liddell. *History of the Second World War.* London: Cassell & Co., 1970.
———, ed. *The Rommel Papers.* London: Collins, 1953.
Hay, Ian [pseud.]. *Malta: The Unconquered Isle.* London: Hodder & Stoughton, 1943.
Hogan, George. *Malta: The Triumphant Years.* London: Hale, 1978.
Judge, Rosa Micallef. "I Remember . . .," *Sunday Times of Malta,* December 18, 1977, 20–21.
Kesselring, Albert. *Memoirs.* London: Wm. Kimber, 1953.
Lewin, Ronald. *Ultra Goes to War.* New York: McGraw-Hill, 1978.
Lloyd, Hugh. *Briefed to Attack: Malta's Part in the African Victory.* London: Hodder & Stoughton, 1949.
Mercer, G. Ellul. *Taht In-Nar: Djarju, 1940–41.* Valletta, Malta: Giov. Muscat, 1949.
Micallef, Joseph. *Rahal Fi Gwerra.* Valletta, Malta: Published by author, 1978.
Mifsud, Richard. *Malta at War.* Marsa, Malta: Jos. Azzopardi, 1979.
Mizzi, Laurence. *Dhahen Tal-Gwerra.* Valletta, Malta: Klabb Kotba Maltin, 1975.
Muggeridge, Malcolm, ed. *Ciano's Diary, 1939–43.* London: William Heinemann, 1947.
Oliver, R. Leslie. *Malta Besieged.* London: Hutchinson & Co., 1944.
Perowne, Stewart. *The Siege within the Walls.* London: Hodder & Stoughton, 1970.
Playfair, I.S.O. *The Mediterranean and the Middle East.* Vols. I–III. London: Her Majesty's Stationery Office, 1954–60.
Poolman, Kenneth. *Faith, Hope, and Charity.* London: Wm. Kimber, 1954.
Ramsay, Winston, ed. *After the Battle: Malta during World War II.* London: Battle of Britain Prints, 1975.
River, W. L. *Malta Story: Based on the Diary and Experiences of Flying Officer Howard M. Coffin, RAF.* New York: Dutton, 1943.
Royal Air Force. *The Air Battle of Malta: The Official Account of the R.A.F. in Malta, June 1940 to November 1942.* London: His Majesty's Stationery Office, 1944.
Samut Tagliaferro, Alfred. "The Malta Convoys of World War II," *Armed Forces of Malta Journal,* No. 27 (April 1977).
Schmidt, Heinz Werner. *With Rommel in the Desert.* London: George G. Harrap & Co., 1951.
Shankland, Peter, and Anthony Hunter. *Malta Convoy.* London: Fontana Books, 1963.

Thomas, David. *Submarine Victory: The Story of British Submarines in World War II.* London: Wm. Kimber, 1961.

Tonna, Emanuel. *First Focus on Floriana.* Valletta, Malta: Progress Press, 1967.

———. *Floriana in Wartime.* Valletta, Malta: Progress Press, 1969.

Trevor-Roper, H. R., ed. *Hitler's War Directives, 1939–45.* London: Sedgwick & Jackson, 1964.

Vella, Andrew. "Intervista Mal-Arcisoof Mikiel Gonzi Divar Il-Karriera Pubblika Tieghu Matul Dan L-Ahhar Nofs Seklu," *Storja 78,* (January 1978), 121–33.

Vella, Philip. "Malta in World War II," *War Relics Exhibition Souvenir Handbook.* Valletta, Malta: Progress Press, 1979.

Weldon, H. E. C. "The Artillery Defense of Malta," *Journal of Royal Artillery,* LXXIX, No. 1 (1952), 15–27.

Winterbotham, F. W. *The Ultra Secret.* New York: Dell, 1975.

Young, Desmond. *Rommel.* London: Collins, 1950.

Index